To
My
POLIS,
With Love

*May Gloucester show the world
the ways of frugality*

The Somist Institute

polis
noun (pl. poleis)
a city-state in ancient Greece, esp. as considered
in its ideal form for philosophical purposes.

Also by Carmine Gorga

*The Economic Process: An Instantaneous Non-Newtonian
Picture* (Lanham, Md. and Oxford: University Press of
America, 2002)

Quality Assurance of Seafood with Louis J. Ronsivalli (NY:
Van Nostrand Reinhold, 1988)

The Somist Institute is dedicated to the study of the theories
and practices of the social man and woman, the civilized person.

To
My
POLIS,
With Love

May Gloucester show the world
the ways of frugality

A COLLECTION OF ESSAYS BY

Carmine Gorga

The Somist Institute

87 Middle Street
Gloucester, MA 01930-5738
www.somist.org

Library of Congress Cataloging-in-Publication Data

Gorga, Carmine
To my polis, with love: may Gloucester show the world
the ways of frugality / Carmine Gorga
p. cm
1. Community economic development-Economic rights and responsibilities-
Monetary policy-Monetary practices. 2. Fisheries development-Gloucester-
Massachusetts-Arts. 3. Justice and peace. I. Title.

ISBN1438288026

Book cover picture by Cristin Bradley

Book Design: Barry Rower

To Saint Peter

the Patron Saint of the Fishermen

who wrote (2 Peter 3:13):

"But we look for new heavens and a new earth according to his promises, in which justice dwelleth."

Table of Contents

Part Two — Essays Published on the Internet

Part Three — Essays Published in Various Scholarly Journals

Preface

by David Wise

I t is a pleasure to offer the Preface to this fine collection of essays by Carmine Gorga. Over the years many Cape Ann residents have read and appreciated the articles he has written for the *Gloucester Daily Times,* but few have had the opportunity to read what he has written for scholarly publications or on the Internet. The selections presented here show us that Dr. Gorga addresses members of the community and representatives of the community of scholars with the same clarity and intent. He wants to build a community of experts at the local level, a community of localists.

Carmine's purpose is to create community through the common goal of economic and cultural growth. He starts from in-depth original research, integrates results into development plans, and participates in building coalitions through personal involvement, debate, and discussion.

The impetus for this collection comes from the need to provide background information for seven suggested resolutions to be presented on September 2, 2008 to the Mayor of Gloucester, Ms. Carolyn Kirk, and the Gloucester City Council. These resolutions are a condensed version of a plan of urban restoration that Carmine and I brought to the people of Gloucester during last year's Sidewalk Bazaar on Main Street. In three days, as pointed out in the text, 425 signatures were gathered, expressing the same aspirations: if enough attention is paid to the needs of the downtown, there will be social and economic rewards.

Born in 1935, Carmine lived through the Great Depression, and World War II, in Southern Italy. He enrolled at the University of Naples to try to understand these two events. He graduated with a Ph.D. in political science. He also received an MA in International Relations from the Johns Hopkins' School of Advanced International Studies (SAIS). He received a Council of Europe Scholarship for his dissertation on the political thought of Louis D. Brandeis and a Fulbright Scholarship.

I met Carmine thirty-five years ago, when he was Director of Planning and Economic Development for Action Inc, the local community action program. We volunteered together on the first Gloucester Community Development Corporation from 1972 to 1975. Thereafter I helped in editing his major published work, *The Economic Process.* And we, as well as our families, have been close friends ever since.

Carmine is certainly a community leader. In his range of contacts, interests, and involvements, he is led by a vision of Concordia, a society built with concord, mutual agreement. He embodies the idea that social progress occurs when the results of in-depth research are integrated into the daily life of people who then share a common goal.

Carmine's work can be divided into three areas: fundamental research, which was guided for 27 years by Professor Franco Modigliani, a Nobel laureate in economics at MIT; action programs he has already implemented; and action programs he hopes to implement.

He has published scholarly articles and two books, *The Economic Process: A Non-Newtonian Instantaneous Picture* (Lanham, Md. and Oxford: University Press of America, 2002) and, with Louis J. Ronsivalli, *Quality Assurance of Seafood* (Van Nostrand Reinhold, 1988). He is now working on a monograph entitled "The Economics of Jubilation: Toward a Regimen of Economic Rights and Responsibilities."

Carmine's work has invigorated the local arts community, perhaps the oldest art colony in America. The first Gloucester Community Development Corporation, founded by Carmine in 1970, supported the nationally known artist and sculptor, Alfred Duca, in a successful community program in the 1970s and early 1980s that used a multi-media approach as a tool to combat issues of addiction among teenagers. Mr. Duca's project, "Channel 1," was replicated across the country.

Carmine's efforts have enriched the fishing industry in Gloucester, MA, the oldest fishing port in the country. Most notably, his work with the Gloucester Laboratory of the National Marine Fisheries Service in the 70s and 80s made it possible for the industry to introduce fresh (as distinguished from frozen) seafood into national supermarkets, with ensuing well-known health benefits for consumers nation-wide.

Working in collaboration with many, he has been instrumental in creating and/or preserving: two Gloucester Community Development Corporations; the Gloucester Fishermen's Wives Association; the Cape Ann Transportation Authority (CATA); Artspace; the Gloucester Maritime Heritage Center; the Gloucester Committee for the Arts; and the Society for the Encouragement of the Arts (seARTS). Some of these organizations have been adopted from other communities; some lend themselves as models to be adapted elsewhere. His past work has received commendation from specialists on the right, left, and center of the political spectrum.

For the immediate future, Carmine is considering opening a Main Street storefront in Gloucester as a community meeting ground for the discussion of a program of urban and economic restoration. This will hopefully promote collaboration with concerned citizens and community leaders to energize the rich economic and cultural tradition of our downtown.

As in the past, if successful, Carmine hopes to encourage a younger generation of community leaders to administer the program. He tells me he then hopes to concentrate his attention on how to do peace — rather than to talk about peace.

All these ideas are presented in detail in the essays you are invited to read. I hope you benefit as much as I have in your review of these essays that Carmine has published over the past twenty-five years.

Introduction

I am a pilgrim: I go where my Lord leads me. More modestly, most days, I consider myself an immigrant. That is the reason why I am especially sensitive to place, my geographic place and my place in society — my polis. Unlike indigenous people (have there ever been such people? Are we not all and always migrants?), I have since childhood been blessed and cursed with the need to move from one society to the next. One day I landed in Gloucester, Massachusetts, USA, and I set roots here.

While not denying the influence of other communities on my development, this group of essays is an expression of my profound gratitude to the people of Gloucester. I will never know, of course, but I'd like to assume that nowhere else in the world could I have done my work with greater ease than in Gloucester. I love the land; I love the inhabitants, both those who are alive and those who are gone. Most days I pass by the Cenotaph on the Boulevard and pay homage to the 5,370 fishermen, and counting, who over the centuries have lost their lives in the sea in pursuit of their magical transformation of fish into food.

I hope my love comes through in these pages.

Part 1 includes articles that editors of the *Gloucester Daily Times* have been gracious enough to publish over the years. Part 2 copies a group of practical programs of action that I have presented on the Internet; they all center in Gloucester, but they will come into full life if they are also applied elsewhere. Imitation is not the sincerest form of flattery; imitation transforms the isolation of the pioneer into a community of shared experiences. Part 3 reproduces a group of articles that originally appeared in a number of scholarly publications. It is by anchoring them in the needs of Gloucester that, I believe, will show their internal cohesion. Part 4 integrates some documents that are relevant to the case presented here. Part 5 gives the details of the petition. Part 6 reduces the entire discussion to a series of resolutions that, ideally, the Gloucester City Council will approve and that the City's Administration will hopefully implement. And Part 7 outlines actions and results obtained so far.

While I am struggling to express the internal cohesion of my thinking in concepts such as Concordian economics, Relationalism, and Somism, I would like to remind the reader that Saint Paul expressed the guiding light of my life's work in simple words. He said: "God has so composed the body that there may be no division in the body, but that the members may have the same care for one another. And if one member suffers, all the members suffer with it; if one member is honored, all the members rejoice with it" (1 Corinthians 24-26). Words so concise and clear have not been uttered to express the deepest possible meaning of Polis.

It never occurred to me to write such a book. It has written itself over the years and has been shaped from different perspectives.

The immediate need for this presentation results from a petition David Wise and I submitted to the people of Gloucester, to Cape Ann's residents, and to tourists during the 2007 Sidewalk Bazaar on Main Street.

In three days, with descriptions of a sustainable and just organization of our community, we gathered 425 signatures that allow us to present the petition to the Mayor and City Council. The petition is in the text. A public hearing has been granted. The essays are meant to offer background material to the Mayor and the City Council so that they might be assisted in resolving the complex questions that confront us now and the days ahead.

The difficulty, as ever, is to find just the right balance between preservation and innovation. May this book be of some help. May our city officials be so inspired that, while each member of our polis "is honored, all the members rejoice" in the process.

July 11, 2008

This day turns out to be Saint Benedict's day. As is well known, disgusted with the last gasps of the decadence of the Roman Empire, Benedict retired to monastic life. At Monte Cassino, he composed his Benedictine Rule and gave birth to the renewal of society. In it he wrote: "No one should follow what he considers to be good for himself, but rather what seems good for another."

Acknowledgments

Harold Bell, who knew a thing or two about people in general and Gloucester in particular, was acute enough to recommend that I thank my wife, Joan, above all and always.

Then I need to thank David Wise. He has been such a staunch supporter and major cheerleader from the first we met in the distant late 60s. He has also been the editor of much of my published work — all for the total sum of $1.00. It is quite proper that his presence should be felt all through this book.

Another expression of personal and private thanks goes to my son, Jonathan, who whenever possible has been a stern and effective editor of my work. For this book he has generously offered his technical skills with computers and his artistic capabilities in the design of the work.

In the same vain I am happy to acknowledge the welcoming hand extended to me by my friends Victor and Giulia Gregory of New York City, my cousins Tony and Ann Zingarelli in Fresno, CA, and Joseph and Phoebe (Eufemia) DiTommaso in Marlborough, MA, and their respective families — and all their friends — who embraced me when, nearly penniless, I reached these shores. They welcomed me with warm open arms, exciting conversation about the new and the old country, and a cornucopia of delicacies that included spaghetti, meatballs, and braciole. It was as if I had died and gone to heaven. Indeed, if I made it to these shores at all it is due to the official sponsorship for Immigration and Naturalization purposes by Harrison Howard and Dr. Angela Falco of New York City. And while in New York and San Francisco they gave me ample opportunities to be bathed in the treasures of modern art. The first time I entered the Guggenheim in New York, I felt an explosion as if the lid of my skull had been removed from my brain.

In the same vain of exciting intellectual experiences, I wish to express my most heartfelt thanks to Professor Raymond G. Torto. As I showed him my revised Keynes' model, he noted: "There is lots of Henry George there!" Is there joy greater than deep human communication? He also sponsored me for induction in the American Economic Association.

The most grateful thanks go to my *intellectual* parents. Professoressa Rosalia Scarlata taught me all the philosophy I know. Professor Vittorio de

Caprariis taught me all the political science I know; and I would be remiss if I were not to acknowledge that he infused in me a deep appreciation for the intellectual life and the intellectual literature of the United States. I can still see him reeling off a long list of American political scientists and constitutional lawyers — presenting us with the unspoken question: "Where is the comparable list of contemporary European intellectuals?" Professor de Caprariis did not only suggest the thought of Louis D. Brandeis as the topic for my dissertation at the University of Naples, he guided my research and even edited my work. For the reader to understand the enormity of his contribution to my intellectual development, I must specify that, for me, Brandeis' thought is the key that unlocks the mystery of how a modern industrial society is put together. Professors Robert A. Mundell, Franco Modigliani, and Meyer L. Burstein taught me all the formal economics I know. Professor Modigliani and Professor Burstein, my only readers for many a year in which the rejection slips accumulated to paper many a room in my house, sustained me morally and intellectually. With readers like that, who needed a larger audience? And Professor Modigliani did something else for my work. He would put right whatever I expressed improperly. He was a true Socratic Maestro. And all that was not enough. I owe to my sister Rosa more than I can ever express: she gave me the gift of the *Collected Works of Saint John of the Cross* with a strong recommendation to read them all. I did that in the 80s and his thoughts spread like balm over my wounded pride: I had changed Keynes' model of the economic system, not in any arbitrary way but by following age-old principles of mathematics and logic, and so few people were paying any attention to me? Mitchell S. Lurio: he taught me the thought of Henry George. Norman G. Kurland: in the late 60s I went all the way to Washington to try to teach him about Louis D. Brandeis; he taught me about Louis O. Kelso. My colleagues at the Society of Catholic Social Scientists (SCSS) have granted me the opportunity to offer formal lectures on a variety of topics that touch upon the core of the teachings of the Magisterium of the Roman Catholic Church. Charles Olson and Vincent Ferrini: they taught me the poetry of community engagement. Joseph E. Garland and Peter N. Anastas: they have taught me the prose of community protest. William C. Rochford: he taught me how to break bread with people and organize them. Rev. Wendy Fitting: she introduced me to the thought of Wendell Berry. David Wise: by keeping an ear on the literature for me, he has introduced me to authors varying from Alexander Marschak to Mark Kurlansky.

Among my intellectual parents, there is another person to single out for undergirding a progressive faith in the value of my work. One day Professor John Kenneth Galbraith coiled down to graciously sit next to me in his studio and in his gravelly voice asked: "What do you mean by national credit?" Nearly terrified, I whispered: "But professor, national credit is the power to create money." Without missing a beat, he shot back: "I like the direction of your thrust."

And then there are the *spiritual* parents: All the theology I know I have learned at the feet of Reverend Richard J. Simeone, Reverend Lyn G. Brakeman, and the incredibly sharp and sensitive acolytes they have gathered around them over the years. My two sisters squared, as my wife calls them, Suor Elia a Vincentian nun and Suor Maria Teresa a Carmelite nun, my Mary and Joseph Community of Secular Discalced Carmelites, and Fr. Albert Sylvia: they strive to teach me about the ineffable.

To my co-authors and co-workers also go special thanks. I like to believe that I have learned something from each one of them. I hope they will recognize themselves in these pages.

Soon after, of course, come my editors who, needless to say, have helped me over the years entirely out of their own goodwill. Here they are: Joan M. Gorga, my wife, Jonathan F. Gorga, my son, David S. Wise, Peter N. Anastas, Janis D. Stelluto, Robert J. Madruga, Esq., my editor-in-chief in matters legal, and Rabbi Myron S. Geller, my editor-in-chief in matters religious.

Franco Modigliani, Meyer L. Burstein, Alan Reynolds, Harry G. Johnson, William J. Baumol, Lawrence H. Summers, Michael E. Brady, Roger H. Gordon, Mark Perlman, Augusto Graziani, John K. Skank, Jeroen C.J.M. van den Bergh, Kevin P. Gallagher, William J. Toth, Otto Eckstein, Wilfred Wolfsma, Steven J. Medema, Frank L. Cooper, Rosanna Marini, John J. Neuhauser, Steve H. Hanke, Michele Boldrin, John C. Médaille, John C. Rao, Stephen M. Krason, Joseph A. Varacalli, Robert Fastggi, Howard Zinn, Robert F. Drinan, Irving Kristol, Michael J. Naughton, Rudy Oswald, Gordon Richards, Buckminster Fuller, Charles T. Wood, Steve Kurtz, Hadi Madjid, Louis J. Ronsivalli, Teresa Arnold, Rabbi Myron Geller, Rev. Thomas J. Marti, Rev. Cassian J. Yuhaus have been the readers of at least one of my papers. To them go my deepest expressions of gratitude for their words of encouragement, when most needed. Without them I might have lacked the stamina to continue in my research.

Whenever proffered, I wish I could direct accolades to them, my intellectual and spiritual parents, co-authors, co-workers, editors, and counselors: Donald Young, Solomon Sandler, Marc Sandler, and Robert

Madruga in legal matters; John Chamberlain in business matters; Howard Frisch in matters of accounting; William R. Collier Jr. in political and religious matters; Walter Johnson in matters of engineering, Joy Chamberlain in human affairs; and Joan M. Gorga in common sense. And how to give thanks to Howard M. Frisch? He started as a landlord, soon became the accountant and continuing adviser to the programs sponsored by the Gloucester Community Development Corporation, and ultimately grew into a mentor. To him is due the link between the Gloucester Interdependence Fund and the New Markets Tax Credit (NMTC) program.

John D. Atwood and L. Denton Crews must have had faith in me at first sight. They hired me without prior experience. And they allowed me to plunge into the mystic worlds of urban planning and community development. The money they paid was not too much; but the intellectual and moral rewards could have not been higher.

Every year at Action Inc., the local agency entrusted with the waging of the war on poverty, I would offer the option of my resignation as Director of the Planning and Economic Development Program. Every year, for five years, they voted to rehire me. Names and characters who are indelibly incised in my consciousness are Enzo Giambanco, Mary Baptiste, Joseph Sheehan, Katherine Brackett, Adam Molinski, and Doris Bayliss. And how can I ever thank Rosalie (Lee) Liquori, my secretary? She was my guide in the mysterious field of Gloucester's local mores.

I might have preached about the need for a Gloucester Fishermen's Wives Association forever (an idea that I got from New Bedford). Without Lena Novello, Mary Ann Moceri, Margaret Favazza, Geri Lovasco, Josie Diliberti, Peggy Sibly, and my assistant Grace Moceri, together with Peter Parsons, this organization would have not come to life.

Behind these and many other indomitable such women there were strong men, both fishermen and fish processors, who consistently exposed themselves to criticism and even possible retaliation whenever I have called for a new approach to solve the problems of the fishing industry during the last forty years. To them my deepest heartfelt thanks of all. Yet to name them is too painful for me and might be too painful for them. All attempts have proven fruitless. Just as to raise a child it takes a village, to solve the problems of the fishing industry takes a whole city.

Although I conceived of the possibility for Action Inc. to take over the collapsed public transportation program on Cape Ann, today's CATA, it was Lionel Klinow who, assisted by Michael Tysver and David Rome, made of it a business success.

With Jo-Ann Castano, Dean H. Harrison, Michele Miller, Susan Erony, Sara Young, Linda Brayton, Lara Lepionka, Annie Melanson, Marty Morgan, Beverly Palmacci, David Benjamin, Paul Cary Goldberg, Scott Harlan, Shep Abbott, Geoffrey H. Richon, Judith Hoglander, Trudy Allen, Carol Amore, Pat Lowry Collins, Jeffrey Schiffman, Val Babson, Mary John Boylan, Ruth Brown, Joy Day Buell, Ruth Mordecai, Heidi Connors, Stan Franzeen, Ellen Gabin, Ellen Leahman, Anna Comolli, Dana Salvo, Jay McLauchlan, Robin J. Hubbard, Sara Stotzer, Jan Bell, Ian McColl, Ann Baylies, Gordon Goetemann, Judith Goetemann, John Orlando, Elizabeth Stacy, Lucille LePage, Richard Earle, Robert Burke, A. Timothy Ewald, Susan White-Shaffer, Veronica Morgan, Martha Oaks, Tom Thurman, Donna O'Sullivan, Marty Krugman, Baraka Berger, Rob & Lori Bradshaw, Nan Cobbey, Alice & Marty Cohen, Krista Cowan, Beth Delforge, Steve Douglas, Patty Dugan, Donald Dunn, Timothy Ewald, Ann Fisk, Lois Gaudette, James Hand, Jeremy Huessi, Jim McDonald, Ethel McDonald, Terry Gallo, Joe & Maggie Rosa, Roz Smith, Joan Swigart, Ed Price, Ethel Price, Rob Amory, Therese Perreault, Deena Prestergard, Jeff Worthley, Katherine Prum, Kathleen Valentine, Henry Ferrini, Christine Lundberg, Joanne Schreiber, Suzanne Silveira, Joan Fowler Smith, Kate Bodin, Harriet Webster, Judy Cox, and many others, I am proud to bask in the glory that surrounds the nearly daily successes of the Society for the Encouragement of the Arts (seARTS), the Gloucester Committee for the Arts, and the Gloucester Maritime Heritage Center. It all started with a community meeting called to order by John "Gus" Foote, the city councilor for my ward, and the then council president Abdullah Khambaty.

For a whole set of rich variegated reasons, thanks go to our former Mayor Bruce Tobey, his community development officer, Dean Harrison, Gracelaw Simmons and the officers of the Sailors' Snug Harbor Foundation of Boston.

How to thank the unrewarded all-volunteer members of the Board of Directors of the Gloucester Community Development Corporation: R. Scott Memhard, president, Gaspar J. Lafata, vice-president, Susan B. Field, treasurer, and former member Joseph Sinagra? How many hours of their lives have they contributed to a cause whose long-term effects might only be recognized in the distant future? Ed Lima helped me set up the program. The professional letterhead for the Gloucester CDC was designed by Giovanna Sanfilippo.

How to thank the all-volunteer Board of Directors of the Gloucester Interdependence Fund? How to thank David L. Marsh, President; Dean W. Harrison, Treasurer; Robert J. Madruga, Clerk; Alan Hagstrom, Director; Robert M. Heineman, Director? For the Gloucester Interdependence Fund, deepest expressions of gratitude also go to the following Gloucester bankers: David Sidon, Peter Anderson, David Marsh, John Pettazzoni, and Harold Rogers. They could have easily dismissed the idea for this fund; instead, they spent much time individually with me and then as a group to vet this program into a feasible proposition.

Franco Modigliani, a Nobel Laureate in economics at MIT, listened to me about the need for Gloucester to have a system dynamics study of the fishing industry; he consulted with Professor Robert Solow, another MIT Nobel Laureate in economics; Professor Solow called me and asked a few pointed questions about the Functional Integration of Management Tasks, and after a few words of explanation he cut me short by saying "I understand, I understand" and went to talk with Dean Smalensee; Dean Smalensee went to talk to Professor Kenneth Morse; Professor Morse invited me to participate in one of their yearly "fairs" where beggars like me make presentations to his students; three of his doctoral candidates — Peter Otto, Sanghyun Lee, and Jeroen Struben — eventually listened to me and decided to accept the challenge; under the guidance of Professor Jim Hines, they prepared the system dynamics analysis of the Gloucester fishing industry that is referenced throughout the following essays. This is how Gloucester acquired a system dynamic study of the fishing industry at no charge, whose value is going to be extracted by the entrepreneur who is going to transform it into a business management plan for the future Gloucester Fish Inc.

A few more people who participated in the making of this study have to be acknowledged here: Seth W. Muriph, Paul O. Perry, Satayan Mahajan, Aliki K. Collins, Jacob Friis, Vivian Fung, Gong Ke Shen, but especially Robert L. Sampson, Captain Joseph Sinagra, Dr. Damon Cummings, Dr. William J. Overholtz, and Dr. Stephen Kelleher. They contributed hard data for the study.

And then I must point out that the roots of this study are deeper still. They go all the way back to my work at Action Inc. in the 60s, when assistance was graciously granted by Professor John K. Shank of the Harvard Business School as well as by Jack Suomela and Forbes Little of MIT Draper Laboratory. Ultimately, it fell upon the broad shoulders of Joseph

G. Wohl of Mitre Corp. to produce a first computer simulation of the New England Fisheries. Damon Cummings, a former professor of hydrodynamics and control theory at MIT, studied this work and said: "This city ought to give a medal to Joe Wohl."

These are some of the political and civic leaders who, listening to one, two or more hour-long presentations of the Program of Urban Restoration (PUR) described in the following pages, have subtly contributed to its formation; whenever their contribution has been substantial, it is more properly acknowledged in the appropriate place: meetings with Augusto Grace and Joan Wasser Gish at the office of Sen. John Kerry, Carolyn Stewart and Gary Barrett at the office of US Rep. John F. Tierney, State Sen. Bruce Tarr, State Rep. Anthony Verga, former Mayor and current Council President Bruce Tobey, former Mayor John Bell, Mayor Carolyn Kirk, city councilors Ab Kambathy and John "Gus" Foote, and Sefatia Romeo, Greg Ketchen, Michael D. Rubin, Louis Linquata, Eliot Jacobson, David Sidon, Peter Anderson, David Marsh, John Pettazzoni, Harold Rogers, Leo E. Bergeron, Bob Gillis, Nina Calomo, Elizabeth Bish, Janice Shea, Austin Connors, Bill Stride, Steve Parkes, Sandy Parco, Pat Legallo, Dave Ellenton, Steve Connolly, Tom Brancaleone, Geoffrey Richon, Kirk Noyes, Robert Burke, Lenny Linquata, Vito Calomo, Peter Sellew, Helen Garland, Joseph Garland, Bill Chapin, Burt Tinker, Vicky Lindsay, Harriet Webster, Robert Sampson, Frank Rose, Marc Sandler, Patricia Kurkul, Kurt Wilhelm, Mark Murray-Brown, Christopher Martin, Bill Strides, Ann Banks, Eliot Jacobson, Jerry Oppenheimer, Bob Gillis, Nina Calomo, Susan Erony, Jay Jaroslav, Janice Shea, Niaz Dorry, Dr. Geeta Pradhan, Priscilla Books, Robin Hubbard, Nancy Goodman, Mike Costello, Fitz Lufkin, David McArdle, Michael Linquata, Carolyn O'Connor, JoAnn Castano, Mark Konecki, David Wise, Dr. Edward Moscovitch, Prof. Henry McCarl, John Orlando, Chief James Marr, Angela Sanfilippo, David Bergeron, David Lincoln, Jeanne Gallo, Kirk Noyes, Janis Stelluto, Michael Rubin, Rev. Wendy Fitting, Rev. Richard J. Simeone, Rev. Lyn G. Brakeman, Fr. Timothy Harrison, Damon Cummings, Valerie Nelson, Carlo Barbara, David Porper, Mac Bell, Bob Whitmarsh, John Sparks, Josh Brackett, John Feener. Now might be the time, my careful listeners, for you to talk to each other.

Nancy Schwoyer and I, and nearly every other social worker in town, have always treated each other at arms length: they work under press to produce immediate result, while I tend to search for permanent long term solutions. The death of Janis Stelluto revealed and sealed the affection that

Nancy and I have grown for each other over the years. Our fingers were locked in tender embrace as we stepped out of the Unitarian Universalist Church on Middle Street the day of Janis' funeral. Silently in that way we paid respect to each other's work and tacitly we prayed for the day in which we can march to the beat of a unified voice to vanquish problems to whose solution we have dedicated our lives.

Deep thanks go to all my brothers and sisters at the St. Vincent de Paul Society attached to the defunct Saint Peter's church for allowing me an up close and personal look into the poverty in Gloucester.

Sinnika Nogelo, the Chief-in-Chief (capo di tutti i capi) of the public programming at the various legal persona of the local cable Channel 12, has over the years been very generous in granting me access to her medium via interviews conducted by Patricia Brady, Jon Ronan, and a series of workshops presented at the Sawyer Free Library in Gloucester in collaboration with many local and national experts in a variety of disciplines during the months of May, June, and July of 2003 on "The Economics and the Environment of Cape Ann and its Future."

David Wise and I wish to thank Kathe German, Jonathan Gorga, Carson AfKlinteberg, and Aaron LeBow for helping us collect signatures and above all we wish to warmly, deeply thank those — some illustrious, all brave — who, both from Cape Ann and elsewhere, signed the petition. Without their active participation, obviously, this opportunity for a wide public discussion of the possibilities awaiting Gloucester might have never found a proper forum for expression. Their 425 names are duly recorded at Gloucester City Hall.

Robert D. Whynott, Jeremy Gillis, and the entire staff of the efficient City Clerk's office patiently sifted through the signatures of the petition and carefully shepherded it so that it eventually overcame all the perils of a difficult bureaucratic journey. Where would we be without valiant administrators?

Thanks, of course, go to Mayor Carolyn A. Kirk, City Council President Bruce Tobey, Vice President Sefatia A. Romeo, and all members of the City Council, namely Joseph Ciolino, Sharon George, Jason Grow, John "Gus" Foote, Steve Curcuru, Jackie Hardy, and Philip Devlin for allowing the official presentation of our petition to be made.

To all poets, artists, and economists on Cape Ann thanks for giving that extra kick to my life and my work. By one of my rough calculations, there are more economists per square inch here on Cape Ann than anywhere else in the world.

To all residents of Gloucester, past, present, and hopefully future, my most sincere thanks. They seem to have consistently appreciated my ideas and they have often expressed private and public words of encouragement for my efforts. They alone, in the end, have made my work possible.

Technical expressions of thankfulness go to various editors of the *Gloucester Daily Times,* of scholarly journals, Robin Hubbard, Chad Konecky and Sheila Ferrini for granting permission to reprint articles included in this collection.

I hope those I have not acknowledged will not feel slighted. I did not neglect them on purpose. I hope they will think they are too deep in my heart and my consciousness to come to the fore.

While errors are mine, whatever glimpses of enlightenment are contained in these pages are due to my spiritual counselors whom I daily invoke: St. Therese of Lisieux, who many years ago gave me a white marble rose; St. Anthony, who searches for the right persons and subjects for me to meet; St. Thomas Aquinas, for infusing intellectual confidence in me; St. Jude, for helping me in my impossible causes; St. Peter, for being the patron saint of the fishermen; St. Paul, for being the first Somist; St. Elizabeth of the Trinity, for teaching me that God is indeed triune; St. Joseph, for not scolding me for lassitude in my work; St. Ann, for writing this book for me; St. Elijah, for teaching me that God is indeed alive; St. Michael, for fighting against all sorts of evil for me; and my Madonna, for her prayers to the Holy Spirit to enlighten me and all those who are in touch with me.

✳ ✳ ✳

This version 1.1 is due to a most careful reading by
Louis J. Ronsivalli, Christian Lehmann, and Jonathan F. Gorga.

PART ONE

Articles Published
in the *Gloucester Daily Times*

It takes a village to raise a child.
Senator Hillary Clinton

Wednesday, February 29, 1984

MY VIEW

To become a Somist

by Carmine Gorga

My self.
My work.
My family.
My community.
My country (and my "old" Country).
The planet Earth.
The universe.

These are the factors that, in their interactions, shape my existence. The closer in harmony I strive to be with all of them, the closer I feel to God's peace; as that harmony diminishes, the heavier the burdens of life weigh.

Left in a "natural" state, those factors do behave harmoniously. Just think about it. To borrow Carl Sagan's phrase, there are "billions and billions of stars in the universe," and from what we truly know about them we must conclude that on the whole they behave harmoniously.

Why can't approximately 5 billion human beings rotate around each other equally harmoniously? We are given many reasons, but upon careful consideration they turn out to be rationalizations. We are told that our planet is too small to sustain 5 billion souls. And yet, if you start from Gloucester and go beyond Marlboro, Mass., you are in almost pristine wilderness — until you reach the Chicago cluster and, after that, the San Francisco-Los Angeles strip. You see this reality clearly if you fly over this country, and nearly every other country in the world.

We are told that "there is not much room at the top," and we abstain from observing how many tree tops there are and how many we do destroy in our passage. Nor do we realize that only a handful of people really want to be at the top; and that the healthy ones want to be there only for a limited amount of time.

We are told that we are made to struggle "to get there." And yet when we do struggle to get there, we do not really enjoy the journey; and if we reach our appointed destination we often find, a' la Gertrude Stein, that "there is no there there."

People who issue these and many other rationalizations simply confuse the struggle to gain power over people, a very unworthy cause, with the struggle to gain control over oneself. This is hard work and there are so few who excel! This is the unbounded life worth living on this beautiful and bountiful planet!

Yet, rationalizations are easy to formulate and to accept. Gullible people who struggle to gain power over people — just like sea gulls — are vociferous, if not always a majority. As the deception of their power catches up to them, they become violent. When the tools at their disposal were relatively few and simple, the damage they could do was comparatively small. Today, the situation has changed so drastically that they can shear and shatter the harmony of the whole world.

Of the thousand little fissures they cause, nothing is more dangerous than their effect upon economic policies and the arms race. It is on these two issues, then, that we should concentrate our efforts.

The road ahead is tortuous, but the hope must grow that somehow we are going to make it. In the final analysis, all it takes is to change those institutions that we know hinder us from becoming SOMISTS: social men and women, civilized persons who strive to acquire control over themselves and are eventually rewarded by becoming creative rather than destructive.

To be a Somist, one must work to fuse the rights of the individual person with the rights of society — namely, other people.

Today, to be a Somist, one must be convinced that the greatest error of contemporary thought is the belief that the dictates of either Individualism or Collectivism are exclusively true and valid and helpful to human beings. Instead, by themselves both ideologies are only half-right because the individual person cannot exist without society and society does not exist without the individual person. Indeed, they are so partially right that they end up being completely wrong: one leads to Babbitt, the other to Big Brother.

To be a Somist, one does not require force to compel people to live harmoniously among themselves and with their environment. One only requires hard thinking and firm action to remove the obstacles, or at least lower the barriers, which, on the mistaken notion that they help us and our friends, we so often put

> BETWEEN
> Our selves
> AND
> Our work
> Our family
> Our community
> Our Country (and other countries)
> Our planet
> Our universe.

Carmine Gorga lives with his wife Joan, a health planner, on Middle Street, "over the shop," from where since 1974 he has run his private consulting firm, Polis-tics Inc.

Thursday, May 3, 1984

MY VIEW

Redefine Power, or Perish - 1

by Carmine Gorga

Editor's note: Carmine Gorga's column this month will be run in two parts. Part 2 will appear tomorrow.

"Do you trust the Russians?"

This is the question, if you are an American. But, if you are a Russian, the question is: "Do you trust the Americans

Ladies and Gentlemen, the answer in unison now please.

"Of course not!"

Stolid people who do not see the irony in this situation are fast transforming it into a supreme tragedy.

We are six minutes away from extinction. With the deployment of cruise and Pershing 2 missiles in Europe, Russia has six minutes to decide whether or not any object in the sky is an enemy missile, whether or not to wait the entire amount of time left from detection to potential impact, whether or not to start immediately retaliating with nuclear weapons.

We impose these severe time constraints on a nation that, whatever the specifics of the case, used two full hours to take the wrong decision on Korean Airline Flight 7!

Dr. Kissinger! The issue is not time. Even with all the time in the world, does America always make the right decision? The issue is that nearly every step we have taken thus far in the field of arms control has only made a perverse situation worse. Evidently we cannot any longer extricate ourselves from these quick sands by facing the situation frontally. We had better approach it indirectly, by attacking the causes of the arms race. We had better think anew about the fundamentals.

Let us, for starters, think very clearly and then act very firmly in regard to power. We still believe that power means "You do what I tell you to do." This is a childish and self-deceiving conception that has consistently bought us trouble.

The two "Superpowers" have too much fear of each other to really apply this conception of power in their mutual relations. They show — each other — who is "the boss" only in their relations with small neighbors and allies! Ironic isn't it?

Mother Russia certainly has shown her "power" in relation to East Germany and Hungary and Czechoslovakia and now Poland and Afghanistan. How is she going to extricate herself from those flash points is something that ought not to concern us directly. Let us rather be concerned with the flash points in which Uncle Sam is at present entangled. These certainly are Europe, the Middle East and Central America. These are situations in which all too often America starts with the illusion of being "in charge," eventually discovers that she is being manipulated by her own allies, and ends up blaming Russia for her troubles. Ironic isn't it?

Only if we identify the correct long term policy toward these and other trouble spots in the world, can we hope to find eminently rational and feasible short term solutions to apparently intractable problems. Some key propositions then begin to emerge: first, stop defending Europe (and Japan); second, stop protecting Israel (or any other nation) whether right or wrong; third, stop imposing democracy on Latin American countries (and other areas of the globe). Remember that, while alliances are transient, the struggle for justice, prosperity and peace everywhere is permanent.

These are necessarily long term solutions, because disengagement from boisterous — if not imperial — commitments of the past will have to take time and great care: risks to us and to other people in possibly conveying the wrong impression must be avoided. It must be made clear that there is lots of strength — moral, economic, and even military strength — with us.

These are long term solutions especially because the rationale for these policies has to become absolutely firm for us and for others as well. People also have to feel comfortable with the many implications of these policies. This is indeed a new — sane and secure — world that we will have to create.

Carmine Gorga lives with his wife Joan, a health planner, on Middle Street, "over the shop," from where since 1974 he has run his private consulting firm, Polis-tics Inc.

Friday, May 4, 1984

MY VIEW

Redefine Power, or Perish - 2

by Carmine Gorga

Editor's note: Carmine Gorga's column is printed in two parts this month. Part 1 appeared yesterday.

How do we create a new — sane and secure — world?

Ultimately, the rationalizations underpinning existing approaches have to be done away with. Strategically, it is hoped that, if the missiles start flying, the American soil will be spared. Entanglements abroad, in this view, represent a first line of defense for America. No one really knows about the future, but — contrary to conventional wisdom — it seems inappropriate to think that a nuclear war will be fought on soil other than the Russian and American one, on a first pass.

Historically, size and arms have had nothing to do with international peace and respect: see the Canadian border, unguarded militarily yet traditionally one of the most peaceful on earth; see San Marino, one of the smallest and yet one of the most independent countries on earth; see Switzerland for a combination of both characteristics.

Commercially, the specter is advanced that, should American wings of war not be spread abroad, markets will disappear. Not true. Pure commercial interests are always mutual. Does not Russia come to the United States to buy, not oil or other raw materials, but a much more essential product, namely wheat?

Psychologically, the notion "Alliances are forever; enemies are forever" is romantic and contrary to reality. The reality is fluid; alliances are floating; enemies are temporary and partial — not total.

A fifth and ultimate rationalization often advanced is that Russia might impose "political blackmail" on those who should fall behind in the arms race. Whatever this expression is supposed to mean, it reveals that the most important lessons from the war in Vietnam have not been learned yet; first, not even the threat of nuclear extinction is capable of bending the will of a determined people; second, it is the will of the people and not arms that constitute the ultimate defense of a country.

But, after rejecting imperialism, do the suggested policies imply isolationism? Not at all. They herald a conception that can succinctly be expressed only with a new word: Earthism. Earthism, or any other such word, implies that the earth belongs to the people who live on it. Theirs are the resources as well as the responsibility of defense from foreign encroachment.

Indeed, provided that the defense of American values is truly at stake, the level of involvement abroad might even increase, although it can never be undertaken unilaterally and the tools for this defense are likely to be completely different from the military ones. In fact, the first line of defense of these values is at home, for their defense abroad to be credible; and it requires passage to a next stage, still a brutish but clearly superior one, in our conception of power: "I do what I want to do." Americans, in other words, have to decide what do they really want — and not what either friends or foes want them to do. Do they want to remain a democracy or become an empire? Do they want to fight Communism or do they want to fight injustice? Do they want to be peaceful or a warmonger?

Beyond this stage, we might eventually get to the point of defining power as "we do together what we both want to do." This is the highest expression of political power. This is civilized power. This is Somist power. This is the only form of power that holds out a glimmer of hope in today's perilous world, because it alone creates mutual trust.

Reaching this stage is not a dream, nor does its achievement conceivably lie that far ahead in the future. Is not Rev. Jesse Jackson using these principles in his call for a "trialogue" in the Middle East? Is not Sen. Gary Hart using these principles in his call for the Soviet Union and the United States to join in a "world crusade" to end hunger among the children of the world? These are glimmers of hope that make one cry out, a la Yogi Berra, we are not doomed until we are doomed.

Ultimately, however, all political power must rest on the solid foundation of personal power — power over oneself. Why? Because, no matter how well intentioned and civilized the parties are, frictions do arise when working with others. The constant temptation to avoid is the conceit that no one is as perfect as we are.

Monday, April 25, 1988

MY VIEW

A Grand Old Dame is Gone

by *Carmine Gorga*

A Grand Old Dame of Gloucester, Mary Baptiste, passed away two years ago. I think the community feels a loss. I know, I do; especially now that she would have been a magnificent *auntie* for our Jonathan.

Mary would frequently make one of her dart visits to our home, tell the latest story, get a glass of water, and never overstay her welcome. But when necessary and possible we also took trips together to Boston. She had gradually become a part of our family.

As one of the first women graduates on Cape Ann, and as a member of the Portuguese community, she obviously had an intense and interesting private life. She was a friend to many — especially to the children in her neighborhood. Above all, she was a poet and a writer. Only a small portion of her literary output was ever published.

Interesting as her private life was, it is the *public* Mary I would like to celebrate, the Mary who taught me and all those who wanted to listen quite a few important lessons. When there was a conflict between her private selfish needs and those of the community, she always served the community. She might have preferred playing bridge or going to the movies. In a society in which most people shun personal responsibility, however, she knew the value of group decisions. She was always ready to join a group that needed her assistance, provided it pursued a cause that was worthy to her. In fact, it is as a board member of the Planning Development Program at Action Inc. that I first met her 20 years ago.

Most important of all, she taught me about the meaning of wealth — both private and public wealth. Many people would have considered her *poor*. She never felt poor. She never was poor. She even fell in love with the idea of a ghost who would come to her rescue whenever she was in financial distress. In truth, the ghost was Mr. Enough. She discovered the importance of living within the limits imposed by reality. She controlled her needs; so whatever she had was enough. And that is indeed the secret of private wealth*. Otherwise, no matter what one has, it is never enough**. One is always poor. One is always in need for more.

But it is on the issue of public wealth that her sense of civilization was most refined. Once she triumphantly announced to the readers of the Gloucester Daily Times that she *owned* the Boulevard. That letter to the editor penetrated deep into my consciousness. It opened new vistas on the meaning of public wealth as well as on interpersonal relationships. Before that, public wealth for me was owned by an invisible institution, The Public. And a potentially inimical institution at that. Who would ever mix with The Public? But, no. Mary taught me that the reality is altogether different. If she owned the Boulevard, it meant that I owned it too. And that I could use and enjoy it too. As an owner, she certainly used and enjoyed that splendid piece of property almost to the end of her life.

I am neither a literary critic nor a poet. So I am unable to pass any judgment on the merit of Mary's work. Fortunately, thanks to the efforts of Mr. David S. Wise, Mary's papers have been preserved and are available for consultation from the Cape Ann Historical Association. Included there is also a short biography of Mary written by her sister, Mrs. Laura Mitchell. I should think that one can learn much from Mary's work. I have read a very little bit of it, and I have liked it a lot.

Carmine Gorga is president of Polis-tics Inc., a community development consulting organization in Gloucester.

* Sentence deleted in published version.
** Sentence deleted in published version.

Friday, October 2, 1998

SYMPOSIUM

Want No Part of Exploiting a Tragedy

Guest column
Carmine Gorga

Here we go again. We were able to withstand one assault of the "Titanic." Will we survive the current one in videotape form?*

My son, who is 11, a few others and I have had no desire to see "Titanic." After the Academy awarded it so many Oscars, we still refused to see it. What is wrong with us?

The amazing thing is not so much that we should refuse to see the movie, but that we should feel under pressure to justify our position. I cannot speak for anyone else, of course, but let me speak for myself. At first, it was just a generalized feeling. Being a cautious man, my mind is very slow to move; and when my feelings enter into the picture, my mind becomes even slower. Without putting things on paper, I had no idea what it was all about.

What were my initial feelings? At first, I thought it was a question of it being "just a movie." But then people began to ask me questions and automatically they told me "everything" about the movie. So my hidden feelings began to well up. I began to realize that it would be very hard for me to get excited about another love story on the celluloid screen. In the back of my mind, I guess, I began to focus on the tragedy of the Titanic. I even read something about the ship's image as The Perfect Machine, The Unsinkable Ship. Aha! Vanity of vanities.

The Tragedy of the Titanic. That was real. And I began to associate it with the series of mistaken, when not disastrous, applications of technology through the years. And my heart become harder and harder against the movie. Queried, directly, why did I not want to see it, I exploded: "Because it is exploitative. It uses a love story to make us wallow in a horrible tragedy. It steals our money and, more precious of all, our time." There.

The question is: Why do we tend to focus so fondly on human tragedies? Why do we tend to wallow in human misery? Certainly the people who help us focus on these stories do it because they want to run all the way to the bank with our money. But is there more? Is it that these people also want to control us?

They do sell addictive material. We see it every day. The more horrible details they give us, the more horrible details they feel they have to give us — otherwise they fear they will not hold our attention.

But at the core of the exploitation there is this reality: There is us. Why do we read those stories? It seems to me that we like horrible stories because they offer us a subtle exultation of our own ways. No matter how bad do I behave today, it is enough for me to read the daily news to say to myself: "I am not as bad as that person, after all."

Thus escapism pulls us more and more into the abyss of our own wickedness.

I leave that issue there, possibly to pick it up on some other occasion. If you try to catch a falling stone, you only get a bump on the head. I need to fortify myself, I need to make some serious preparations before I can touch that issue in a serious way.

The question to consider is this: How do the people who sell those stories justify their positions to themselves? It would be naïve — and ultimately very ineffective — to simply believe that they are exploitative and they are conscious about their exploitative acts. No. I firmly believe that they are in a daze. I believe that they live in a cocoon larger than themselves, and it is this cocoon that lets them sleep rather peacefully at night.

Proofs of the validity of this position have been exploding one right after the other. James Cameron, accepting his Best Director award, yelled: "I'm king of the world!" Yes, Sire.

True to form, moments later, accepting the Oscar for Best Picture, Mr. Cameron ordered us to observe "a few seconds of silence" in remembrance of the fifteen hundred people lost in the tragedy of the Titanic. Did I resent being bossed around? No. I fell for it at a deeper level than you might think. "There," I said, "there his soul is coming through after all. He knows precisely what he has done. He has exploited a human tragedy."

But he did not know what he was doing. The final proof rang as clear as a bell. How did he come out of those few seconds? What did he suggest that we do? Mr. Cameron spurred us to "party till dawn." A horrifying non-sequitur?

Hardly. He was coming from a different position than most people, and he lectured us about it. The tragedy of the Titanic, he preached, urges us to enjoy the moment. There you have it. There is the cocoon of the culture that envelops us all. The cult of "the pursuit of happiness."

I will not stop at Jefferson, the Father of our country who changed Locke's formula concerning the right to "life, liberty, and property," by erasing the word property and substituting it with the pursuit of happiness. No. I need to go farther back in history to Lorenzo Il Magnifico, the Florentine leader who is one of the Fathers of our modern culture. He wrote a madrigal saying, in part: "Chi vuol esser lieto sia, del doman non c'é certezza (Who wants to be happy, let him be happy. There is no certainty in tomorrow.)"

Mr. Cameron was not original after all.

What is wrong with the pursuit of happiness? Is this not one of our inalienable rights? Am I trying to be a spoil sport, or worse, am I attempting to destroy the foundation of such an inalienable right?

None of this at all. Gentle reader, do not entertain such dark suspicions for a moment longer. While I am a pleasure seeking machine second to none, perhaps, I am also in relentless pursuit of the truth. I believe that our culture is misguiding us by looking at only half of the truth. "Tomorrow is not certain" is a half truth. To get to the whole truth, one must go to the Shakers. Remember their motto? Their motto is: "Live as if you were to die today — or if you were to live a thousand years."

That is the whole truth.

And that is a fundamental truth. It is a truth that made the Shakers enrich our culture with their unique heritage of beauty and efficiency: Shaker music and Shaker songs, Shaker furniture and Shaker architecture, Shaker machinery. To imbibe Shaker culture is to experience deep pleasure indeed.

Living as if there were no tomorrow, we have been mostly leaving a trail of tragedies in our wake: from the Religious Wars to the genocidal colonization of primitive cultures, from Marie-Antoinette and the French Revolution to Hitler and Stalin, from obliteration of the "other" who might become a — real or imaginary — obstacle to the pursuit of our happiness to the destruction of ourselves in the pursuit of immediate gratification achieved through drugs and addictions.

I am very proud of my son, Jonathan. I am very thankful for the D.A.R.E. program that is carried out by police officers in our school system.

He took the challenge. No assurance about the future, as I say to all those who want to hear, but for now Jonathan has so internalized the message of the need to resist peer pressure in order to ward off badness that he has not only written about it in an award-winning essay. Most important of all, he has internalized the lesson by resisting peer pressure — and, lately, he tells me, even his own inner temptation — to see "Titanic." My hat's off to you, Jonathan!

Carmine Gorga is president of Polis-tics, Inc., a community development firm that can be sighted at www.polis-tics.com.

*Changed in the published form to "Will we survive the next one?"

Wednesday, May 29, 1996

MY VIEW

Just Compensation

by Carmine Gorga

There are those who are concerned that in order to curb the excesses of exorbitant executive pay one must have government intervention. This is an expression of the poverty of the current political discourse, according to which one is supposed to be either a rugged individualist or a rabid socialist. Let me try to enrich the discourse by using a new word.

There are not two forms of justice, and two methods of achieving it, but three.

Winner take-all-justice is the first. Ultimately based on brute force of the rugged individual, this form of justice eventually leads to a Dickensian world of abject poverty and moral squalor.

The second is fiat-by-government justice. Ultimately based on brute force-by-association of rogue individuals, it eventually leads to horrors of the Gulag Archipelago.

The third form of justice is based on analysis, hard decisions, and civilized discourse. I like to call it Somist justice.

Some of the details of Somist justice are these. Somist justice starts from an ideal of justice. Not abstract justice. But concrete, perfectible justice. Justice interpreted as the common good. Justice as determined by the Thou and the I. Not by the government, nor by the I or the Thou alone; but by the I and the Thou together.

And since the I and Thou are not always equal, in today's world Somist justice fully recognizes the need for labor unions — labor unions, it adds, without their traditional excesses, furthermore, labor unions that work toward the recognition of the importance for workers to accept the rewards as well as the risks of ownership rather than shortsighted, highest possible compensation for their labors.

What do the I and the Thou who are in fair balance of forces do? They engage in conversation. They discover that $500 million compensation for

Mr. Milkin does not come from the sky. It comes from wages that are below the living standard for thousands of workers.

Nor should this be the only concern at the heart of their discussion. There should also be concern for invention, innovation, and the future. How many R&D projects are being scrapped because of the downward pressure applied by tapping into the wishing well of stratospheric executive compensation?

As it can be seen, the discussion will concern itself with very concrete alternatives. At the heart for the discussion, however, one finds that the issue is one of moral fiber. When there are so many vital unmet needs, no executive should have the chutzpah to ask for exorbitant compensation; and no corporate board of directors should indulge in complacency and grant such a compensation.

There is also an issue of self-interest. The gap created by lack of jobs, the gap created by wages below the living standard will not be filled exclusively by human sufferance. It will also be filled by direct or indirect contributions by the majority of us. So we have a stake in the decisions of corporate boards. So we have the economic right to ask corporate boards to analyze all the consequences of their actions. Today, they live in splendid, but dangerous isolation.

Somist justice recognizes this broad reality and assumes that when people meet in a condition of fair parity* they discover something that is quite exhilarating. They discover what is just. And, when they see it, they will want to be just. There is no prodding them; and no stopping them. There is no force, no government intervention in letting the parties do what is right.

Unrestrained executive compensation is an irresponsible flight of the imagination. It is a flight from reality. Moral restraint is a call to each one of us.

Dr. Gorga is a Gloucester resident. He is president of Polis-tics Inc. He believes he has been blessed with the opportunity to work toward the creation of a civilized world.

*This word was published as "poverty".

Tuesday, November 26, 1996

MY VIEW

In Defense of Alma Mater

by Carmine Gorga

Note: This is a Mr. Gorga's account of a conversation he (CG) had with his Alma Mater (AM). the University of Naples.

AM: Aren't you going to defend me?

CG: I don't have time for that sort of thing. That was a preposterous attack. Am I supposed to be a socialist because Naples got a socialist administration years after I left the city?

AM: The attack is, not against you, but against me. I am the one who is accused of fostering socialism. You *are in situ*. Are you going to defend me?

CG: Well, I suppose you are right. But how do we go about it? Any suggestion?

AM: Just the facts, son. Just the facts.

CG: About 800 years worth of facts?

AM: Well start with the teachings of one of my earliest and dearest sons, St. Thomas Aquinas (1225-1274). This is an easy case. With my Greek (Naples means New Polis) and Roman roots, in the warm splendor of the Southern sky, I taught him how to respect the truth and the past.

CG: Yes, I know. He is the one who reconciled Aristotle with the Christian tradition. He is the one who made it easy for Dante to so powerfully visualize the effects of virtues and vices.

AM: That is well known. What is not known is that St. Thomas was a staunch defender of private property. He justified the acquisition of private property on the basis of efficiency of procurement, stability of maintenance, and social order "if each one is contented with his own." This is far away from socialism. Isn't it?

CG: Yes, Mother. But with all due respect, it seems to me you are skirting two issues. One is how well understood and respected has St. Thomas's thought been even within Catholic circles. The other is the issue of the use of property. Didn't St. Thomas suggest that an individual owner of "superfluous things" ought to be "ready to communicate them to others in their need"?

AM: Yes. But you do not add that this is supposed to be a wholly voluntary decision on the part of the owner, and that the obligation is of a moral, not legal or political, character. What would you expect? What is proper? What is moral? What are riches for, if not for one's own needs and the needs of others? As to implementation, the issue is even more complex.

CG: How?

AM: People have to be free. Free to commit their own mistakes. Free to learn from their own mistakes. Only if there is liberty, there is morality.

CG: As you say, this is a complex issue. Is there any easier way to put the issues clearly?

AM: Yes, there is one fundamental way. That is if you mention the work of Giambattista Vico (1668-1744), one of my most favorite sons. Ah, if people had listened to his thought!

CG: Yes. Yes. He is the one who built his thought not only on the ideal of liberty, realism, and truth, but especially on the fact that in history one does not find linear developments. Rather history proves that we proceed by the way of loops: "Corsi e ricorsi storici" is the way he put it.

AM: If people had listened to him, people would have been immunized against thoughts brewed in the frigid mists of Northern climates. People would have been immunized against the "historical determinism" of Karl Marx as well as the linear descent into hell of Charles Darwin. No Communism, no dEvolution. [GDT changed it to Evolution.]

CG: Hard to imagine what the right set of ideas can do, one way or the other. But this is rather old history. Let me tell you of what I have read recently. A book by Robert H. Nelson has constructed a lineage from Marx and Darwin to Freud, Hitler, and Stalin.

AM: So I hear. So I hear. The lineage I, instead, want to emphasize is that from St. Thomas to Vico to Croce.

CG: Yes, of course. Benedetto Croce (1866-1952). "History is history of freedom." Did he not build his thought around this formula? Of course he did. But, once again, what you are telling me is a series of what ifs. A series of potentially different historical developments if people had listened to the teachings of your sons.

AM: Oh, no! I am not talking of past history and of ifs and buts. I am talking of vital, current, live and living history.

CG: Where, where?

AM: Right under your nose. Right in the United States. The Fathers of the United States Constitution did listen to the teachings of my people. They studied Rome, they studied Greece. They studied the Old and the New Testament. And they put it all together, just as St. Thomas had done. They studied the history of liberty, as Vico, and later Croce, did. Liberty! Liberty for all — not libertinism for the few. And they established a framework in which you all live. A res publica; not a res privata. "A republic, if you can keep it."

CG: Yes, who said that is my only hero, an individualist — if there ever was one — with a spectacular sense of community, a sense of the polis: Benjamin Franklin.

Carmine Gorga graduated from the University of Naples in 1959 with a doctorate in Political Science. He is the president of Polis-tics Inc. Since 1970 he has lived and worked on Middle Street, where — in the bosom of the Universalist Church — religious Liberty was born.

Wednesday, August 7, 2002

MY VIEW

Sketching Art's Impact on Gloucester

by Carmine Gorga

Where the arts thrive, commerce thrives — and, as eventually we will see, industry follows. The chain of events has been validated by an ongoing study conducted by Americans for the Arts and is supported by the latest insights into the field of economic development.

Conventional wisdom would have us believe just the reverse; that when industry thrives, commerce thrives and the arts follow.

Not so. A preliminary study of the economic impact of nonprofit art institutions on the local, state and national economies released by Americans for the Arts reveals that "nonprofit arts are a growth industry in the U.S." Spending by these organizations has increased from $36.8 billion in 1992 to $53.2 billion in 2000 — a 45 percent increase.

What is even more significant is that the secondary effects of these expenditures outweigh the direct expenditures. Event-related spending by audiences amounted to $80.8 billion in the year 2000. It was estimated that attendees at such events spend an average of $22.87 above the cost of attendance. This is the first time that this type of information has been gathered.

Needless to say, nonprofit arts organizations are only a fraction of the total arts and entertainment industry. What is excluded is the panoply of individual artists, arts, and craft organizations that are organized for profit — whether they make a profit or not.

U.S. Rep. Louise M. Slaughter, who chairs the Congressional Arts Caucus, has made this persuasive point as quoted in a pamphlet recently released with the study by Americans for the Arts: "What's good for the arts is good for the economy. The mayors of cities with strong economies tell us that the arts have helped their communities thrive." It takes only a glance to see the crowds in downtown districts where the arts are alive.

It is for this benefit that the Gloucester Community Development Corporation, in collaboration with SEArts, a coalition of local cultural institutions, has become a partner in the national study conducted by Americans for the Arts. Our participation calls for sending out survey forms to all nonprofit arts organizations in Gloucester and then collecting 750 responses from attendees at cultural events in order to gather audience expenditure data. The survey packets were sent out last year, and again this year to those organizations that have not filled out the forms yet. We hope to obtain a fair and representative participation.

Americans for the Arts is a national organization with offices in New York and Washington, D.C. It is the leading nonprofit organization for advancing the arts in America, with a 40-year record of objective research in its field. It is "dedicated to representing and serving local communities and creating opportunities for every American to participate in and appreciate all forms of the arts."

In 1994, it produced a benchmark study entitled "Jobs, Arts and the Economy." This study was a powerful tool that contributed to preserving the National Endowment for the Arts, through which many arts institutions are kept afloat. The title of the ongoing study is "Arts and Economic Prosperity."

Many of you have already seen people with clipboards asking questions at local cultural performances; you will see a few more such questionnaires carried around in the next few months. Please, fill out this two-page simple survey. The survey solicits the input of residents as well as tourists and visitors from other towns.

When our portion of the study is completed, we will receive a detailed analysis of the importance of the arts to the Gloucester economy. We can then compare our position in relation to other cities and towns in the United States and gather a better appreciation for the impact of the arts on our economy. Gloucester, after all, is the home of the oldest arts association in the country, the North Shore Arts Association. As we see it, the very participation in this study is a way of gaining a strong tool for making the case for the arts and for keeping the name of Gloucester and its artists in front of a national audience.

The benefits of commerce are only one set of benefits reaped by the community when the arts thrive. The most important and everlasting is the benefit that befalls the practitioners of the arts. Most often, artists are the leading lights. For better, and sometimes for worse, they are like the canaries in the mines. If they thrive, they offer assurance to the rest of us that all is well. Where artists — and scientists — are today is most often where we will be tomorrow.

In an age in which so much is going wrong, do not the arts and sciences provide a ray of hope that we can all live a better life, a more human, self-fulfilling and enlightened life, in the future?

Saturday, July 22, 2005

MY VIEW

Gloucester Cooperative Bank, Sorry, but No!

by Carmine Gorga

As fathers and mothers, sons and daughters, even as friends, we all experience that revelatory moment in which we are compelled to say to the other person: "I am sorry. But no! For your own good, I cannot give you this."

This is the moment I have reached with my neighbors, the officers of the Gloucester Cooperative Bank. No matter how painful it is to me — and to the rest of my family — I have to say to them: "Sorry. No. For the bank's own good and the good of the city as I see it, I cannot give you my permission to carve a three-lane highway on your premises, to tear down stores on Pleasant Street and make room for a new exit road, to place a parking lot along Main Street, and to double the size of your building. This project shatters our 400-year-old neighborhood." Indeed, I urge all other citizens, friends and members of official bodies here in Gloucester to gather the strength to take the same position.

What are the economics of this project? From various presentations, we have learned that it will take 40 years for the proposed building to become fully occupied. That means that the expenditure for this project is not going to bring in a fair return for many years to come. That can't be good for the clients or the owners of the bank. Much retail space is being lost. That can't be good for the city's finances.

My neighbor bankers seem to be so concentrated on the request of some of their customers to have an ATM drive-through facility on their premises that they are discounting all other factors. Have they calculated how many customers they are going to lose, because they are antagonizing so many people with conflicting needs, such as merchants whose means of livelihood rely on downtown pedestrian traffic? Have they calculated how many clients will be deterred from reaching their premises because of the dangerous traffic patterns they are going to create in their parking lot?

My neighbor bankers have heard the call of some of their customers for a drive-through ATM window, but have they listened to the screams at their proposed three — repeat, three — entrances and exits, from mothers and fathers of toddlers who yell: "Stop! Stop! How many times do I have to tell you that you have to stop when crossing the street?" Any objective bystander will notice that the kids are not in the middle of a street, at all. They are on a city sidewalk interrupted by a drive-through!

Whatever fascination we attach to cars — whether it is power, autonomy or sheer convenience — there is no getting away from the fact that cars have so far destroyed our cities and they are gradually destroying our suburbs. Worse, they are our mortal enemies. Last year, they killed 42,800 people. That many people were taken away from their families and friends, in the most horrible of ways.

Against this tragedy, new benefits from walking are being discovered today. We knew that walking was good for us. But who knew that walking cuts certain health risks in half? So why does the bank listen only to its car-driving customers?

Here is a suggestion. Rather than sinking their investment into a three-lane highway, a super-busy parking lot, and a building planned to remain partially vacant for the next 40 years, why not put a challenge to the community? Why not set up a loan fund for $4 million to invest in the fishing industry — provided other banks and private investors put in their own share? We all know that unless we rejuvenate the fishing industry we are not going to have a stable local economy. A study done by analysts from the System Dynamics Program at MIT proves that there are immediate, handsome financial rewards — let alone many long-term benefits — to be gained from such an investment.

There is an even bigger challenge that my neighbor bankers can present to the community as a whole. Rather than favoring this car fetish, why do they not spearhead a civic effort to transform the downtown of Gloucester into a full-fledged pedestrian economy in which their self-interest will thrive?

The choice is clear. Expected results from these different approaches are well-known. They were starkly made by a recent article in The Boston Globe comparing two cities. Worcester favors the car and suffers from an ailing condition, while Providence favors a pedestrian culture and shows a vibrant economy.

To be sure, to create a pedestrian economy requires much work. Why not engage in it? There are many encouraging new ways of taming the car and fostering civilized urban behavior. Another word for civilized behavior is the search for the common good.

Carmine Gorga is president of Polis-tics Inc.

Saturday, November 12, 2005

MY VIEW

Fish and Future

by Carmine Gorga

Fish will always be with us. And that is a good thing, because fish is good for us. As more and more research proves, eating fish at least once a week reduces — to repeat — reduces our cholesterol levels; reduces our risk of Alzheimer's disease; reduces our risk of stroke. Eating fish, such as salmon and tuna, which are rich in omega-3 fatty acids, has been shown to prevent heart disease. Some studies even suggest that eating fish fights osteoporosis; and other studies indicate positive effects on certain forms of cancer. "Eat Fish; Live Longer" was an earlier slogan suggested by the many health benefits of eating fish at least once a week.

Fish makes us live longer and live better. Eating fish postpones age-related mental decline by three to four years, suggests one of the latest studies. This research provides further evidence that a fish-rich diet helps keep the mind sharp. "Eat Fish; Stay Young" is the new slogan launched by Ann Shriver, the executive director of the International Institute of Fisheries Economics and Trade.

Those who make a living from the ocean are not lone rangers. While at sea they tend to be in constant contact with each other — visually and, today, electronically. While on land they tend to be stable members of compact communities. Thus fish is sociologically good for us.

Fish is sociologically good for us, we realize, also if we look at ourselves retrospectively. Fish is such an intrinsic part of our heritage that it defines who we are. Say that you hail from Gloucester, and most people in the world recognize not only who you are — that you share some part of an age-old fish story; they will also know which part of the world you come from. People do not say, "Gloucester, where?" So you cut down on the idle talk and can immediately engage in more serious conversation.

Fish is economically good for us. A dollar's worth of fish feeds more mouths than a dollar's worth of trade or services. Its multiplier effect is higher, because it creates wealth anew. A dollar's worth of fish feeds the butcher and the baker, and the oil maker — and the banker and the insurer.

Indeed, fish is good for the nation as a whole because, if we do not produce fish, we are so hungry for it that we import fish from abroad — in large quantities. And we put our nation more heavily in debt with foreign nations. Now we have to remember that a dollar sent abroad is a claim on our wealth at home. Sooner or later, those dollars will be converted into control over our resources at home.

That fish is good for us is indisputable. Doubts today are planted as to whether fish will always be with us. Are not most commercial species of fish depleted? Yes, in part. But this answer does not look at the entire biomass. While some species are depleted, others are superabundant. Scary headlines insist that cod and other bottom fish are depleted; yet, mackerel and herring — the pelagics that live in the middle of the water column — are still superabundant.

It is only by looking at the entire biomass and the relationships among predators and preys that we might be able to find lasting and equitable solutions to the future physical utilization of the harbor. So far, we have identified one major predator-prey relationship: bottom fish and pelagics are in such a relationship. This is clearly visible as soon as one abandons the static, linear, pyramidal conception of the biomass. Predators are not always predators and preys are not always preys. At times predators become preys and vice versa.

The relationship is this. The larvae of the bottom fish need to go to the surface of the ocean in order to obtain food — plankton — and light. While they go up, they become a feast for the pelagics. When those larvae that survive become codlings, they want to go back to their friends and relatives. While they descend to their native habitat, they become a second feast for the pelagics.

In collaboration with volunteers from the MIT Systems Dynamics program, at the Gloucester Community Development Corporation we have quantified these relationships and published them on the Internet at www.gloucesterdc.org. Dr. Peter Otto and Jeroen Struben have also published part of this study in the prestigious System Dynamics Review (Winter 2004). This study makes it clear that, if biological limits are not respected, the situation can be reversed — and the bottom fish can become so superabundant as to threaten the existence of the pelagics.

A collapse of the pelagics would of course affect especially those migratory fish that rely on the pelagics for their feed: especially tuna. Yet a superabundance of the pelagics is definitely not good for the bottom fish. The evidence is overwhelming. Codlings have been found in the stomach of herring and mackerel. The first predator-prey model was developed by a biologist and a mathematicians studying the fishing industry in the Adriatic in early 1900s. The validity of the predator-prey model has been confirmed by chaos theory. The predator-prey relation has been found in nature in all living species, even in trees, even in lemmings.

Those who have memory of local history will remember that when Lippman Marine was in existence converting pelagics into chicken feed, and thus helping maintain a balance in the predator-prey relationship in the ocean, the bottom fish was in good health.

This history and this research lead to only one conclusion. Local fishermen are unjustly accused of overfishing the oceans. When looked in the context of these relationships within the total biomass, the overfishing is clearly done — not by fishermen — but by the natural predators of the bottom fish. And certainly this research does not excuse the fishermen for such well established negative practices of the past as using too small mesh sizes, for uprooting the bottom floor of the ocean, for fishing while and where fish are spawning, for harvesting bottom fish while fishing for pelagics, and the like. Nor is this research a call for over-exploitation of the pelagics. The issue, as usual, is an issue of balance. All rights have to be established and respected on the basis of corresponding responsibilities.

There is not one fishing industry in Gloucester. There are at least three such industries: bottom fish, pelagics and tuna — let alone lobstering, sportfishing and whale watching. All these interests have to be taken into account. They are all entitled to their share of the fruits of the ocean. But none is entitled to control over the entire ocean.

The question for Gloucester then is not: Will there be fish in the future? If we respect the natural balance among those various natural and economic interests, there will be fish. That is for sure. The real question is: Will Gloucester be ready for fish?

Gloucester became a "hub" harbor, an infrastructure that serves the interests of the entire New England fishing industry — including, to repeat, pleasure boating and sportfishing. It took about 400 years to develop this infrastructure. It can easily be destroyed. It cannot easily be rebuilt.

The question is: Will Gloucester be ready for fish, when a balance in the use of the oceans' resources for the benefit of human beings is re-established in the future?

Carmine Gorga is president of Polis-tics Inc.

MY VIEW

One of the Merits of My Plea

by Carmine Gorga

One cannot say everything at once. In my plea, published in the Gloucester Daily Times of July 22, 2005, to the officers of the Cooperative Bank next door, I pointed out this alternative: "Rather than favoring this car fetish, why do they not spearhead a civic effort to transform the downtown of Gloucester into a full-fledged pedestrian economy in which their self-interest will thrive?"

They preferred not to listen. So we are now arguing these issues in court. In their advertisement to the public, published in the Gloucester Daily Times of Jan. 24, officers of the Cooperative Bank take rather strong issue with the legal suit I am in the process of joining as a last ditch effort to let them reconsider their project and see the damage that their project, if carried out, will inflict upon the community. They claim the suit is "meritless." The community will be interested to know that what follows below outlines one of the merits of my effort.

In a recent New York Times column, Nicholas Kristof has followed this line of reasoning: "President Bush is slated to discuss health care in his State of the Union address tonight. It's about time: It's scandalous that babies born in the United States are less likely to survive their first year than babies born in Slovenia. But the solutions to the health crisis lie less in reorganizing medical treatment than in improving public health ..."

After emphasizing that some of the biggest advancements in improving Americans' health over the last generations have nothing to do with traditional forms of medicine, he asks: "So what can we do? In my last column, I praised Gov. Mike Huckabee of Arkansas for leading a series of initiatives to confront obesity and lack of exercise. Health experts suggest a variety of others ..." The suggestion he advances that is most pertinent to our situation in Gloucester is the following one:

"Promote jogging and biking. Since we pay for all the consequence of inactivity (like those heart bypasses), we should encourage exercise. We should build more bicycle paths and turn more streets over to bikers, skaters and pedestrians — starting with Sixth Avenue in Manhattan."

If evidently there are people who can conceive of a pedestrian Sixth Avenue in Manhattan, should we recoil at that thought of a pedestrian Main Street in Gloucester?

Picking up from Mr. Kristof's final plea, I might add, "Granted, a War on Sloth isn't as dramatic" for the Cooperative Bank as imposing its presence on Main Street. But there is perhaps no better way of serving its own self-interest as well as the interest of the community than to nest this project into the culture of a pedestrian economy rather than building a three-lane highway, three entrances and exits, and parking lot in the midst of an ancient neighborhood.

It is not too late. Now one needs only change a design. A built design — no matter how ill-conceived — will stay with us for generations to come.

Carmine Gorga is president of Polis-tics Inc.

Friday, September 15, 2006
Tuesday, September 19, 2006
Friday, September 22, 2006

MY VIEW

A Procedural Proposal

by Carmine Gorga

Forty years of observation have led me to conclude that the administrative procedure on how things get built in New England is a lawyers' paradise. I have observed this procedure as an urban planner and a community planner; as a developer of specific public and private projects — as well as a private citizen and, for many years, as a member of the Gloucester Historic District Commission.

Unlike Shakespeare, I love lawyers. So I am not going to suggest cutting them out of the proceedings. No. They have an important role to play. They keep procedures orderly. That alone would justify their continuing presence — but not as prima donnas to guide the proceedings toward their predetermined goal. No. They have a major role to play, as Justice Brandeis used to say well before he acceded to the Supreme Court of the land. They have a major role to play as the people's attorney — no matter who pays them.

How to achieve this feat, while private lawyers are obviously being paid by private parties?

The solution lies in making the community the center of attraction. And to keep the community in focus, we need to quicken the pace and shorten the tempi of the administrative procedure — from months and even years, to one to four months at most.

But, while shortening the tempi, will the lawyers see their paycheck shortened as well? Well, not necessarily so. As we will see, while the time of public exposure for lawyers would be shortened, the time for private preparation of the proposal would be extended because of the very nature of the proposal under consideration.

Here is the core of the proposal. It calls for a modification, not in the substance, but the timing sequence of the procedure. All parties that need to be consulted would still be consulted; all committees and commissions that need to pass upon a specific proposal would still need to give their vote of approval or disapproval; all neighbors who need to be listened to would still have the opportunity to speak up and have their input taken into consideration.

All issues of power content and power relations would remain unaltered.

All that would change would be the sequence of events. Rather than presenting the proposal to one commission at a time, all commissions that today have to pass upon a specific project would be consulted at once. So, instead of being approached as if in a maze, all members of all commissions that need to pass upon the project would all be in one big room. Members of each commission would have an opportunity to educate themselves about all the needs of the community, by going beyond their narrow specialization and listening to what members of all other commissions have to say.

Each member of the various commissions will still vote only as members of their commission. So they would not lose the advantage that the focus of their narrow specialization affords them. Yet, they would also have the opportunity, before voting, to look at the project from all other points of view — because the lawyers presenting the case, having studied it with their client from every possible point of view, will educate the entire community as to all the benefits of their project.

This proposal would not turn the procedure into a shootout at high noon. There would be — at most — three votes taken: one vote per week (or month), with a week (or month) off as cooling-off time. Some of these hearings might stretch for more than one session. Unless approved or definitely denied sooner, the proposal would come up for final approval or denial on the fourth week (or month) — with still all members of the various commissions present and each member independently voting on the proposal.

The vote on the first week could be the first and last vote in case of decided approval or rejection of the project.

Most likely, each member of the various commissions is ready to give only conditional approval to a project. So, the vote in the first week would serve to specify those conditions. Again, if all reservations are taken care of, the project could be approved on the second hearing.

However, some members of the various commissions might want to reassess the case in light of the modifications brought to a plan. They might then want to specify further details as conditions for their approval and for transition to the last stage, with a cooling-off period in between. At the last hearing, the project is voted up or down.

The project is approved if, as today, it receives approval from a majority of the members of each commission. The City Council — as the ultimate authority in a city like Gloucester — could either be present at the first and third hearing or only at one ad hoc session to pass final judgment on the project.

No more the waning of the months. No more the lawyerly procedure to narrow down the project to fit the specialized knowledge of each commission, with the hope — and often the explicit promise from lawyers — that the specific awkward issue can be overlooked by one commission because the next one will take care of it. No.

Each member of the various commissions would see the first week whether that awkward issue is indeed taken care of by the next commission — or falls by the wayside into the interstices of the specialized knowledge that each commission brings to bear on behalf of the community as a whole.

The final consequence of the lawyer's paradise that prevails today is that John Q. Public is ultimately so aroused as to appeal the decision of some specific commission — and the project is shepherded by lawyers in front of boards of appeal and even the courts for years at a stretch.

This is not a proposal set in stone. Many modifications can be attached to it at any one end of its major aspects.

Another basic consideration to keep in mind is that this proposal could be put into practice in one or two test cases — in one or two cities or towns at a time — and eventually modified at the school of hard knocks. The proposal should also be looked at as a reversible procedure once implemented on a test basis.

The most important consideration to keep in mind perhaps is this: Things are not working right, they are not working to the benefit of the community as a whole, and it is highly arguable whether they are working to the benefit of any private concerns. This is basically only a call to put the present administrative procedure on how to get things built under the microscope and search for possible better alternatives.

With the current procedure no one ultimately wins. One community after another is being gutted at its core as well as at its periphery. But this is another spiel from which you must, please, stop me from entering right now. The "suburbs" should stop being interested only in the suburbs. Downtown people should stop being interested only in the downtown.

It is the community as a whole that suffers from these splits in visions and specializations.

Carmine Gorga is president of Polis-tics Inc. and former member of the Gloucester Historical Commission.

Friday, December 8, 2006

MY VIEW

From a Hole in the Ground to Holy Ground

by Carmine Gorga

The wheels of justice grind fine but grind slowly. About nine months ago, I petitioned the Essex County Superior Court to join a legal suit to stop the present plans of the Gloucester Cooperative Bank from being built.

The Judge in his wisdom denied my bid to join the suit only a couple of weeks ago and I am in the process of determining whether to appeal that decision. By one estimate, it will take perhaps two more years for this case to be heard.

In the meantime, I am frequently asked: "How do you like the hole in the ground on Main Street?" In pain, my answer is: "Not a bit."

Here is a proposal on how to turn that hole in the ground into holy ground — because, make no mistake about it, that is where the heart of the city is: That is holy ground. To reach a speedier solution than can be reached in court, it will take a concerted effort not only on the part of the officers of the Gloucester Cooperative Bank, but of the City and the community as a whole. Here is a proposal:

It does not matter who takes the initiative for the first step. But the honor of the first step belongs by right to the mayor. If legally necessary, after all the ground work is laid out, Mayor John Bell might want to call one extraordinary meeting whereby in a single audience all the various aspects of the case are discussed and resolved.

All city officials, from Community Development to Police Department, who need to be present, ought to be present; all city boards, from the Planning Board to the Downtown Committee, ought to be there (interestingly, the Historic District Committee might not need to be there); so that the officers of the Bank will need to make only one unified presentation and be ready to answer all questions at once. The mayor, of course, does not necessarily need to preside over the meeting. A professional facilitator might be another choice.

The gist of the presentation might run along a couple of scenarios. First scenario. The Gloucester Cooperative Bank requests all necessary permits to build a brand-new building all along its property on Main Street to rent or to sell to local merchants.

Second scenario. The Gloucester Cooperative Bank requests all necessary permits to build a brand-new building all along its property on Main Street where, upon completion, it will move its headquarters. I trust that in this case the officers of the Bank will keep their promise to offer retail space on Main Street, because a 500-foot span of bank windows might not be too appealing to the tourist, let alone the local passerby.

In either scenario, the building will fill the hole on Main Street by joining the building of Sovereign Bank next door and curving along Pleasant Street.

In either scenario, the bank might also want to consider the possibility of building a third floor, as officially allowed, and reserve it to residential — perhaps even condominium — use.

The cost for the architectural renderings for this presentation can be reduced to zero, if the officers of the Bank should promise to adopt any standard architectural style and subsequently adhere to it in their construction.

Perhaps reference to the style of one or more of the surrounding buildings on Main Street could be acceptable to all concerned. The structures seem to be versatile and elegant enough to accommodate an appropriately spacious see-through lobby for the bank.

In the rear of this new building there will be as ample a parking lot as necessary — as well as room for an ATM drive-through window. The lot would be entered from Pleasant Street and exited from Middle Street or, vice versa, entered from Middle Street and exited from Pleasant Street.

As suggested by other people, the present headquarters of the Gloucester Cooperative Bank could be either rented or sold. Prominent among the institutions in town that are ready to spend millions of dollars to build new facilities is the Cape Ann Historical Association.

Also the city might be willing to consider using the building as a City Hall Annex. Either singly or jointly, these institutions could become part of the solution to the puzzle of the hole in the ground on Main Street.

It seems to me that, if this plan is presented by the bank and accepted by the city, the legal suit would become moot — and construction could start the day after.

It seems to me that this proposal, especially in its second scenario, meets a number of prerequisites at once. The Gloucester Cooperative Bank would have the exposure on Main Street that it has sought for years and its requested ATM drive-through window as well.

Main Street would have one less missing tooth in its façade, the missing tooth represented by the current bank driveway.

The continuity of the sidewalk would be re-established as in the olden days and the safety of the sidewalk recovered. The West End of Main Street would be joined with the newly rejuvenated East End of Main Street.

The city would start collecting a sorely needed penny in taxes from the hole in the ground. And the city, who knows, perhaps might even be spurred to design a new approach to its customary long, drawn-out and costly building permit procedure.

What do you think, People and Institutions of Gloucester? Is there not still much spunk and spirit left in this Old Town?

Let us all work together and do it!

Carmine Gorga is president of Polis-tics Inc.

Editor's note: Gorga, whose home in the Downtown Historic District is adjacent to the existing bank building on Middle Street, served on the Historic District Commission and recused himself from deliberations on the bank's application before resigning in October 2006.

Thursday, May 24, 2007

MY VIEW

What a Difference

by Carmine Gorga

What a difference does a different perspective make. Looking at her motives from the outside in, some people have found a variety of negative explanations for Louise Palazzola's objection to the proposed Gloucester Cooperative Bank's construction plans.

Some people have found in her "selfishness;" others have found "frivolousness" and even "spite." The fear that her motives are driven by selfishness is easy to dispel. What type of selfishness exposes one's financial resources to a steady drain and to substantial loss if one loses in court?

The issue of spite is too psychological to be addressed here. But the issue of frivolousness can be discussed.

How frivolous is it to object to a plan to build a three-lane highway from Middle Street to Main Street: Two lanes around the proposed ATM window stand and one passing lane so as not to inconvenience any driver; three entrances and three exits from the proposed parking lot; a wall on Main Street; and a veneer of commercial space along Pleasant Street and Main Street? Make no mistake. This is the plan.

If we look at Louise Palazzola's objection from the inside out, we reach a different conclusion. She is led by two forces: First, she is resisting the negative effects of the present plans if they ever get carried out. These can be easily recounted again: Bad urban planning (the plan might be good on a highway, but it is not good in the downtown of an old city); bad transportation planning (in the downtown you want to encourage pedestrian, not vehicular circulation); bad economics (vehicular circulation goes hand in hand with exhaustion of non-renewable natural resources and air pollution: both very costly phenomena); bad aesthetics (Main Street does not need another toothless gape, it needs to envelop the visitor as warmly as possible).

Were all negatives unavoidable, one should make peace with the plan.

They are not. Indeed, this is Louise's vision of what could be: Close the front of Main Street with the planned addition to the bank and extend the construction with retail space curving along Pleasant Street; let one continuous flow of cars run from Middle Street to Pleasant Street; place the drive-through ATM window in the middle of the parking lot — which is now enclosed and not exposed to Main Street; and link the two buildings with an aerial pass-through just like the one that connects various terminal buildings to the parking lot at Logan Airport.

Officers at the bank reject this solution, which Louise proposed to them as soon as they aired their plans to the public, because it is more costly than making the new building an extension of the existing bank building. Considering that any new construction lasts at least for four to five generations, if the bank cannot afford the expense then perhaps it should not undertake the enterprise.

Second, there are fiscal mechanisms available to a city like Gloucester that, used properly, will greatly absorb the extra cost.

These are very large issues that cannot be reduced to a tug of wills between two parties. There are many people who have objected to the bank's plans from the very beginning. They should encourage the bank to do the proper thing.

Carmine Gorga is president of Polis-tics Inc.

Editor's note: Gorga, whose home in the Downtown Historic District is adjacent to the existing bank building on Middle Street, served on the Historic District Commission and recused himself from deliberations on the bank's application before resigning in October 2005.

Saturday, June 09, 2007

MY VIEW

Don't Sell the City — Own it Instead

by Carmine Gorga

Gloucester Crossing is a wonderful project, but . . .

You have heard all the objections before, so I will not repeat them. I will rather try to suggest a location for this project that will eliminate all legitimate reservations against its current presentation. The location I'm going to suggest is downtown, but not a downtown as it is today. Rather, a restructured downtown.

To incorporate all the positive aspects of Gloucester Crossing in our downtown, we need to make a few changes in the management, the legal structure, and the physical structure of downtown. I hope to show that these are relatively small intellectual changes, and that we can make them with a minimal effort of our individual and collective will. Here they are:

We all speak of downtown as a unit, because it is an economic unit. As we all know, it mostly stands or falls together. Yet, there is no corresponding managerial entity to represent this reality. With Mr. Sam Park's consent and the consent of downtown owners, Gloucester Crossing might become this managerial entity. All we need is a formal — not a substantial — change in the legal structure of downtown. This is how. Also, the extent of the "downtown" will have to be determined: Does it cover the Fort, where a splendid hotel/assisted living complex might be located?

Today, the various owners who make their living downtown operate as independent entities — while they actually live in an interdependent economic unit. That can change only if we change the legal structure of downtown. All downtown owners can become the component parts of Gloucester Crossing by giving up their individual ownership and acquiring corresponding shares of stock in Gloucester Crossing Inc. in accordance with the amount of their current ownership values.

Lawyers and accountants know very well how to do this. The kicker that will make this structure work is a lease/management back agreement as right of first refusal given to present owners and managers, so they will be assured that nothing changes in their lives. What changes is this: Rather than being individual owners, they will be owners of a larger legal entity: Gloucester Crossing Inc. In other words, from owners of small units, they will become owners of the whole downtown — and share this ownership with other present owners. All successful managers of downtown properties can be assured they will continue to manage those properties. And if the plan cannot be carried out through voluntary effort, is there enough political will to use the power of eminent domain that has lately been granted to communities?

The general manager of Gloucester Crossing will be Mr. Sam Park and his legal, marketing, architectural and management team. Thus the administrative costs incurred so far will be mostly recovered — and, of course, the plan requires adjustments and adaptations; but it can be made urban and fun. His Board of Directors will be enlarged to include all present owners whose power will be granted as stockholders of Gloucester Crossing Inc. in accordance with the share of value of their present property. Enough of these legal and management questions. A few more explanations can be found at http://polis-tics.com.

Let us see now the physical changes that are necessary to make this revised conception of Gloucester Crossing a reality. First, parking. Parking is the word that encompasses it all. Everything in the downtown, in the age of the car, starts and stops at the magic word: parking. Of course, we are not going to do away with our car. So, the next question is: Where do we park it? Well, the answer is this: under an elevated Rogers Street. A more comprehensive answer, as part of a more comprehensive plan of urban restoration, can be found at *http://polis-tics.com.*

Where do we find the money for all this? The answers are many. The first answer is that the money is to be found precisely where Mr. Park is looking for it, in the private capital market combined with public funds. A more exciting answer to raise funds and invest them locally can be found at http://polis-tics.com. Indeed, a few more plums can be gathered today than when I first developed this plan of financial interdependence, which tries to implement the suggestions of a slogan I designed a few years back: Do not sell Gloucester. Own it!

Today the implementation of the Gloucester Interdependence Fund can be enormously helped by recent developments in our national fiscal policies. The structure to look at is called new market tax credits. Indeed, with powerful assistance by outstanding local leaders such a plan was submitted to the U.S. Treasury Department a few years ago. The answer came in the official debriefing document concerning our application that, in part, reads: "The Applicant's strategy for serving communities of high economic distress is excellent ... ." Yet, the application was denied because we had no sufficient administrative experience to implement the plan.

If we truly work as a community, led by all Gloucester banking institutions as in its original conception, this plan of financial interdependence will indeed allow us to own Gloucester, not sell it. Individually, as many leaders who have individually been approving of these ideas in the past few years will attest, we are all powerless. It is when we act as responsible members of groups working within the specified framework of a common goal for the common good that we all regain our innate powers.

Carmine Gorga is president of Polis-tics Inc.

Saturday, July 21, 2007

MY VIEW

Three Pleas Regarding Gloucester Crossing

by Carmine Gorga

I sat through a session of the Planning and Development Standing Committee of the City Council recently. It was an inspiration. There was one element that very strongly unified all people present, those who spoke in favor of the Gloucester Crossing project, those who spoke against it, as well as the three councilors who had the official responsibility to make a decision on the issues. This was an intense love for Gloucester. This feeling seems to have been present at the full Council meeting as well.

The meeting inspired me to issue three pleas.

The first plea is to the people of Gloucester and especially the abutters of the Gloucester Crossing project. Please, free Mr. Park of his current financial obligations. Buy the land back from him. Is it too much to hope for the arrival of a knight on a white horse, just like the one who appeared to help the Rockport Arts Association? Or to hope for the collection of the pledges for the proposed expansion of the Sawyer Free Library? If these hopes come to naught, I am convinced that if we pool all our financial resources, we will have enough cash to buy the property back. Through these efforts, and the efforts of the local banks, the Gloucester Interdependence Fund might even become a reality. For some of the characteristics of this proposed fund, please see *www.polis-tics.com.*

The second plea is to Mr. Sam Park. Please Mr Park, why don't you consider becoming the James Rouse of the 21st Century? You remember Mr Rouse. He is the real estate developer who had the vision to transform Quincy Market in Boston, a rather sore downtown spot, into Faneuil Hall Marketplace. The project was a financial success, an act of historic preservation, and an anchor for urban revitalization. If you go down to Boston, you will see that Faneuil Hall Marketplace is still a vibrant urban core.

Mr Park, you can do the same here in Gloucester. You already have assembled a brilliant team of experts to achieve this goal. You already have done much of the marketing work to make the project flourish. You already have a brilliant name for it, Gloucester Crossing. And, incidentally, the name Gloucester Crossing would perfectly fit the spot. The location you have selected now is more like Gloucester Woods than Gloucester Crossing. The out-of-town people whom you hope to attract might never see Gloucester. And, in fact, your request for a traffic light on Route 128 Extension assures that most people visiting your proposed shopping center would never see Gloucester. And the large majority of people coming from Gloucester that you plan to attract would only drain more resources from an already deeply wounded downtown. Remember, parking is a great pall on downtown development. Many shoppers will certainly prefer to find free parking space at your proposed project. I can even envisage some downtown merchants giving up the struggle and joining you up there in the Gloucester Woods.

In the meantime, such a flow of shoppers and merchants would most certainly drain whatever energy is left downtown. You as an individual developer might benefit from this drain, but Gloucester would not. Without a daily injection of shopping money, the local merchants would gradually close even more shops. Blight would set in. But the place would still need to be protected against fire and against vandalism. The City coffers would only suffer a drain but would not be replenished by a dwindling tax base.

If I were you, I would not touch the Gloucester downtown either. As it is today, the place would only scare me away. However, as I pointed out in the Gloucester Daily Times of last June 9, there are *major innovations* that under your leadership the City could sponsor. As I said, you have to see yourself as the next James Rouse. Do you think he had an easier task ahead of him?

My third plea is to the abutters. Please, see yourselves as the developers of an industrial park. As you know, the land in the Blackburn Industrial Park is exhausted. Your lot could be the next area open for industrial development. Success is nearly assured. Are there not more applicants than parcels of land in the existing industrial park? People love to come to Gloucester, you know. The industrial park will gradually be filled. Well, to assure your success, you already have a potentially appealing name. You could use Blackburn Crossing Industrial Park.

Carmine Gorga is president of Polis-tics Inc.

Saturday, September 22, 2007

MY VIEW

Unified Downtown
Would be Stronger and Wealthier

by Carmine Gorga

A young open mind, Joel Messier, has spurred me to suggest what are the specific incentives for the establishment of a Gloucester Downtown Corporation (or any similar formal legal association) as outlined in my previous posts in the Gloucester Daily Times of June 9 and July 21.

Incentives are innumerable. Here are a few of them.

The most important one for the current owners, managers and workers downtown is this: You shall live — and not die. And you shall live more, not less, independently; stronger in every sense; and wealthier.

If you become part-owners, managers and workers of Gloucester Downtown Corporation, you are going to get rid of a false sense of independence. How independent are you today? Be honest; be clear-minded.

In social and economic life, the reality is not independence but interdependence. Start thinking about going to gather your coffee beans in the morning and grinding them. And this is just for coffee.

Once you give up your false sense of independence, you will grow more economically interdependent. Instead of a voice in the wilderness, you can join your voice with those of others with similar economic interests.

Rather than owning 100 percent of a pittance with decreasing value you will own a share of a great and increasing value. The share will be in proportion to the value of your assets today in relation to the assets of your neighbors. And your voice will be raised in the same proportion.

You will remain the owners and the managers of Gloucester Downtown Corporation.

Once you give up on your false sense of independence and organize yourselves as members of GDC, you will discover the many benefits you can gather by working together in a unified downtown. Let us first talk about money. Don't you think you will have a better chance of securing a loan if you are part of a thriving downtown unit?

And then insurance. You can buy one health care plan to be shared in common; one liability insurance plan; one fire and theft insurance plan. Insurance will not only be available to you; it will be available at a lower cost.

And then there are energy costs. You can have one contract with the electric company, share the costs in accordance with your relative use and pocket the benefit of an assured lower cost. Indeed, you might even consider the possibility of buying one electric generator to serve the entire corporation.

As I have explained more technically at http://www.polis-tics.com/id21.htm, if you do become a part of GDC, you will get rid of all your administrative aggravations and you can concentrate on your direct area of expertise: merchandising.

Speaking of enticing new customers and holding on to current ones: We are so accustomed to thinking of vertical buildings that we do not see the possibility of building one hotel, wisely interspersed with restaurants, on the second floor of the south side of Main Street. Do you see the stupendous views of the harbor that you are going to offer your visitors? And on the north side of the street, added to the street level space, we could have continuous retail space to accommodate more than one merchant. In addition to the old Brown's Building, we have quite a few imposing structures to satisfy the needs of the most demanding "modern" merchandise complex.

One final benefit in the form of question: Have you ever tried to have your voice heard in the political arena? Just imagine what would be the response to a question you might ask of any politician, if you ask it as a representative of Gloucester Downtown Corporation.

Carmine Gorga is president of Polis-tics Inc. of Gloucester.

Tuesday, December 04, 2007

MY VIEW

A Cape Ann Experience —
and What a Trip It Is

by Carmine Gorga, Special to the Times

Do I dare, do I dare make a bold suggestion to our friends and neighbors in Rockport?

Dear friends and neighbors, with whom we share the unique and blessed land that is Cape Ann, as you know we in Gloucester are going through a very rough patch.

Would you explore the possibility of becoming the fulcrum to turn our situation around? If you do, you might discover that the proposed solution will in turn greatly help you as well in the end.

This is a bold proposal. Please take a deep breath and consider it.

Would you consider a new location for your proposed Shalin Liu Performance Center? I will not repeat the shortcomings of the downtown location you have chosen. I will only try to point out some of the advantages of a different location.

This is the location I would like for you to seriously consider. The location is on Blackburn Circle in Gloucester. At the very center of Blackburn Circle.

State Sen. Bruce Tarr promised some time ago to work diligently, as is his wont, to convince responsible state authorities to grant an appropriate use of this location to any worthy cause.

All for one dollar.

Your Rockport Chamber Music Festival might qualify as a worthy destination of such an opportunity.

Blackburn Circle is huge and it is one of the tallest spots on Cape Ann. If you were to build a three- to four-story high, circular building there, you would see the ocean all across the horizon. The outer structure might form a series of scalloped eyes, to suggest that we do keep an eye on the world and that we do want the world to keep an eye on us.

The scalloped shape of the outer building would, of course, remind everyone that we do live in a fishing community. The outer shell could be made of glass, or it could offer deep balconies on each floor all around the perimeter of the building.

Inside, the structure could give hospitality, not only to a regional-national art performance center to include the chamber music orchestra and a regional theater but also a convention center and a community center.

The outer ring might even play host to some lawyers' and architectural offices.

The facility could be built on a modular basis, so to expand as needed over time from the inside out — without ever tearing down what was first built.

In front of the center, there would be only a drop-off lane. Parking could be gradually built by filling in the ravine cut into the rock to create Route 128 extension. We could have there a multilevel parking structure.

The outer edge of the parking structure could be extended over time to catch the summer tourist traffic. In its ultimate design it should attempt to reconstruct the rounded shape of the original hill. Eventually, at each outer edge of the structure there could be a balcony overlooking the ocean and even some apartment structures.

Eventually, a people-mover or a shuttle bus would take people from this parking structure back to the visitor/arts center. And from there one line of jitneys could take visitors to Rockport and another line would take them to Rocky Neck and downtown Gloucester.

Visitors could be encouraged to walk all through the trails of Dogtown Common. And if a stairway is ever built to connect Blackburn Circle to downtown Gloucester, as (if memory serves) a Harvard-MIT Joint Center for Urban Studies design proposed years ago, then visitors would be encouraged to walk up and down the stairway, which would afford incomparable views of the ocean. Planters and flags would enliven the walk.

Walkers then could extend their *passeggiata* by joining with a dropped-down promenade to be built along an elevated Rogers Street, which would shelter parking facilities for Main Street shoppers.

Wait, is that a surimi plant and Omega-3 oil complex we see? Let us get down to visit it. We proceed down a short stairway located every couple of blocks along the promenade overlooking a park punctuated by lively benches and kiosks. We cross this park that replaces today's many parking lots along Rogers Street to reach the working harbor or we walk on to Main Street.

Main Street would only be pedestrian, as in Joseph M. Orlando's vision (Times, May 25, 2007). And, well of course there could be an open-air fresh fish and produce market on the infamous I4-C2 lot as well, as envisaged by Ronn Garry (Times, May 10, 2007). That is truly a terrific idea!

Our walkers could be taken all around the Fort area hugging the shore but protected by a thick Plexiglas tunnel that would allow visitors to experience first-hand the working waterfront, such as the operation of loading ice on fishing vessels at Cape Pond Ice — and, eventually, visitors could even go through an underground Plexiglas tunnel hugging the ocean floor next to the shore. That would indeed be a natural aquarium. Our walkers could then explore the Boulevard and perhaps go all the way to the Magnolia Woods.

What a trip.

Upon a return to the Shalin Liu Performance Center, visitors would then be ready to sit in plush chairs to listen to stupendously transporting chamber music.

Carmine Gorga is president of Polis-tics Inc. of Gloucester.

Tuesday, December 11, 2007

MY VIEW

Oh, the Power of Wrong Ideas

by Carmine Gorga, Special to the Times

Wrong ideas do incalculable damage.

The tendency is to attribute bad ideas to malice and foresight. More often than not, wrong ideas only stem from ignorance. At least that appears to be the case in relation to the fishing industry in the United States. Repeat after me: Overfishing is done by the natural predators; overfishing is not done by the fishermen.

The depletion of traditional bottom fish species is attributed to the behavior of fishermen. Wrong. The depletion of traditional bottom fish species is due primarily to their natural predators, the pelagics — herring and mackerel — that live in the middle of the water column.

This dynamic becomes incontrovertible as soon as one stops sponsoring the wrong conception of a fixed, linear and pyramidal food chain, a line whose starting and end points are entirely arbitrary. The reality is that the line is constantly in flux, and the predators of today become the prey of tomorrow.

Herring and mackerel are not the constant prey and feed of bottom fish, needing to be protected from being caught by the fishermen. At times, the opposite is true. Herring and mackerel are the predators of bottom fish. Ours is still one of those times.

Herring and mackerel are abundant because, rather than being the feed of the bottom fish, they are fed by them.

When herring and mackerel are in abundant supply, they provide a barrier for bottom fish, keeping them from going up and down the water column. And they need to go up and down the water column because, when bottom fish spawn, the larvae need to go up toward the light and the food — the plankton — that exist at the very top of the water column.

And once they grow up, the codlings want, indeed, they need, to go back to their habitat among their friends and relatives to reproduce, enjoy life and savor better food than plankton.

It is when they go up and down the water column that bottom fish become a feast for the predators: herring and mackerel.

The only way to provide for a natural replenishment of the bottom fish is to catch the pelagics. It is to take them out of the water column.

All this is elementary. All this is proved by history and by statistics. Just now that some herring and mackerel are being caught again in New England waters, the stocks of bottom fish are rebounding at an accelerating rate. When, 40 and more years ago, pelagics were caught by Lippman Marine for use as fertilizers and chicken feed (ouch!), the bottom fish were in abundant supply.

And yet, just as a balance is gradually being restored through the increasing catches of herring and mackerel, the New England Fisheries Management Council is now being pressured to curb those efforts. Limits, of course, there have to be; one cannot pass from one extreme to the other.

But the numbers indicate that we are still a long way from helping form a natural balance between natural prey and predators. Pelagics still need to be taken out of the water.

All this is not even simply elementary any longer. There are reams of science that prove the existence of these natural cycles. And yet, all this knowledge is being neglected by those who are urging a stop to the catch of herring and mackerel in New England waters (hereinafter, "the herring lovers" for short).

It is as if the herring lovers had never heard of the Lotke-Volterra model — the first predator-prey model, developed for fish caught in the Adriatic Sea by Lotke, a mathematician, working in collaboration with Volterra, a biologist. That is not undigested news. This is a model that was developed just about a century ago.

It is as if the herring lovers had never heard of chaos theory. This is a complex development in mathematics and geometry that has occurred during the last couple of generations and has revolutionized most of our stale linear thinking processes.

It is as if the herring lovers had never heard of a study published in Science a few years ago that even lemmings do not live and die all by themselves. They do not periodically go down a cliff just for the fun of it.

Rather, they are being subjected to the same forces as all other living creatures. When their predators are in short supply, they multiply incontinently. And then, once their own food supplies begin to dwindle, they are weakened and their predators get the upper hand: Their stocks collapse temporarily.

It is as if the herring lovers never had listened to a lecture by our magnificent national park rangers, who instruct us that even trees are subject to the same interrelationships in their natural habitat as fish and other living creatures.

Balance one ought to search for. The golden mean is the ideal to tend toward. Let us shy away from all extremes.

Try as I might, I never find evidence of recognition by the herring lovers that herring and mackerel are also the predators of bottom fish. Hence, some herring and mackerel must at times be taken out of the water to re-establish a balance among the species.

To follow their recommended policy — to stop taking herring and mackerel out of the water at this time — is to condemn local fishing communities to a perpetual state of crisis.

Carmine Gorga is president of Polis-tics, Inc. of Gloucester.

Monday, December 17, 2007

Do We Love the Paint Factory?
Then Let Us Prove it

by Carmine Gorga

The most important lesson I came away with a few years ago after reading "The Seven Habits of Highly Effective People" by Stephen Covey is that love is not a feeling.

Love is an action, or a set of actions through which the feeling of love is engendered and fostered. So, if we say we love the Paint Factory, we have to prove it by concrete actions.

Perhaps it might be good to summarize the reasons why many of us do indeed love the Paint Factory, that unique icon on the Gloucester waterfront.

Those who love history have the easiest time expressing their love for that building. It represents much of the history of Gloucester and much of the history of the fishing industry.

Then there are the esthetic reasons. The Paint Factory is important as a symbol and as a physical anchor, a mass of space that seems to have been there forever to provide ballast for the structure of the harbor.

As a symbol, the building not only represents history and the past, it also captures the present, and heralds possible shapes of the future. It speaks to us, and we speak to it. For instance, we ask: Will you be there in the future? Will we raze you? Will you be there as a solid massive unit that speaks of the industrial origin of the building or will we perforate you with windows that speak of a service and tourist future?

For those who know the arguments, and by now there must be very few people in and around Gloucester who do not know them, the present of the Paint Factory represents, in full, the state of agitation in which we live in this community. The state of agitation derives from uncertainty in relation to what to do, not only with the building, but with our harbor as a whole: Should it be reserved for maritime and fishing interests as in the past or should it be converted to the interests of the service and tourist industry? Or should there be a compromise solution? It is indeed quite reasonable to assume that as the Paint Factory goes, so goes the harbor.

The difference between the two approaches is fundamental. It is captured in a pithy expression of our beloved Lena Novello, one of the grand dames of Gloucester. Repeating the ancient wisdom of her father, she used to remind us, "Boats build homes. Homes do not build boats." This is the difference between production and consumption. After the expulsion from the Garden of Eden, we are bound to produce first before we can consume.

Thus we see that the issues surrounding the destiny of the Paint Factory become bigger and bigger and go to the very essence of our society. The fishing industry has provided livelihood for countless generations year-round; the service industry is, at best, seasonal; and private residences do not earn money — they cost money for their upkeep.

As distinguished from the service industry, the fishing industry not only provides many people with steady income, it also helps keep the nation solvent. We eat fish because it is tasty and is good for us. If we do not catch fish, we import it from abroad — and we inflict further damage upon our balance of payments.

Then there are psychological, legal and political angles to the Paint Factory. The psychological angle is easy to figure out. It can be reduced to a single sentence: "Are we capable of making up our minds as one community, or are we forever going to be split into at least two factions, those who are for the preservation of the building and those who might want to change course at almost any cost?"

The legal is one of the most important angles, because it is joined with the political angle. Are property rights absolute? If they have to have limits, what are they? Having placed more and more restrictions on the exercise of property rights to accommodate legitimate concerns for the health, safety and welfare of the community, there are some among us who are ready to extend restrictions to cases in which the bulk of the benefits are public.

On whose shoulders should the financial costs of esthetics and history and urban amenities fall? Assume you own the building and have faced taxes and insurance costs while receiving no income from that property for any number of years. How long will you resist the pressure to put it to any use, or even to tear the building down and reduce your expenses?

The reasonable answer is inescapable. It consists in not quibbling over details. It consists in accepting the limits of the present owners and relieving them of the pressures they are under.

The essence of reasonableness and fairness consists in recognizing that, since the benefits are shared by all, the costs also ought to be shared by all. The short-term solution lies in empowering any institution that is primarily interested in the heritage of Gloucester to purchase the building at fair price.

It is here that all issues are fused together — and love flows in. If anyone really loves that building, the love has to become concrete. The love has to be manifested in contributions of money, time and other resources in accordance with personal capabilities and in correspondence with the amount of love one holds in the heart for that building.

Let us pass the tin cup around.

Carmine Gorga is president of Polis-tics Inc. of Gloucester.

Thursday, February 21, 2008

MY VIEW

In Search of Common Ground — and Common Prayer

by Carmine Gorga

From my windows, I used to see the majestic structure of the temple; from my windows, I saw the inferno that destroyed it on the night of Dec. 14; from my windows, now I see the black heap of scarred timber left behind.

Did Shiva's fire of destruction engulf Temple Ahavat Achim and the Lorraine Apartments to create a void in our landscape and our hearts? Must the loss of the one life, fortunately only one valuable life, be in vain?

I believe in the living God. I believe in the God of love. I know that no one can hurt me as hard as God, but that he hurts me not for his good or someone else's good. He hurts me for my own good. He wants to bring me to a more elevated state of consciousness, a more refined appreciation of life.

I believe there is a lesson to be learned from this tragedy. Might God want the Jewish people and the whole of Gloucester population to grow stronger in love and appreciation of each other? Love and appreciation of each other already exist in Gloucester aplenty. That is why Gloucester is a community.

The Universalist Church has opened its house of worship to the Jews in this time of trial. One ecumenical service did take place there. The spirit of giving is alive and well. The Jewish temple will be rebuilt.

But is that enough?

Is God pointing his Jewish people, and all of us in Gloucester, toward a higher calling? Perhaps each one of us ought to ask ourselves this question. Perhaps all of us ought to come together one day to compare the answers that each one of us has found.

The answer I have received is this. We have to build one temple to the one living God. How we are going to go about it, I have only the scantiest of ideas. Of one thing I am absolutely sure: we have to focus on what unites us all.

Whenever I have had the opportunity and the need to follow such an inquiry in the past, I have constantly been astonished. On nonessential questions I have discovered infinite variety; however, on the essentials I have hardly found any difference at all among all religions and even among all serious expressions of atheism.

Brahma, Shiva and Vishnu form the triune expression of the single God-head, just like the variegated shades of our more familiar monotheistic religions' Trinity.

At the next step, we run into a stumbling block that is not a stumbling block: the Messiah. What is the reality? All three monotheistic religions believe in the Messiah. Christians believe that the Messiah has already come. Jews believe that the Messiah is still to come. The followers of Allah have the most difficult task of all. Shiite Muslims believe in Vali Asr, the revered Hidden Imam, whose appearance someday will establish the perfect Islamic political community.

How can these huge differences be bridged?

I believe what spans the chasm is the conception of the Spiritual Messiah. Most Christians are — or, indeed, ought to be — ready to concede that they are in active expectation for the arrival of the Spiritual Messiah in their hearts. The more spiritual the Christian, the more desirous one is of the coming of the Spiritual Messiah.

Is not the more spiritual Jew expectant of the coming Messiah?

The Jesus who came on Earth as my personal Messiah did not ask for any prayer to be directed to him. The prayer he taught us is the Our Father — your father, my father, as well as his father.

And what can a firm believer gain from the understanding of nonbelievers? The great Buddhist masters and serious atheists follow a profound method to arrive at their convictions. As soon as we say what God is for us, they urge us to reconsider. And if we are serious, we must admit that we can never be sure of any aspect of the substance or the essence of God. The more seriously we go through the process, the more we subtract qualities we may have mistakenly attributed to God and then the closer we get to the true God.

Hence, we must thank Buddhists and atheists for helping us reach a closer relation with God.

Once we get as close as possible to God, we get into a personal relation with God. And is not that what God wants? Is not that what any religion strives to achieve?

So, let us strive for a renewal of the spirit on Cape Ann. May we enter any church, temple, mosque and synagogue and feel that we are entering into the spirit of our own personal God.

May we feel capable of joining any congregation in their prayers and may we be capable of inviting any individual into our congregation. Let us make their prayer our own prayer.

Carmine Gorga is president of Polis-tics Inc. of Gloucester.

Tuesday, May 27, 2008

MY VIEW

Three Integrated Ideas
for Gloucester's Resurgence

by Carmine Gorga, Special to the Times

We have just heard the first salvo in the discussion: The expected level of cuts in city services is "pretty brutal." We shall soon hear of strong attempts at raising revenues, whether by raising taxes or by appeals to state and federal government to replenish our exhausted financial resources.

There is a third rail that most people will avoid to touch; this is the alternative of enlarging the tax base of our community. The time to consider it is now.

It takes time and lots of care to expand the tax base of a community. Gloucester is certainly not wanting in ideas, plots, and plans. Here are three projects that would go a long way to putting our community on the path of personal wealth and fiscal health. They have been discussed for years, but now perhaps is the time to put some muscle behind them. These are the three projects:

• **The creation of Dogtown Village**. Many communities have done a lot more with much less history than we have. Gloucester is not only rich as the oldest fishing port and the oldest art colony in the nation; Gloucester also has the remains of one of the oldest urban settlements in New England. Near the center of Dogtown Common there are the ruins of many house foundations. It is there that our early ancestors settled. It is from the safety of that huddled environment that they ventured to farm the surrounding land and to fish the vast expanses of the waters surrounding our Cape Ann peninsula.

Who were these people? Where did they come from? Where did they ultimately go? How did they live while they lived in Dogtown? Their homes could be gradually reconstructed. Their stories could be presented on tablets dispersed along bucolic pathways through which one could reach the reconstructed village. These tablets could also explain much of the rich variety of flora and fauna that existed then and still exists today on this glorious terrain.

How much sense of the past would we recover? How much deeper would our appreciation for life be? While visitors' lives would be enriched by imbibing a chunk of real life, we might get a sorely needed penny in our pockets. Not a bad trade-off for everyone involved.

• **A surimi plant**. Surimi is a 1,000-year-old Japanese technique to extrude relatively long-lasting protein from highly perishable fish. A modern update of this technique — designed by Dr. Herbert Hultin and Dr. Steven Kelleher, two scientists with a long string of successes — would allow us to take a small amount of herring and mackerel from the water and transform them into three saleable products: Surimi from the flesh of the fishes, fertilizers from their scales and bones, and then fish oils — especially the well-known omega-3s.

The direct advantage of this plant would be not only to create a new fish plant on the waterfront, it would also offer a new outlet for the sale of herring and mackerel — fishes still in such abundant supply that they are only minimally regulated. Indirectly, taking herring and mackerel from the water would benefit the very traditional species of bottom fish that are depleted today. Herring and mackerel are the natural predators of the depleted cod.

Overfishing is done, but not by the fishermen; it is done by the natural predators of bottom fish. The natural predators of bottom fish such as cod and haddock and flounder are herring and mackerel. Living in the middle of the water column, they fatten on cod larvae going up toward the sun and the plankton; and then they fatten on codlings going back to their friends and relatives on the bottom of the ocean.

Gradually, the surimi plant — which of course can use cod and haddock just as well, when they become more abundant again — could expand its operations to produce consumer products derived from surimi: shrimp and lobster analogs. Then, we would witness the rejuvenation of our waterfront and use it as nature intended it: for industrial marine-oriented activities that are active year-round, rather than for hotels and restaurants that produce mainly low-paying summer jobs.

Among the many advantages of this project, we would cut down on the importation of foreign fish, and thus help our struggling balance of payments.

• **A downtown restoration project**. If Dogtown Village is restored, it will undoubtedly attract many more tourists than we attract today. What would we do with them?

The first thing would be to embrace them at a welcoming center that invites them to leave their cars in a garage to be built on many levels by filling in the ravine created by the construction of Route 128 Extension. From this multi-level garage, at whose edge one could encompass a panoramic view of most of Gloucester, tourists would go back to the welcoming center — a facility that would also function as a community center, a convention hall, and a regional theater on top of Blackburn Circle, the highest point on Cape Ann.

Tourists who like to walk could either go to Dogtown Village or take a stairway to downtown Gloucester. Or they could take a shuttle buggy that would take them either to Rockport, Rocky Neck, or Main Street. Main Street would be closed to traffic. Gloucester cars and the cars of a few tourist escapees would be parked under an elevated Rogers Street, with an attached walkway from which to observe the Inner Harbor.

These are not three disjointed pieces. They are three pivotal components of an integrated plan of urban restoration.

Readers who know my work know that these pieces are also integrated into a set of financial plans through which Gloucester can be owned by those who contribute to its growth.

Carmine Gorga is president of Polis-tics Inc.

Wednesday, July 9, 2008

MY VIEW

It's Time for Drastic Action on Fishing Regulations — and Regulators

by Carmine Gorga, Special to the Times

Last Nov. 21, the Times published a story headlined, "Yearlong federal probe roils the waterfront."

Five days later, Capt. Paul Cohan felt free to detail the deepest reason for the state of disturbance that prevails on the waterfront in Gloucester and New Bedford. Capt. Cohan, a highly respected member of the fishing community, pointed out that the investigation was being conducted with tactics that showed no respect for the constitutional rights of fishermen.

Such tactics included "Armed local, state, federal, and military agents rifling through your personal possessions with no warrants, no probable cause, no justification except your profession."

On April 16, another highly respected fisherman, Sam Frontiero, in a letter to the Times, added to the long list of indignities to which fishermen are subjected daily: They are monitored when they go to work; they are monitored when they come back from work; they are monitored where and while they are at work; they have to buy expensive permits to go to work; for certain species of fish, they are allowed to work only 40 days a year and they can land only a few hundred pounds of fish per day; if they land more, they are subjected to heavy fines and the danger of losing their licenses; hence, they throw fish overboard — all the while, they "see the starving kids all over the world."

There's more, he noted: "While driving around, you may be pulled over to be detained for hours after your long day to have your papers checked out and have the car fleeced for any part of what brings you your income."

Fishermen are being treated like criminals because at times they are caught working without carrying with them cumbersome and conflicting letters of authorization; and because at times they land a few pounds of fish above draconian limits. This is fish that is already dead and they are required to toss it overboard, rather than even donating it to charities as they have innumerable times proposed.

These allegations deserve the widest possible formal investigation. The investigation ought to be swift and thorough, since the law enforced affects the livelihood of many local fishing communities. And if the allegations turn out to be true, the outcome of the investigation ought to be drastic.

It might not be sufficient to mend the misguided tactics of our law enforcement officers, however. Law enforcement tactics are open to interpretation. Since they are enforcing a misguided law, the federal Magnuson-Stevens fishery law, there is only one ultimate solution to this intolerable state of affairs. It is the law itself that must be amended — or done away with.

The law stands on an untrue and unjustifiable premise. The premise is that overfishing is done by the fishermen. While this tall tale has been thrust upon the fishing community because of the weak political standing of its easily divided victims, reams of science and statistics prove otherwise. They prove that overfishing is done by the natural predators of fish.

This dynamic becomes incontrovertible as soon as one stops sponsoring the wrong conception of a fixed linear and pyramidal food chain. The reality is that the line changes over time, and the predators of today become the prey of tomorrow.

To the very least, the Magnuson-Stevens fishery law must be amended to incorporate this simple verity: Overfishing is done by the natural predators of fish. When this simple verity is incorporated into the structure of the law, 90 percent of today's draconian measures will appear for what they are: unnecessary and counterproductive.

The predator/prey model is not anyone's theory; it is a standard understanding in all respectable scientific circles today. It is not the large bottom fish that are the prey of herring and mackerel; rather, it is the larvae of bottom fish when they go up toward light and food-the plankton-that exist at the very top of the water column. And once they grow up, the codlings need to go back to their habitat to reproduce and savor better food than plankton.

It is when their offspring go up and down the water column that bottom fish become a feast for the midwater predators: herring and mackerel.

This is not a theory, but proven fact. Codlings were found when stomachs of herring and mackerel were opened up for inspection.

All this is not simply elementary any longer. All this is proved history. Not simply ancient history that is buried in volumes of statistics. Just now that some herring and mackerel are being caught again in New England waters, as they used to be in the past, the stocks of bottom fish are rebounding at an accelerating rate.

There are reams of science that prove the existence of these natural cycles. The first predator-prey model was developed for fish caught in the Adriatic Sea by Lotke, a mathematician, working in collaboration with Volterra, a biologist, about a century ago.

As one of the direct consequences of that first discovery, the complex chaos theory that has unfurled in mathematics and geometry during the last couple of generations has revolutionized most of our stale linear thinking processes. At the very core of that theory, the predator/pray model has been proven to affect all living creatures.

Have we not read in *Science* that even the lemmings are subject to the same dynamics?

And yet, administrators of the Magnuson-Stevens fishery law and environmentalists, of all people, show no evidence of recognizing that herring and mackerel are the predators of bottom fish. In their unholy catering to (or is it dominance of?) federal administrators of that law, they have built a solid barrier to understanding. To admit the existence of the predator/pray model would be tantamount to admitting that all the unconscionable hardship imposed upon the fishing community in the past has been all unnecessary.

No. That is not all. To cover their past mistakes, vociferous members of that unholy alliance now have the gall to call for greater restrictions on the catch of herring and mackerel.

To follow their recommendations is to condemn local fishing communities to a state of perpetual crisis -in a perpetual state of fear of enforcement of misguided rules and regulations.

Carmine Gorga is president of Polis-tics, Inc.

MY VIEW

Land Holdings, Taxation a Key to Economic Justice

by Carmine Gorga, Ph.D.

Concordian economics is a theory in progress of development. The attention is focused not on a simplistic observations of markets, but on the economic effects of the inner workings of economic justice.

To best understand Concordian economics, one has to relate it to the conditions of the modern world. The essentials of this condition can be put quite simply. While the followers of Don Quixote (artists and the literati) chase windmills, the followers of Galilei (scientists and technologists) build windmills; and a chosen few — the oligarchs — concentrate on owning the windmills.

The numbers are impressive. Summarizing the results of numerous studies and official government reports, Paul Krugman, the noted Princeton economist and columnist, has specified in the New York Times of Feb. 27, 2006, that, between 1972 and 2001, the wage and salary income of Americans at the 90th percentile of the income distribution rose only 34 percent, or about 1 percent per year. So being in the top 10 percent of the income distribution, like being a college graduate, wasn't a ticket to big income gains.

But income at the 99th percentile rose 87 percent; income at the 99.9th percentile rose 181 percent; and income at the 99.99th percentile rose 497 percent. No, that's not a misprint.

Just to give you a sense of who we're talking about: the nonpartisan Tax Policy Center estimates that this year the 99th percentile will correspond to an income of $402,306, and the 99.9th percentile to an income of $1,672,726. The center doesn't give a number for the 99.99th percentile, but it's probably well over $6 million a year.

Aren't you at least a little bit curious as to how the oligarchs do it?

Hint: They do it legally.

Double hint: They do not corrupt judges and legislators.

Triple hint: These results have nothing to do with the laws of supply and demand, but with the workings of the economic process as a whole.

What does economic justice recommend? The way I read it, economic justice recommends that one should be neither a Luddite, I do not believe in smashing the windmills; nor a socialist,

I also do not believe that "the state" will ever help us wrest the ownership of the windmills from the oligarchs. I do believe in the power of these four economic rights and responsibilities to set things right in the modern world:

1. We all have the right of access to land and natural resources. This is a natural right. It belongs to us just in virtue of our humanness. The oligarchs control an enormous portion of land and natural resources because they do not pay fair taxes on them.

2. We all have the right of access to national credit. Since national credit is the power of a nation to create money, and since the value of money is given by the value of wealth left over by past generations and the creativity of every person in a nation, national credit is the last frontier: the last commons. Capital credit liberates, while consumer credit enslaves us.

3. We all have the right to the fruits of our labor. This right should not be limited to the right to obtain only a wage. It should be extended to the right to the other major fruit of economic growth over time: capital appreciation — as well as being subject to capital loss, of course. While workers receive the pittance of a diminishing wage, the oligarchs receive the blessings of capital appreciation.

4. We all have the right to protect our wealth. It used to be that the oligarchs would make money on money, now they use money to buy and sell entire corporations.

I must say that there is not a stitch of originality in these principles. They all stem from the thought of Benjamin Franklin, Henry George, Louis D. Brandeis, and Louis O. Kelso. Read them in rapid succession, and you discover that one picks up from where the other left off. Individually, they do not stand; but together they form a very sturdy compound; together they shape an unassailable, comprehensive, all-American economic policy concerning (1) land and natural resources; (2) money; (3) labor; and (4) physical capital.

We at www.concordians.org are not simply talking about these principles; we are starting a movement to implement them. Here are some of our guidelines. Feel free to create your own.

Do not fight City Hall; rather, ask your city councilors to gradually shift the tax burden from buildings onto land. That is all that they have to do. For details, see www.urbantools.org.

Do not fight the oligarchs; rather, join them. Ask them not for a wage, but for a share of the profits — a share of the ownership of the corporation in which you work — and assume the risks of doing so. Gradually transform the Labor Movement into an Ownership Movement. For details, see www.nceo.org.

Do not fight the conglomerates; forget about becoming a globalist; rather, become a localist. Hold those pieces of the conglomerates that happen to be in your community to the fire of truth, economic justice, and economic freedom for all.

Carmine Gorga, Ph.D., is president of Polis-tics Inc., based on Middle Street in Gloucester. He is also founder of Concordian Economics, and the author of "The Economic Process: An Instantaneous Non-Newtonian Picture" (University Press of America, 2002).

Tuesday, September 23, 2008

MY VIEW

Finding Money Close to Home to Support Innovative Ideas

by Carmine Gorga

I can hear it. I can hear the question, "You have such big ideas; beautiful ideas, perhaps; but, where is the money to implement them?"

I hope to show that the question of money is a stumbling block only to the uninitiated.

Please enter with me into the marvelous mystery world of money. The money is in three locations. Here in Gloucester, in Boston, and in Washington. Today, let us look at how we can access the money that is in Gloucester. In following pieces over the next few days, I will address the other dollar sources.

Just as the power of a wrong linear idea (the idea of the pyramidical food chain) makes the fish disappear in the ocean, so the power of a wrong linear idea (competition or the rat race) makes money disappear from our coffers.

Correspondingly, as the right set of ideas manifested in fisheries — managed in accordance with the organic multi-species predator/pray model — makes the cod larvae survive the onslaught of the midwater hordes of herring and mackerel, so the right set of ideas concerning our financial affairs makes the money appear within our reach. The big idea about money is that the world of economics is not dominated by competition, but by interdependence. If you have any doubt, to straighten your thinking process about economics you do not need to read my book on The Economic Process; you only need to dip into a magisterial essay by Leonard E. Read entitled "I Pencil" at http://www.fee.org.

The linear thinking of the rat race, the linear thinking of competition, literally kills us and destroys our financial resources in the process. The right set of ideas concerning the understanding and implementation of interdependence makes us live in a world of economic peace and harmony — a world in which we all have all the money that we ever need.

We will still compete: we still want to excel; but the competition is against ourselves.

Rather than going on much longer about the abstract characteristics of the financial and the economic world, let me cut to the chase: The tool to access the money that is in Gloucester is the Gloucester Interdependence Fund (GIF).

Once organized, each one of us will keep ownership of that portion of our personal financial resources we contribute to the fund; but we will let people who really know how to manage and use money have temporary control of the money.

I can hear the rush of questions whirling around these statements. We can attempt to deal with a few of them right now; many others are treated at http://www.polis-tics.com/id23.htm." Without a doubt, many others can be treated in the future — and, I trust, by those who have a much deeper level of expertise in finance than I do.

So, from a sample of questions, here is the first one: How much money should we contribute to the GIF?

A fantastic handle on this question was given to me by Bill Ellis, in a personal communication from the Institute for Global Communications. He spoke of capital tithing, rather than income tithing. So, to follow tithing's traditional meaning, we should contribute to the fund just 10% of our capital. Our capital today is mostly in stocks and bonds handled by unknown hands on Wall Street. Let us cash in 10% of the value of those stocks and bonds and entrust the proceeds to the GIF. A brief aside. The first time I came up with the idea of this fund was in 1999 — just before the tech bubble burst, and $8 trillion went up in smoke. Just about $8 trillion, give or take a few million dollars.

Can you imagine how much money we would have personally saved? Can you imagine how much money would have been made available to entrepreneurs in Gloucester, had we started the fund then? Before leaving this subject, just remember that we are in the very midst of the bursting of the housing bubble. A word to the wise ought to be worth a thousand-page dissertation.

Who should administer the GIF? Time ago, I came up with a simple idea: a committee of Gloucester bankers. You and the eventual owners of the fund might have a better idea.

Who are the entrepreneurs who would qualify to obtain preferably loans, rather than equity positions, from the fund? The first essential pre-requisite, to my mind, is that the entrepreneur should be ready to do primary business in Gloucester. (Indeed, for any other community far or near to accommodate their own financial needs, I would recommend that they establish their own Interdependence Fund.)

The second most important requirement to obtain any loan from the fund is that the entrepreneur establish either an ESOP or a cooperative. We want worker-owned enterprises, because they can be both most efficient and most just organizations; they are also the most effective legal means to spread economic benefits as widely as possible.

The third most important characteristic of any such loan is that they should be issued at cost — a formula that does not destroy the incentive of profit, but keeps the profit of the original investor within reasonable bounds. The real profit to the investors in the fund will be derived by conceivably being themselves the owners of the new enterprises.

What type of enterprises ought to be funded? Especially at the beginning of the fund, when resources will certainly be limited, the GIF ought to give precedence to existing or new enterprises involved in year-round, preferably marine-oriented enterprises. A Surimi plant, perhaps? If there is going to be a democratically developed master plan for the economic development of our community, the management of the GIF ought to take the lead from suggestions in that plan.

The overall motto might be: Let Gloucester people own Gloucester. Let us make a declaration of economic interdependence. Only then will we become truly independent. Only then will we extend our political independence to embrace the field of economic independence.

Is there scarcity of money? I don't think so. There is only poverty of right ideas.

Carmine Gorga is president of Polis-tics, Inc. of Gloucester.

Thursday, September 25, 2008

MY VIEW

Getting to the Money in Boston

by Carmine Gorga

This title is a bit mischievous, as you will see.

But I like the idea of letting a bit of shiver and excitement run down the spine of our political and economic leaders in Boston. In the end, they will also benefit from this search for money in their neck of the woods.

The pot of money I am talking about today is administratively held in Boston, but conceptually in Washington. Never mind the details. The Fed is in Boston and it administers our money in the Northeast region. So, ultimately, to Boston we have to go.

Notice, I said "our money." That is what the Fed administers — our money. The money is not the bankers' money. It is "We, the people" who give value to money with our sweat and tears. The Fed and the bankers simply administer our money.

Just think about it. A banker can have all the money in the world and, if it remains in the bank's vaults, it is simply a long scroll of printed paper. The paper acquires its power as soon as it is borrowed by someone. It is this someone who has an essential quality that brings money to life. This person has credit. This person is creditworthy; this person has the credibility to repay the loan. This person has the ability to use the notes in such a way as to create the value of the capital borrowed and even add new value that can go to repay a reasonable amount of interest.

Simply keep in mind that, while consumer credit enslaves us, capital credit liberates us.

Benjamin Franklin wrote a brilliant essay on this quintessential American conception of money in 1729 when he was barely 23. Its title is "A Modest Enquiry Into the Nature and Necessity of a Paper-Currency" and it is today readily available on the Internet. In it he recovered the Biblical conception of money as a social good, extricating it from the corrupt European conception of money as a private good, a good created by the bankers.

Indeed, in the United States, thanks to the clearness of mind of our forefathers this is recognized to be not only an economic fact, but even a legal fact emblazoned right there, in the First Article of the US Constitution, Section 8, Paragraph 5, where it is heralded to the four winds that Our Congress has the power to "coin" money, the power to create money.

In-depth contemporary historical research on these matters is demonstrating that, while American colonists indeed objected to "taxation without representation," what drove them to open rebellion was the request of the Bank of England to sell its script to people who for about one hundred years had tasted the exhilarating experience of creating their own money. Massachusetts was the first political organization in modern times to create such script for its people; Massachusetts might as well become the first state to reaffirm this essential power of true independence. Political freedom has to embrace economic freedom. The shot that was fired at Concord, once heard around the world, gave us political freedom. We are more civilized today: an intellectual shot fired here in Gloucester might enlighten the world to the splendor of economic freedom.

That is what the Fed can do; that is what the Fed ought to do. An entrepreneur goes to the local bank to borrow money, and the bank does not go to its depositors; rather, it obtains the money at the discount window of the Federal Reserve System.

Thus the monetary authority creates the money as an asset, not as a debt.

There is a valid objection to the American conception of money. The objection is based on historical fact. Whenever a legislature has been left free to print money, the legislature has created so much money as to fan the flames of inflation and thus destroy the value of all money in circulation. Current money holders, unsurprisingly, have resisted the temptation of the legislature to create money.

What is to be noted is that too much money has often been created by the bankers as well. The monetary history of the world does not offer any basis for preferring one method over the other.

Also to be noted is that man is the only creature not to be bound by history.

In any case, monetary policy is so important that it bears experimentation. The legislature has never worked with well defined rules. As I have pointed out in a number of presentations, three such rules, if applied consistently, will eliminate the danger of inflation and provide just as much money as necessary.

First, money has to be issued as a loan; the money borrowed has to be repaid. If money is seen as a pool of common resources, then money does not belong to anyone in particular. The use of money can be entrusted only to those who give an assurance that they are able to repay the loan and thus reconstitute the integrity of the pool of common financial resources.

This assurance is stronger if the loan is issued only for the creation of new real wealth — and not for the purchase of consumer goods, or financial paper, or goods to be hoarded. Hence these latter activities do not qualify for access to our national credit.

Second, the loan has to be issued at cost. It is indefensible for a public agency to make money on money.

The third rule is that the loan ought to turn to the benefit of every citizen. Since not everyone is an entrepreneur who can wisely make use of money, the applicability of this rule bears additional restraints. It means that the loan ought to be issued only to individual entrepreneurs, to entrepreneurs who are ready to extend the benefit to all who participate in the enterprise by creating ESOPs or cooperatives, and to governmental agencies with taxing power.

If we follow these three rules, we will gradually take the economic power away from Wall Street and turn it back to Main Street, where it all started and where it properly belongs. From a means of control by the few over the many, money can gradually be transformed into a means to build community among the many.

Carmine Gorga is president of Polis-tics, Inc. of Gloucester.

Saturday, September 27, 2008

MY VIEW

Fed Money Is Ours —
and Can Help Our City's Revitalization

by Carmine Gorga

Washington, of course, is a jungle — a true jungle.

The alphabet soup of governmental agencies was invented to give us crumbs so that, a' la Hansel and Gretel, we can disperse them behind us if we ever hope to find our way back to sanity. This morning I will pick up two such crumbs: HTF and NMTC.

The Highway Transportation Fund (HTF) is a fund we can access if we want to restore the integrity of our landscape here in Gloucester to the status it exhibited before it was carved by the combined action of urban renewal and the construction of the highway through town: one left us with the devastation that still today is Rogers Street; the other left us with the ravine that is Route 128 Extension. These two holes in the ground must be filled.

Rogers Street can be elevated and thus taken out of sight as a physical interruption of the landscape that naturally devolves from Main Street toward the harbor; the Route 128 Extension ravine can be filled with a multi-layered structure that restores the curvature of the original hill. Under the elevated Rogers Street and within the multi-layered structure of 128 Route Extension we can have car, and truck, parking facilities.

Attached to the elevated Rogers Street, at a dropped-down level, we can have a Gloucester Promenade with stairways to go down to a park that can be created by eliminating the scattered parking lots that exist today between Rogers Street and the harbor.

The HTF is the agency in Washington ideally suited to give us fiscal resources to satisfy our needs. And make no mistake about it. The money we are requesting is not Washington's money.

It is our money. We send it for safe keeping to Washington whenever we buy a gallon of gas to go grocery shopping or to work. This is money that the entire country keeps in common for community needs. Helped by our congressional delegation and the goodwill acquired by our own capable CATA administrators, we ought to be able to satisfy the requirements of HTF for the release of our funds to implement our badly needed public transportation projects.

There is another Washington agency in control of our children's money that could be of great assistance in filling in needs that straddle the public-private line of demarcation. This is the New Markets Tax Credit (NMTC) program. Both Republicans and Democrats, gathered in a near unanimous agreement, created this special pot of money. Gloucester can access it because of the depressed condition of its economy.

A tax credit, again, is not Washington's money; it is our children's money. We simply shift the burden onto their shoulders. The wisdom of such an action can be judged only on the basis of the results. If we leave our children with a richer heritage, they might be able to afford the expenses. Very few would deny that if we build a visitor's center, convention hall, regional theater on top of Blackburn Circle and set up a fleet of jitneys to let visitors get to Rockport and to Rocky Neck or downtown Gloucester rather than using their private cars to infest the atmosphere and clog our streets; and if we build a Surimi, omega-3 oils, and fertilizer marine-industrial complex on the waterfront with the help of NMTC funds, our children might be glad that we burdened them with additional taxes. They will know that we had to spend the money in order to make the money.

Of course, I am not recommending that we neglect all other honey pots that exist in Washington. Many of them are being fully utilized by a number of local private or public institutions. But these activities seem to cover expenses for essential day-to-day programs. What I am calling for in this overall program of urban restoration is to pay attention to rather long-term vital needs of our community and our neighboring Rockport, needs that under the press of present exigencies might be neglected at the peril of losing our particular identity given to us by past people of Gloucester and by our God-given renewable resources.

Our way to sanity, of course, can be found only when we forget about Washington, organize our money intelligently, and then we give it a last kick: We then organize the Mutual Assurance Fund. This again can become a fairly complex apparatus. Yet, the intention is to keep it as simple as possible. For ways out of complications, please see HYPERLINK "http://www.polis-tics.com/id17.htm" www.polis-tics.com/id17.htm.

Here is the straightforward complexion of this fund. Get a small group of friends together who really care for each other, religious congregations ought to be ideal assemblages of such people — and definitely keep the group small. Whenever any member feels the urge to spend some money foolishly, this person is offered the opportunity to put the money into (your) Mutual Assurance Fund. Any person who needs a fiscal transfusion should feel free to access the fund — and replenish it, if and when possible. No questions asked; no explanations offered. If we organize such funds, then the realization will come to us: Money is everywhere.

Money is in Gloucester. (the Times, Sept, 23). Money is in Boston. (the Times, Sept, 27). Money is in Washington. If we have credit, and if we have friends, money is everywhere we are. Money should never stop us from reaching our potential. The way to develop our potential is to nurture common goals. Debtors shall then walk hand in hand with creditors.

Carmine Gorga is president of Polis-tics, Inc. of Gloucester.

Thursday, October 02, 2008

MY VIEW

The Financial Bottom Line: Waste Not, Want Not

by Carmine Gorga

Jack Sheedy (many readers will remember him as the peaceful, perfect image of true power) disabused me of an idea that still finds currency in many quarters.

I was a gung-ho idealist/realist with a head full of steam those days in late 1968 or early 1969. At my first meeting with Jack, the head of the Housing Authority, I found myself reeling off to him a long list of programs that could be brought to bear on the War on Poverty here in Gloucester. One of my points of leverage was the idea that the money I was talking about was not coming from Gloucester, but from Boston and Washington.

He was very polite, but very firm. He asked me only one question: "Where do you think the money in Boston and Washington is coming from?"

He stopped my spiel in mid-course. I was in the process of telling him that if we did not get that money, other communities would. "My" idea is still in vogue today: It is a very fallacious and dangerous idea.

It is fallacious because, whether tax money goes to Boston or to Washington, it still comes out of our pockets. There is no way of arguing the contrary.

Unless the money is created by the national monetary authority, it all comes out of our pockets. And even the money put in circulation by the monetary authority on the basis of national credit, even this money, if it should exceed the bounds of need to create new wealth, the extra money will also come out of our pockets in the form of inflation.

When two inflated dollars buy the same item we used to buy with one dollar, an additional dollar comes out of our pockets. The inflation process might take longer to be felt, but the result is identical to the action of the tax man. We pay.

The idea that we had better avail ourselves of any money that has been accumulated in Boston or Washington because other communities might get a hold of it before us is very dangerous, because it fosters irresponsibility. Just because our money has gone to Boston or to Washington, we cannot disassociate ourselves from it. It is still our responsibility to care that it be spent wisely, whether it returns here to Gloucester or goes to another community.

The weasel approach of justifying any type of expenditure here in Gloucester, because if we do not get the money, some other community will get it, is the height of irresponsibility.

If this is the best justification we can come up with for any proposed public expenditure, it does not take many calculations to conclude that the proposed project does not offer the best possible use of that money.

The proof of the pudding is quite elementary. If Boston money and Washington money is not spent wisely, it is wasted.

Waste not, want not. There is the proof in the pudding. Our ancestors knew better.

Waste is especially painful under two conditions: when the current use of the money or the use of any other resource is frivolous and occurs in the presence of real needs whose urgency is palpably evident. Our ancestors knew that, if our tax money is wasted, we have to come up with more money for essential expenditures: collapsing bridges, educational systems always wanting for essential tools — both in teachers, teacher salaries, and material aids. The list is endless.

And when the tax man hits us for more money, then it is too late to complain. Let us remember that.

Is it not much wiser to curb our urges for conspicuous consumption whether in the public or the private sphere? Are we not coming to an end of profligacy in the use of our monetary and natural resources? Let us concentrate our attention for a moment on the waste of our natural resources. The larvae of bottom fish that we leave to the predators are a waste; the predators we do not harvest are a waste; the fish that we throw overboard because of absurd fishing regulations are a waste; wasteful use of the land is not tolerated by natural forces. We might still be in the nick of time. To avoid fiscal bankruptcy and ecological collapse we might want to give some serious thought to exploring the world of creative frugality or even frugal capitalism. The terms sound like oxymorons today. But perhaps they point the way to recovery of our inner and outer riches.

Jack Sheedy, may his soul rest in peace, knew it well way back then. I am still thankful to him for teaching me such an important lesson — a lesson in economics, a lesson in morality, a lesson in reality. His patient gentle teaching helped me sharpen my mind. It helped me avoid the pitfall of shortcuts. I hope you will benefit in equal measure.

This is the last in a series of four related columns on the accessibility of money to develop and advance new economic and other ideas for Gloucester. The others appeared on Sept. 23, Sept. 25 and Sept. 27.

Carmine Gorga is president of Polis-tics Inc. of Gloucester.

PART TWO

Essays Published
on the Internet

It takes a child to raise a village.
Senator Clinton Hillary (in reverse)

The Way

How to transform the American Dream into daily reality!

One suggestion is that the dream can indeed be implemented by following:

The Way of Concord

The Way of Concord is the way of jujitsu. When faced with over-whelming force, it is not wise to stay in the way of your opponent. You ought to use the art of weaponless self-defense developed in Japan many centuries ago. Jujitsu is a science that uses throws, holds, and blows as well as the power derived from the attacker's own weight and strength.

This strategy can be applied to contemporary political, social, and economic life by discovering common goals and convincing your opponent to work with you on the achievement of the determined common goals. This strategy can be called the Way of Concord. It can be reduced to the following four fundamental tenets.

Do not stay in the way of militarism; realize that the military are in search of peace; hence, transform the power of the military by creating a parallel force for peace.

Do not stay in the way of racism; realize that the racist wants everyone to be like him; hence, transform the racist into a member of the human race.

Do not stay in the way of globalism; realize that the globalist wants to bring the good life to other countries; hence, transform the globalist into a localist.

In the United States, do not stay in the way of either Democrats or Republicans; realize that both parties want the best for their country; hence, transform them both — as well as any Independent — into Concordians. Greens and other "minority" parties are certainly included in this invitation.

In their soul, party members, dissatisfied with the polarization of the modern political world, might already be Concordians. And if they are not, the large number of people who do not seem to be able to join either party, the Independents and those who do not vote, certainly are very close to being Concordians.

To become a Concordian, you need to take the Pledge of Concord.

The Roots of the Concordian World

The roots of the Concordian World extend very deep into the best traditions of the world. I was raised in the Catholic tradition, so it is easier for me to recognize those roots — from Jesus to Thoreau. But I can also see many other traditions, from Buddhism to Hinduism to "Americanism" (the way of Native Americans) in the propositions that make up the Way of Concord and Pledge of Concord. So, in brief, for me:

A Concordian is a person who rediscovers his or her true inner soul and tries to infuse it into the modern world.

Whereas the modern world, in general, is mechanistic, materialistic, and reductionist — individualistic, atomistic, isolationist — hence empty and rather shallow, the Concordian world is holistic, organic, associationistic, and, in the end, very satisfying and very real.

CG July 8, 2004

A Pledge of Concord

Concordian Politics	Concordian Sociology	Concordian Economic Practices
1. Unity in diversity	Declaration of Economic Interdependence	1. We all have the right of access to natural resources — and the responsibility to pay taxes for the exclusive use of those resources
2. Popular sovereignty		2. We all have the right of access to national credit — and the responsibility to repay loans
3. Democratic equality		3. We all have the right to the fruits of our labor — and the responsibility to offer services equal to our compensation
4. Rule of law		4. We all have the right to protect our wealth — and the responsibility to respect the wealth of others

Bill Collier & Carmine Gorga, October 16, 2002

Fully appreciative of the many blessings of the Declaration of

Independence *it might now be an appropriate time to draft a*

A DECLARATION OF ECONOMIC INTERDEPENDENCE

Whereas the Declaration of (Political) Independence has, without open discussion, been transformed into a Declaration of Personal In-dependence;

Whereas this ideology has given rise to the Age of Entitlements, an age dominated by the conception that there can ever be rights with-out responsibilities;

Whereas the lack of personal and civic responsibility has generated the conception of

Life as

One-Against-All

Whereas this emphasis on our own welfare — independent, if not at the expense, of the welfare of our fellow citizens — has created economic insecurity for everyone, rich and poor alike,

we affirm that our greatest political need

is

to build a society

in which

the reality of

Economic Interdependence

is fully acknowledged.

In this society, we declare, the fundamental conception of Life is

One-With-All

— and we trust that the effect will be

economic jubilation for all.

In order to build such a society

we are called upon to realize the political ideals of

Liberty, Justice, and Goodwill toward one and all.

In order to build such a society

our challenge is

to deny

all structures of individual and societal selfishness

and

to affirm

THE PRINCIPLES OF ECONOMIC JUSTICE

as enunciated in

A Bill of Economic Rights and Responsibilities

✳ ✳ ✳

This work has uniquely been assisted financially by "The Joan M. Gorga Foundation" and editorially by Stuart-Sinclair Weeks.

First penned by
Carmine Gorga
September 25, 1996

For a fuller explanation of the reasoning on which this Declaration is based, see a volume entitled *The Economic Process: An Instantaneous Non-Newtonian Picture.*
By Carmine Gorga. Lanham, MD, and Oxford: University Press of America, 2002.
The best explanation of economic interdependence that this writer has found is an article by Leonard E. Read entitled "I, Pencil: My family Tree".
It is available from The Foundation for Economic Education, Inc. at www.fee.org

A Bill of Economic Rights and Responsibilities

"We need an Economic Bill of Rights."

Martin Luther King, written in 1968 just before his assassination

* * *

**"We'll never revitalize our market economy till ...
every single American is protected by
an economic bill of rights."**

Jerry Brown, "We the People, Take Back America"

* * *

**"I ask the Congress to explore the means for incrementing this
economic bill of rights (a second Bill of Rights) — for it is
definitely the responsibility of the Congress to do so."**

**President Franklin D. Roosevelt
State of the Union Message, Jan. 11, 1944**

* * *

**"At the United Nations, the Pope urged the rich to show
solidarity with the poor. His social teaching has emphasized
that this moral commitment should not be done by dole
that creates dependency, but by empowering
the poor to become full participants in economic life."**

George Weigel, President, Ethics & Public Policy Center

A Working Draft

Article 1

We all have the right to receive economic justice; we all have the responsibility to grant economic justice to others.

Article 2

We all have the right to peace and to the economic benefits of law and order; we all have the responsibility to pay for the instrumentalities of peace, law and order.

Article 2a

We all have the right to equal pay for equal or comparable work; we all have the responsibility to provide equal or comparable work for equal pay.

Article 2b

We all have the right to associate in unions to even out our status in arguments for the reception of our share of the fruits of economic life; we all have the responsibility to keep membership in our unions open to all potential co-workers.

Article 2c

We all have the right to associate in cooperatives and corporations to assure our role in the production and distribution of our share of the fruits of economic life; we all have the responsibility to keep membership in our cooperatives and corporations open to all potential co-producers and co-consumers.

Article 3

We all have the right of access to natural resources; we all have the responsibility to pay taxes as compensation to the rest of the community for the exclusive use of those resources.

Article 4
We all have the right of access to national credit; we all have the responsibility to repay the loan issued on the basis of national credit.

Article 4a
All communities with taxing power have a right of access to national credit for the financing of public works programs; communities have the responsibility to repay the loan issued on the basis of national credit.

Article 5
We all have the right to own the fruits of our labor; we all have the responsibility, if working with and for others, to offer services commensurate with the value of the reward received in the form of stocks — eventually, no longer wages.

Article 6
We all have the right to protect our wealth; we all have the responsibility to respect other people's possessions.

Article 7
We all have the right to healthy air, water, and food supplies; we all have the responsibility to accept the higher prices that result from the provision of those qualities.

Article 8

The poor have the right to society's surplus; the poor have the responsibility to accept society's surplus.

Article 9
The government has the right to raise taxes to administer peace and justice; the government has the responsibility to administer peace and justice.

This work has uniquely been assisted financially by "The Joan M. Gorga Foundation" and editorially by Stuart-Sinclair Weeks.

First penned by
Carmine Gorga
October 12, 1995
Last revised: March 15, 2005

An Introduction to
Concordian Economics

CONCORDIAN ECONOMICS is a theory in progress of development. It is based on the revision of Keynes' model of the economic system, a work that was notably assisted for 27 years by Professor Franco Modigliani, a Nobel laureate in economics at MIT, and for 21 years by Professor M. L. Burstein, a Professor of economics at York University..

So far, its founder, Carmine Gorga, Ph.D., has produced a book and, at times in collaboration with others, a series of papers. The book is entitled *The Economic Process: An Instantaneous Non-Newtonian Picture* (University Press of America, 2002). In it, the writer transforms the linear world of supply and demand, the world of the "dismal science," into an organic and dynamic set of human relationships: How do people produce wealth, how do they divide the ownership of that wealth among themselves, how do they use money to buy and to sell goods.

The attention then is focused not on a simplistic observations of markets, but on the economic effects of the inner workings of economic justice.

The most important papers are reprinted at *http://www.carmine-gorga.us/id34.htm.*

To best understand Concordian economics, one has to relate it to the conditions of the modern world. The essentials of this condition can be put quite simply. While the followers of Don Quixote (artists and the literati) chase windmills, the followers of Galilei (scientists and technologists) build windmills; and a chosen few — the oligarchs — concentrate on owning the windmills.

The numbers are impressive. Summarizing the results of numerous studies and official government reports, Paul Krugman, the noted Princeton economist and columnist, has specified in the *New York Times* of February 27, 2006 that

> Between 1972 and 2001 the wage and salary income of Americans at the 90th percentile of the income distribution rose only 34 percent, or about 1 percent per year.

So being in the top 10 percent of the income distribution, like being a college graduate, wasn't a ticket to big income gains.

But income at the 99th percentile rose 87 percent; income at the 99.9th percentile rose 181 percent; and income at the 99.99th percentile rose 497 percent. No, that's not a misprint.

Just to give you a sense of who we're talking about: the nonpartisan Tax Policy Center estimates that this year the 99th percentile will correspond to an income of $402,306, and the 99.9th percentile to an income of $1,672,726. The center doesn't give a number for the 99.99th percentile, but it's probably well over $6 million a year.

Aren't you at least a little bit curious as to how the oligarchs do it?
Hint: They do it legally.
Double hint: They do not corrupt judges and legislators.
Triple hint: These results have nothing to do with the laws of supply and demand, but with the workings of the economic process as a whole.

❊ ❊ ❊

I am biased, of course, but that in a nutshell is the reason why I recommend my book so highly to any reader who is interested in what goes on in the world today. If one wants to understand what goes on in the world, one must understand the inner workings of the economic process. No, the above vignette of our economic condition is neither a new development nor a new revelation. The process has gone on for the last four hundred — if not four thousand — years.

❊ ❊ ❊

No book stands alone. *The Economic Process* is the pivot of Concordian economics, a set of propositions that builds a seamless canvass out of economic theory, policy, and practice. The book itself has its roots in a new/old system of logic and a new/old epistemology, fields that I believe contain the basic rules of civilized discourse. In turn, the book prepares the way for the implementation of economic justice.

And what does economic justice recommend? The way I read it, economic justice recommends that one should be neither a Luddite, I do not believe in smashing the windmills; nor a socialist, I do not believe that "the state" will ever help us wrest the ownership of the windmills from the oligarchs. And that would be wrong in any case. I believe in the power of economic justice. I believe in the power of producing, distributing, and exchanging wealth in accordance with the principles of economic justice from this moment on. I believe in the power of these four economic rights and responsibilities to set things right in the modern world:

1. *We all have the right of access to land and natural resources.* This is a natural right. It belongs to us just in virtue of our humanness. Land and natural resources are our original commons. They belong to us all. This is an essential right, because without the possibility of exercising it, we are deprived of the possibility of participating in the economic process. And without participation in the economic process, we are marginalized; we are made dependent on the good will of others. The most direct way of securing this right is through the exercise of *the responsibility to pay taxes* for the exclusive use of those resources that are under our command. Hoarding idle land is the economic link between the tax on that land and the right of access to that land and its natural resources. Paying taxes on land and natural resources gradually encourages dis-hoarding and correspondingly opens up the resources of that land to all those who need them and can make use of them. Worrisome hoarding is that which occurs both downtown and in the belt surrounding major cities and towns: it is to leapfrog over this belt that people go to the suburbs in search for affordable land, thus creating overlong commuting lines and overstretched lines of communication and protection. Paying taxes on land values is a most fair form of taxation, because it implies returning to the community part of the value that is created, not by the individual owner, but by the community. And still there is no compulsion in this policy: pay more taxes and keep control of more land.

Quick decoding key: The oligarchs control an enormous portion of land and natural resources because they do not pay fair taxes on them.

2. *We all have the right of access to national credit.* Since national credit is the power of a nation to create money, and since the value of money is given by the value of wealth left over by past generations and the creativity of every person in a nation, national credit is the last frontier: the last commons. Without access to credit today one is made economically impotent. Worse, since this advantage is automatically granted to the few — the so-called prime dealers — it is automatically denied to the majority of

the population who are henceforth condemned to pay a higher rate of interest, if they obtain credit at all. Of course, a loan should be extended only on the basis of *the responsibility to repay the loan*. And these loans will have a high chance of being repaid because they are issued at cost and are issued exclusively for capital formation, for the creation of new wealth — not to buy consumer goods or financial papers or goods to be hoarded. Capital credit liberates, while consumer credit enslaves us.

Quick decoding key: The central bank creates money for the benefit of the oligarchs and then borrows money from them.

3. *We all have the right to the fruits of our labor.* This right should not be limited to the right to obtain only a wage. It should be extended to the right to the other major fruit of economic growth over time: capital appreciation — as well as being subject to capital loss, of course. The only justification for reserving the right to capital appreciation to the stockholders, the owners of a corporation, and excluding the workers from it, can be found in the fact that today loans are given only to owners of past wealth (the catch-22 of today's economic reasoning). But from now on this right can be extended to people who do not have prior wealth through the right of access to national credit — especially by legally transforming workers into owners through individually owned enterprises, ESOPs, and cooperatives. Of course, this right should be extended only in correspondence with *the responsibility to offer services* equal to projected compensation. And there will be an outpouring of such services because, while in a command and control economy workers are requested to check their brains at the factory entrance, in a Concordian — and chaordic — economy owners are legally and psychologically empowered to exercise their brains at their work post.

Quick decoding key: While workers receive the pittance of a diminishing wage, the oligarchs receive the blessings of capital appreciation.

4. *We all have the right to protect our wealth.* This right seems to be universally accepted, except in one case that matters most: in the case of the trustification process, the process originally conceived to create corporate trusts and repeated in a hundred subtle variations in industrial growth. There are two ways in which most corporations grow: one is through internal growth, and this manifestation ought to be protected in no uncertain terms; the other is growth by external purchase, and this manifestation

ought to be prohibited in no uncertain terms. Why? Because this prohibition is the only certain way to protect the wealth of present owners. And if it is assumed that most stockholders of the modern corporation are happy to have their shares bought and sold on the market, it must be granted that growth-by-purchase takes wealth away from workers who have contributed to create that value — and many times, in the trustification process, lose their work site as well. All in the name of efficiency — a misnomer that stands for private financial gain garnered at the expense of shifting costs of living onto the community. Of course, this right ought to be purchased only at the cost of *the responsibility to respect the wealth of others*. These are two way streets. We cannot even attempt to restrain the Pac-Man economy, while we use Pac-Man instruments.

Quick decoding key It used to be that the oligarchs would make money on money, now they use money to buy and sell entire corporations.

A disclaimer. Apart from necessary technical innovations and the glue that holds the various pieces of the canvas together, I must say that there is not a stitch of originality in these principles. They all stem from the thought of Benjamin Franklin, Henry George, Louis D. Brandeis, and Louis O. Kelso. Read them in rapid succession, and you discover that one picks up from where the other left off. Individually, they do not stand; but together they form a very sturdy compound; together they shape an unassailable, comprehensive, all-American economic policy concerning (1) land and natural resources; (2) money; (3) labor; and (4) physical capital.

❋ ❋ ❋

We at *www.concordians.org* are not simply talking about these principles; we are starting a movement to implement them. Here are some of our guidelines. Feel free to create your own.

Do not fight the Federal Reserve System; rather, show them that it is possible to have a different conception and administration of money by starting a Mutual Assurance Fund with your friends and progressing to the establishment of a community-wide Financial Interdependence Fund. Then pass on your very own Concord Resolution. For details, see *www.polis-tics.com*.

Do not fight City Hall; rather, ask your City Councilors to gradually shift the tax burden from buildings onto land. That is all that they have to do. For details, see *www.urbantools.org*.

Do not fight the oligarchs; rather, join them. Ask them not for a wage, but for a share of the profits — a share of the ownership of the corporation in which you work — and assume the risks of doing so. Gradually transform the Labor Movement into an Ownership Movement. For details, see *www.nceo.org*.

Do not fight the conglomerates; forget about becoming a globalist; rather, become a localist. Hold those pieces of the conglomerates that happen to be in your community to the fire of truth, economic justice, and economic freedom for all.

✳ ✳ ✳

Buy the book, if you can. Read it at the library, if you wish. Borrow it from a friend. Somehow get acquainted with the basic propositions of Concordian economics. If you have read thus far, you have already made a good start. Above all, join us in the effort to change the world — in any way you can. Join us in the effort to create a Concordian world. There is plenty of exhilarating work to be done.

CG April 18, 2006

A Modest Proposal
A Mutual Assurance Fund
For Your Organization

(YourYami)

When Jonathan, our son, went through Miami more than once, he asked: This is MY Yami; where is Your Yami?

by
Carmine Gorga

In consultation with David S. Wise

February 2004
Revised March 2005

1. What is the Mutual Assurance Fund?
The Fund is a pool of common wealth; it is wealth that belongs to all members of YourYami.

2. How is the Mutual Assurance Fund constituted?
The Fund is constituted through voluntary contributions by any person or institution whether or not a member of YourYami.

3. How can the Mutual Assurance Fund be managed?
The Fund will be managed as a separate line item within YourYami budget; no funds raised by YourYami for its own mission will be used for the purposes of the Fund.

4. But there are always expenses...
True. And it is also true that by depositing in a bank the proceeds of the Fund, the Fund will earn some interest which-for ease of administration-will be added to the revenues of YourYami. In any case, if with the passage of time the

administration of the Fund should become too onerous, decisions will have to be made: the Fund can cut down on its activities, or cover its expenses through its own funds, or raise ad hoc resources.

5. Who can access the Mutual Assurance Fund?
Only members of YourYami can benefit from the Fund.

6. What are the procedures for accessing the Mutual Assurance Fund?
Any member of YourYami who may need assistance from the Fund will have to secure approval from two (2) members of YourYami, hereinafter called the Approval Committee.

7. Who appoints the Approval Committee?
The person who requests the assistance has the responsibility to create the ad hoc, case-by-case, Approval Committee.

8. What are the conditions for approval of the request?
There are no conditions, except those dictated by the honor system: requests are expected not to be too frivolous; not too frequent; and with a reasonable expectation of a refund.

9. Are there external limits to the amounts approved?
Yes. The Approval Committee cannot authorize expenditures in excess of the amount available at any moment in the Mutual Assurance Fund. And, in case of conflicting requests, the "first-come, first-served" rule ought to be of assistance.

10. Are there internal limits to the amounts approved?
Yes. There are many internal limits to the amounts approved. The amounts will have to be established at the discretion of the Approval Committee. One expects the exercise of prudence in respect to many factors: since the Fund is a pool of common wealth, one expects that a number of concerns be manifest in each decision of the Approval Committee such as concern for the present and future needs of other members of YourYami; concern for the replenishment of the Fund; concern for the "good name" of the Fund.

11. Are there limits as to the number of times a person can ask for contributions from the Mutual Assurance Fund?

This is another area where the discretion of the Approval Committee has to prevail. It is possible to envisage cases in which one person will be denied a second time around, while another person will receive approval innumerable times-depending on specific circumstances. A person who uses the common pool of resources for frivolous reasons, and is not forthcoming in restoring the integrity of the Fund, will not likely be approved a second or third time. Instead, a person raising young children, for instance, might be approved to receive reasonable funds for a reasonable number of years.

12. What are the operating procedures of the Mutual Assurance Fund?

Once the treasurer of YourYami receives a voucher (any piece of paper will do) signed by the Approval Committee, a check is issued to the person who requests the funds. The name of the recipient is kept confidential; but the names of the members serving on the Approval Committee(s) will receive an honorable mention at the subsequent Board Meeting.

12b. Any other procedure?

Perhaps, once the organization grows-and the demands on the Mutual Assurance Fund grow-it might become necessary to appoint a Review Committee to assist the treasurer in sharing final responsibility for the wellbeing of the Fund. A Review Committee of 3 might be appointed by the board, for instance, to review single applications that might consume more than fifty percent of the resources available at any time in the Fund.

13. What are the operating procedures for the collection of funds?

As an integral part of the budget report, the treasurer of YourYami will deliver a written report to the Board outlining expenses as well as totals raised each month divided into two categories: anonymous donations and attributed contributions by name of donors.

14. Lists, lists... and yearly summaries

Yes. The treasurer of YourYami — or any other member appointed by the Board — will in effect keep three lists (and yearly summaries) on an accrual basis: a list of expenses; a list of contributors, divided as to number of anonymous contributors and named contributors; and a list of participants in the various ad hoc Approval (and Review) Committees.

15. How will the Mutual Assurance Fund be reconstituted?

There will be three sources of funds: the generosity of the members of YourYami: the honesty of the borrowers/grantees; and possible outside grants.

16. What does the generosity of the members ultimately require?
Oh, the usual virtues of prudence, justice, temperance, and fortitude. Wisdom, science, and understanding will certainly help. The indispensable ones are hope, faith, and love. Ultimately, these are the internal resources that each member of YourYami will have to call upon.

17. And what else?
A spirit of self-sacrifice, is that the expected answer? Well, no; not a spirit of sacrifice, but a spirit of self-fulfillment.

18. What is the ultimate purpose of the Fund?
The ultimate purpose of the Mutual Assurance Fund is to offer a moral choice to the members of YourYami. Faced with the temptation to hoard wealth, one will have the opportunity to face this fundamental choice: "Will I catch more happiness from hoarding this wealth or from adding it to the Fund?" Better still. Faced with the temptation to incur an expense for a dispensable item, one will have the opportunity to ask: "Will I catch more happiness from pursuing this expense or from adding to the Fund?"

19. Who are the ultimate administrators of the Mutual Assurance Fund?
The administrators of the Mutual Assurance Fund are all the members of YourYami who, acting just like the leprechauns of old, will never leave the pot full and never leave it empty.

Guidance

The Parable of the Talents: Do not hoard.
Mt. 6:26, 28-29
Look at
  the birds of the air;
  they neither sow
  nor reap
  nor gather
  into barns,

and yet
your heavenly Father
feeds them.

Consider the lilies
of the field
how they grow;
they neither toil
nor spin;
yet, I tell you,
even Solomon
in all his glory
was not arrayed
like one of these.

Precedents

Corn left at the edge of the corn field for people in need to collect freely and other forms of charity (i.e., love) as recounted, for instance, in *Tzedakah, A Way of Life* ed. Azriel Eisenberg, New York, N.Y.: Behrman House, 1963.

The Sabbath for the Lord on the seventh day, for seven weeks every year, the seventh year, and the forty-ninth year-rest and forgiveness for people, land, and debts (Lev. 25-1-4; Is. 65; Lk. 4) as presented by, e.g., Maria Harris, *Proclaim Jubilee!* Louisville, KY: Westminster John Knox Press, 1996

Maimonides' Eight degrees of charity

The Guilds

St. Vincent's Society

Microfinancing

At the suggestion of David S. Wise, the Harvard Class of 1955 established a fund in 1991, replenished through voluntary contributions, for the purpose of assisting "a class member facing financial, physical, or psychological hardship through the receipt of a morale-building 'unexpected' material or monetary gift" (David S. Wise, "Class Assistance Fund Report", in the 45th Annual Report of Harvard Class of 1955, p. xv).

Acknowledgments

Thanks go especially to
> Judy Cox
> Gordon Goetemann
> Lara Lepionka
> Michele Miller
> Ruth Mordecai

January 1999

A WORKING PAPER ON CAPITAL TITHING

The Gloucester Interdependence Fund

An Indirect Venture Capital Fund

by
Carmine Gorga, Ph.D.
President, Polis-tics, Inc.

NOTE: Two complementary structures might make the plan feasible: from a legal point of view, JMPSO or Joint Municipal Private Securities Offering™ and, in a low income community such as Gloucester, MA, from a financial point of view, NMTC or New Market Tax Credits.

AN OVERVIEW IN POWER POINT

Functions
Entrust to us 10% of your capital
Together, we will make it grow
Together, we will find success through the work of our hands

Characteristics of GIF
A Special Case of Capital Tithing
An Indirect Venture Capital Fund
Lending at Cost / Insuring Loans

Comparative Advantage

Fosters the enterprise of its borrowers
Sells shares worldwide
Lends only within city limits
Has direct knowledge of fundamentals

Benefits to Stockholders
Constant liquidity
Many indirect benefits
Steady capital appreciation

Sources of Anticipated Increase in Shares Market Value
Interest earned by deposits of the proceeds of the sale of shares
Interest earned by deposits of the proceeds of loans made
Interest earned by deposits of proceeds of grants
Consulting fees and other fees the Fund may charge for its various administrative, legal, and accounting operations
Possibilities of traditional income tithing

Other Benefits to Shareholders
From combining all shares together
From borrowings obtained on the strength of the Fund as a whole
From insuring borrowed or lent funds
From the amounts of grants and other donations that can be obtained by the fund
From the social and political leverage that can be acquired by pooling resources together

Constant Benefit
Shareholders will benefit from the insulation of their wealth from the vicissitudes of the stock market
The value of the Fund can, at the very least, be expected to even out the highs and lows of the stock market

Long Term Benefits
From an increase in the value of buildings and land one may own in the city
From the increase of the value of one's business operation owned in the city

From the increase of one's wage income

Conditions of Loans
Only for Creation of New Real Wealth
For the Benefit of All Participants in the Borrowing Enterprise
Loans Are Issued At Cost

Benefits to Borrowers
Greater availability of credit
Lower cost of credit

Here ends the power point presentation and starts a more detailed description of the Fund

This brief introduction to the Gloucester Interdependence Fund presents an overview of the nature, purpose, functions, and structure of the organization, a description of procedures to be followed by the Fund, and — given certain assumptions — a survey of effects upon shareholders, borrowers, banks participating and banks non-participating in the organization of the Fund, as well as effects on the community as a whole.

Nature and Mission of the Fund
The Gloucester Interdependence Fund is an indirect venture capital fund, with a restrained internal capital growth policy. The Fund purposefully restrains its growth potential by lending to, rather than investing in, business enterprises. The Fund also restrains its capital growth potential by lending at cost. This policy is adopted in order to serve the Fund's mission, which is to foster the business enterprises of its borrowers.

Comparative Advantage
The Gloucester Interdependence Fund has a comparative advantage over other growth funds because, by focusing its operations on lending within city limits, the value of its shares is based — not on psychology and hear-say — but on direct knowledge, economic fundamentals, and genuine human interest.

Purpose and Functions
The primary purpose of the Gloucester Interdependence Fund is to

gather credit, become its steward, and to channel it at the lowest possible cost.

The Gloucester Interdependence Fund acquires and disperses funds at the lowest possible cost because, working in cooperation with the market, it performs the following essential functions:

- It offers constant liquidity;
- It offers the prospect of steady capital appreciation to its shareholders;
- It offers loans at cost;

The market will gradually recognize that Gloucester Interdependence Fund (GIF) shares, because of their exceptional functional value, have a financial value greater than the accounting value of the Fund's assets;

In order to provide the benefits analyzed below, the Gloucester Interdependence Fund reduces expenses to a minimum. Hence, the GIF is set up as a growth fund that does not offer interest or dividend payments on the shares of the fund, because the administrative costs are too high, and the benefits to the shareholders would be minimal;

Other savings will come through an immediate use of all cyberspace capabilities. For instance, we will study the feasibility of developing a GloucesterCcard™ to perform Fund's capital credit tasks, as well as a cyber auction to set the market value of its shares. As in credit unions, shares might be bought through automatic payroll deductions;

Short and long term returns to all stakeholders are detailed below.

Organizational Structure

An Independent Entity

The Gloucester Interdependence Fund is organized as a for profit corporation under the laws of the Commonwealth of Massachusetts.

The tasks of the Fund are: to sell shares, issue loans, and administer grants.

The purpose of the fund is to offer more commercial credit at lower price to the local business community.

The initial value of the shares is one US dollar per share; the shares will not earn interest or dividends; the shares are constantly redeemable into cash, at market value at the moment of redemption.

The sources of anticipated increase in the market value of the shares are:

- interest earned by deposits of the proceeds of the sale of shares;
- interest earned by deposits of the proceeds of loans made;
- interest earned by deposits of proceeds of grants, subject to stipulation with the granting authority, be it public agencies or private foundations and donors; consulting fees and other fees the Fund may charge for its various administrative, legal, and accounting operations.

Current All-Volunteer Board
David L. Marsh, President
Dean W. Harrison, Treasurer
Robert J. Madruga, Clerk
Alan Hagstrom, Director
Robert M. Heineman, Director

Procedures
Yearly Assembly of Shareholders
Each person investing in the Fund is entitled to one vote: The principle of One Person, One Vote is based on the recognition of the relative sacrifice involved in the investment of one's funds.
There is one yearly assembly of shareholders.
The functions of the Yearly Assembly are: Election of Plenary Board, Setting and Ratification of Policies of the Board.

Eventual Board Composition
Procedures for the election of the Plenary Board will be adopted as the Fund grows.

There are two classes of Board Members: Ex-Officio members and freely elected members.

The initial Plenary Board is composed of Present *and* Past City "Fathers & Mothers," namely, Mayor(s), President(s) of City Council, City Councilors, Chair(s) of City Boards and Commissions, State Senator(s), State Representative(s), President of Each Bank, Representative of Each Industry and Each Major Socio-economic Organization in the City (Chamber of Commerce, Council on Aging, Rotary, Legion, Elk's, Knights, Moose, Gloucester Fishermen's Wives Organization, Action, Wellspring, Gloucester Initiatives).

Board Meetings — Executive and Plenary Sessions

Plenary Sessions

The Board Meets, publicly, in plenary session whenever there is a decision to be taken concerning the use of public moneys. The Board will also meet in plenary session whenever a project is of such complexity, magnitude, and significance as to be potentially able to affect the entire economic life of the city. As the life of the Fund unfolds, the Board will determine whether a project under consideration deserves a plenary session of the board. But it is wise to decide on a threshold figure from the outset. Let us say that every project involving the expenditure of more than $4.9 million deserves to be discussed in plenary session and this figure will be automatically adjusted in relation to the value of the money. Alternatively, one can establish that the Board will meet in plenary session whenever 51% of its members decide that the project deserves to be discussed in plenary session. One more alternative to consider is that a plenary session can be called by 40% of the members of the Executive Board.

Whenever the Board meets in Plenary Session, it will have to consider the need for three separate sessions, or three iterations of its procedures, involving, respectively, **Planning, Financing, and Implementation** for each one of the projects under its jurisdiction.

Detailed procedures for these events will develop as the Fund grows.

Executive Sessions

The Presidents of banks sponsoring the creation of the Gloucester Interdependence Fund form, *ex officio*, the Executive Council. The Executive Council meets regularly to oversee the management of the Fund. And it meets in private session in all cases that do not require a plenary session.

Separate Administration of Grants

Funds that are received from public or private agencies as grants and donations are administered through a separate ledger. The Fund will receive a set of fees, stipulated with each funding agency, for the management and administration of these funds.

Selling Shares

Shares of the Fund will be sold worldwide. Shares can be underwritten by the banks participating in the organization of the Fund. The slogan that might be adopted for this sales campaign is: "Entrust to us 10% of your capital. Together, we will make it grow. Together, we will find success through the work of our hands."

Formula for Deposit of Proceeds from Shares, Fees, and Grants
There are two procedures for the selection of the banks where funds are deposited. The first procedure involves a voluntary selection by each shareholder at the time that the shares are purchased.

The second formula involves the distribution of deposits of proceeds from sales on non-committed shareholders, fees earned by the Fund, and grants received from private or public agencies and donors.

Proceeds from sale of non-committed shares, borrowings by the Fund, and grants will be deposited in each bank operating in Gloucester in accordance with the value of shares purchased by their depositors and shareholders.

Lending
Funds raised by the Fund are lent out. They are not invested through the purchase of shares or other direct participation in any individual or corporate enterprise. Loans will be issued only to individual entrepreneurs and corporations operating within City limits, in accordance with the following three fundamental principles:

I. Loans Are Issued For Creation of New Real Wealth
Loans are issued only for the creation of new real wealth. This policy implies that no loans will be issued for the transfer of ownership of existing wealth, for the purchase of financial instruments, for the purchase of wealth that is then hoarded, and for the purchase of consumer goods.

II. For the Benefit of All Participants in the Borrowing Enterprise
Loans issued by the Fund are issued at the lowest possible rate on interest. For the members of the shareholders to bear such burden, they will need to know that their sacrifice of immediate income — in terms of interest and dividends — is due to the purchase of community-wide benefits. The procedure to secure such benefits are these: loans will be issued to sole proprietors who operate without any hired help — or sole proprietors who include their help in a fair share of the rights of sole proprietorship. Loans that are issued to corporate enterprises will achieve the same public purpose if the corporation receiving the loan is a cooperative or has estab-

lished an Employee Stock Ownership Plan (ESOP).

III. Loans Are Issued At Cost

Loans are issued with interest at cost. Loans will not bear the profit segments of any interest charge. But the interest at cost will have to recover all expenses of the Fund.

Effects

The legal and institutional procedures described above will create special effects

- *on Shareholders*
- *on Borrowers*
- *on Participating Banks*
- *on non-Participating Banks*
- *on the Local Economy*

These effects are investigated below.

Analysis of Effects

on Shareholders

The prospectus will stipulate that shareholders cannot expect benefits in the form of interest or dividends. The prospectus will clearly state that shareholders will have to *wait* for their rewards, and that tangible rewards will come in a variety of forms.

The first rewards will come through an expected steady growth in the capital appreciation of the value of the shares. The sources of the expected steady increase in the value of the shares are:

- whatever consulting and other fees the Fund might charge for its various administrative, legal, and accounting operations;
- interest earned by deposits of proceeds of sale of shares;
- interest earned by deposits of proceeds of loans to the Fund;
- interest earned by deposits of proceeds of grants, subject to stipulation with the granting authority, be it public agencies or private foundations;
- income tithing from private donors and especially people who benefit from the operations of the Fund.

If the shareholder happens also to be a borrower, the shareholder will immediately reap the benefit of receiving loans at cost.

Immediately, any shareholder will benefit from acquiring control over a much lager portion of wealth than one's own share participation. This increase will come from these sources:
- from combining all shares together;
- from the increase in the Interdependence fund holdings to be achieved through borrowings obtained on the strength of the Fund as a whole;
- from the financial advantageous terms that can be gotten in borrowing funds by pooling resources into a Interdependence fund;
- from the amounts of grants and other donations that can be obtained by the fund;
- from the social and political leverage that can be acquired by pooling resources together.

In the short term, shareholders will benefit from the insulation of their wealth from the vicissitudes of the stock market. The value of the Fund can, at the very least, be expected to even out the highs and lows of the stock market.

In the long term, shareholders can be expected to benefit from these sources:
- from an increase in the value of buildings and land they may own in the city (this value will gradually and partially have to be shared with the public at large through higher taxes on land and lower taxes on buildings);
- from the increase of the value of the business operation they may own in the city;
- from the increased wage income they may receive in the city.

on Borrowers

A Interdependence fund can acquire a comparative advantage over banks and other financial institutions. Apart from equity dilution, banks and other financial institutions cannot be expected to receive funds, under any legal structure, without paying interest or dividends — as the Gloucester Interdependence Fund will be able to do. Thus the Gloucester Interdependence Fund is able to pass this benefit along to its borrowers.

on Participating Banks

Participating banks will lose some business accounts that they might have otherwise funded. These losses will be offset by the following benefits:

Participating banks will benefit from fees for underwriting and/or gradually selling shares in the Fund:

Participating banks will benefit from the increase in deposits that will occur from sale of shares outside the local community, the creation of new money for the purchase of those shares; and from the inflow of funds from loans to the Fund as well as from the deposits of grants:

This increase in bank deposits will allow for an expansion of consumer credit. (In order to fully exploit this benefit, participating banks might *in the long run* want to consider the creation of a new joint venture — outside the realm of the Fund. This joint venture can be defined as the creation of a GloucesterCard™. This new consumer credit card would help keep funds and benefits from the use of these funds within the local community.)

on non-Participating Banks

Non-participating banks, just like the participating ones, will lose some business accounts that they might have otherwise funded.

Non-participating banks will lose deposits if their customary depositors and stockholders close or reduce the amount of their deposits and redeem stock with whose proceeds they purchase shares in the Gloucester Interdependence Fund.

These losses will be offset by partial and indirect benefits from an increased welfare of the overall local economy that will accrue to non-participating banks as well as to the participating banks.

on the Local Economy

To the extent that there are bankable ideas that cannot be executed because of lack of loanable resources or because of the high cost of these funds, to that extent the existence of the Gloucester Interdependence Fund will benefit the community at large.

With the Gloucester Interdependence Fund, the local economy receives a boost toward a fuller utilization of all its human and natural resources, including the resources of the sea. Fuller employment has a tendency of improving the general welfare of the community. If projects are selected that would not otherwise be selected and become operational with the fullest possible respect for the esthetic and environmental qualities of the community, to that extent the community will be better off. This effect is particularly to be expected if all issues are openly brought to the fore by representatives of all interests in the city at the three key stages of planning, financing, and implementation of community-wide projects.

Other benefits that can be expected from the establishment of the Gloucester Interdependence Fund result from insulating the local economy from vicissitudes of the national and world economy as much as possible — and thus gaining more autonomy and more control over one's lives.

Assumptions

This survey of potential effects is based on a number of financial, economic, and procedural assumptions. Changing any of the assumptions, one changes the effects to be expected. The overall project might still prove feasible on a different set of assumptions.

THE (GLOUCESTER, MANCHESTER, YOUR YAMI, MY YAMI, WHATEVER)
Concord Resolution

Public Money for Public Projects

To determine whether the Town (City, State, Nation) will borrow *public money* to fund duly authorized *public works* projects.

The Treasurer is authorized, with the approval of the Board of Selectmen (or other appropriate body) to borrow public money by accessing national credit, rather than the private bond market.

Loans are thus obtained at cost, rather than at exorbitant interest charges.

The Federal Reserve System will thus use national credit to create money as an asset.

The loan will preferably be repaid from proceeds of increased taxes on land and natural resources (while correspondingly reducing taxes on improvements and other assets).

For theoretical background, please see:

Gorga, C. "Concordian Economics: Tools to Return Relevance to Economics," *Forum on Social Economics* (May 2008).

Gorga, C. *The Economic Process: An Instantaneous Non-Newtonian Picture,* Lanham, Md. and Oxford: University Press of America, 2002.

Gorga, C. "The Productivity Standard: A True Golden Standard" (with Norman G. Kurland), *in* Dawn M. Kurland (ed.), *Every Worker an Owner: A Revolutionary Free Enterprise Challenge to Marxism,* Washington, D.C.: Center for Economic and Social Justice, 1987, pp. 83-86.

For much pertinent — and some impertinent — additional information, please see:

    www.concordresolution.org
    www.monetary.org
    www.webofdebt.com/articles/minnesota-bank-proposal.php
    www.prosperityuk.com/prosperity/prosperity.html

See also:
money site:youtube.com
Money As Debt (1 of 5)
www.youtube.com/watch?v=DU7E3jMVtjI

CG June 9, 2008

BOTTOM-UP MONETARY POLICY

There are two essential forms of monetary policy.

One is the European form, the top-down monetary policy.
The second is the American monetary policy.

This is the bottom-up monetary policy.

The first American to advocate for it formally was Benjamin Franklin, in a brilliant paper he wrote when he was barely a 23-year-old lad! He was simply defending a practice initiated by Massachusetts colonists in 1690. The American Revolution, it is now becoming clear again, was fought to preserve the power of the colonists to create the money they needed for industry and commerce against threatened infringement from the Bank of England. This power was inscribed in the very first article of the United States Constitution. The most vigorous attempt to exercise this power was made by the greatest of American presidents, Lincoln.

This policy has never quite taken hold in academia because it seems to have no inner restraints, and it has indeed been put into practice many times without any established restraints. The limits within which this policy can be safely implemented are listed below; they were first more formally presented in the paper on the "golden standard" that is reproduced in this collection and that I wrote in collaboration with Norman Kurland.

The Definition of Money

Economic theory has no definition of money. It distinguishes among the functions of money; but functions are not definitions.

Money is a legal institution with economic effects. Money is a contract. It is a contract between the holder of whatever form money assumes and the rest of society. It is a mutual obligation.

The most important obligation of society is to preserve the value of money.

The most important obligation of the individual person is to create the economic value that money represents: real goods and services.

The Administration of Money

Ever since time immemorial, it has been found useful to grant the administration of money to an official Monetary Authority, be it the King, the Central Bank, or a Federal Reserve System. It is the function of monetary policy to determine the functions of the Monetary Authority.

The most important determinations of monetary policy concern the modality of the creation of money; the flow of the money; and the quantity of money.

Two Forms of Money Creation

Money can be created either as a debt or as an asset. When the Monetary Authority borrows money from the public and lends it to a government agency or a private institution, the MA puts money in circulation as debt. It basically lets the banks or other private institutions create the money. The MA creates money as an asset when it "discounts" a note from the public, a note that represents the value of (current and expected) real goods and services. The MA then does not borrow money; it lends money out. The MA then creates money as an asset.

Alternative Flows of Money

The flows of money are better followed through the following figure:

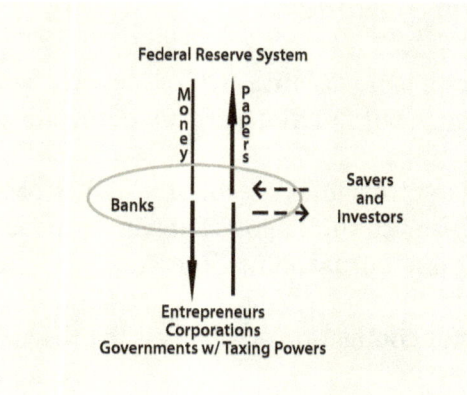

Alternative Money Flows
Figure 1

As it can be seen from this figure, the Central Bank either creates money or allows banks to create money. This fact is rooted in the very nature of money and credit. Money starts as an "I Owe You" (IOU) note between two people. When the IOU note is accepted by a third and a fourth party, the note becomes a "public" note; eventually, it becomes legal tender, i.e., a contract between the holder of the note and society as a whole. And with this transformation, it becomes necessary to go beyond the question of private trust between two parties into the issue of public trust. With this transformation, the nation acquires the **responsibility** to guarantee the value of the note and the **right** to create notes.

The United States Constitution and the legislation that created the Federal Reserve System give entrepreneurs, corporations, and governments with taxing powers the right of access to national credit; the Discount Window was created for this purpose.

In a Trickle-Down Monetary Policy, or the European conception of money, the Discount Window is used as a last resort. In a Bottom-Up Monetary Policy, or the American conception of money, the Discount Window is the preferred use to create money and put it into circulation.

The advantages of a Bottom-Up Monetary Policy are numerous and extremely important. Money is created in perfect correspondence with the need of the nation to create real wealth (national credit, i.e., new money, is not created to purchase consumer goods or other financial instruments); money is created at cost (not at an arbitrarily changing interest rate); money is created to benefit those who create real wealth (not those who create financial wealth, paper wealth).

CG July 23, 2008
October 16, 2008

Functional Integration of Management Tasks

by Carmine Gorga

Background: This plan is an outgrowth of extremely successful work done in the 70s and 80s by Polis-tics, Inc. in collaboration with the Gloucester Laboratory of the National Marine Fisheries Service. NOAA, US Department of Commerce. The work led to the introduction of fresh fish into the chain of national supermarkets . Supermarkets had since their inception been against the introduction of fresh fish into their distribution system. Fresh fish interfered too much with the main stay of supermarkets: meat products. So the Gloucester Laboratory designed a way to prepackage fresh fish. Since fresh fish only loses quality over time, the work involved a close collaboration among three pillars of the distribution system of fresh fish: fishermen, seafood processors, and supermarkets.

We set up a controlled experiment though a series of pilot projects and analyzed the results in a number of published papers and eventually a book by Carmine Gorga and Louis J. Ronsivalli entitled Quality Assurance of Seafood (van Nostrand Reinhold, 1988). The major results were that consumers were ready to pay $1.00 more per pound for products of assured quality than for products whose quality was not assured; all the technical details necessary to assure the quality of fresh fish to the consumer amounted to an increased cost of 10 cents per pound; thus the project yielded a 90 cents benefit per pound.

With our means of communication, we whispered these results to the industry. With subsequent work done through Joe Slavin and Associates we were able to use the megaphone of the Food Marketing Institute, and the program took off like wildfire. Fresh fish entered the supermarket chain — and hence the national diet. Fresh fish, as is well known, contains dietary elements that are quasi vital in relation to a large number of benefits, from reduction of cholesterol levels though positive effects on certain forms of cancer to osteoporosis. Seafood in the diet goes very well with the lean and exotic cuisine to improve the physical fitness and wellbeing of the nation.

If the enormous success of this program was due to the hard work of seafood technologists at the Gloucester Laboratory of the National Marine

Fisheries Service, the social cauldron mixed all the right ingredients at the right time: Julia Child was extolling the subtle flavors of seafood to awaken the American palate; the scientific community was discovering one after another the many therapeutic values of seafood; and then the jogging craze was just starting and it required a lean cuisine that seafoods could best provide. Yet it was the economic analysis that added magic to the mix and made it all come alive: we proved that, while the added costs were minimal, the consumer was willing to pay one dollar more per pound for fish whose quality was assured by the interdependent actions of fishermen, processors, and marketers.

* * *

When all was said and done, this was a ragtag effort, relying entirely on happenstance relationships. The question then became: How can we institutionalize the program? How can we make sure that the program will not die but be extended to other industries? It was then that the ideas constituting the model of Functional Integration of Management Tasks were born.

* * *

The topic of Functional Integration of Management Tasks is very important. There is much to be said. For the time being, I can only add a few notes to an excerpt from one of my papers entitled *Fisheries Renewal: A Renewal of the Soul of Business* [The Catholic Social Science Review, Volume II (1997) 145-161.] Stuart B. Weeks was the co-author of this paper.

We need to create new institutions in conformity with a new principle, a principle that we like to call Functional Integration. This is a form of organization that attempts to obtain the complementary benefits of vertical or horizontal integration as well as those of total independence. The Functional Integration (FI) Model attempts to gather activities together that are already related in accordance to their function. This is a new form of organization that is designed to lead to *social harmony and civic responsibility*. After all, do we not all share a common goal? Simply put, is not this goal the achievement of a civilized society?

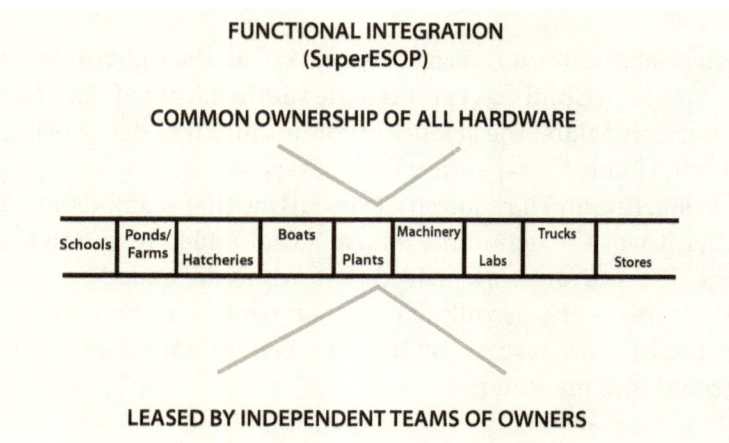

Functional Integration Within the Seafood Industry
Figure 3

Figure 3 suggests the forms this type of integration might assume within the seafood industry. Let us conceive of all participants in the seafood industry as owning in common all the hardware: From fishing boats to seafood processing plants; from institutes for the industry to educate the consumer, and be educated by the consumer, to laboratories for the research and development of all possible means of utilization of renewable marine resources; from trucks to stores. The hardware would be under the stewardship of a group of people organized into a SuperESOP, whose Board of Directors is elected by all the owners. The owners exercise all the rights and enjoy all the privileges of owners, as the stockholders of democratic organizations do and ought to do. The SuperESOP would attend to the financing and maintenance requirements of the hardware, and independent teams of entrepreneurs would be making that hardware operational, by leasing it — from whom? from themselves. If each team organizes itself with the assistance of individual ESOPs [Employee Stock Ownership Plans], so much the better. The essential point is that the independence of each team is fully preserved *by concentrating the operation of functions, rather than concentrating control over people.*

The nearest equivalent to this type of social integration is a shopping mall that would be owned by all owners and employees of stores operating within the mall. This is in contrast to the conventional structure in which the malls are owned and operated by independent concerns, in which instance stores simply rent space within the mall, pay rent, and are provided with all the services that are needed in common. In this case, quite rightly, all capital gains (or losses) that accrue from the operation of the mall belong to the owners of the mall. In the FI Model, capital gains or losses accrue to owners of the hardware; and whatever profits accrue from the rental of the hardware belong only to the teams that rent the hardware. Beyond the legitimate concerns of health, safety, and public welfare, the state, or the public in general, has no say on any of the operations of the FI Model.

This structure might not be born full blown. It might be necessary to assemble it piece by piece. And there might be two or more SuperESOPs for each port. But, clearly, the more trust, the more cohesion, the more benefits. If, through a SuperESOP, the participants in the industry own as much of the hardware as possible, many things can be done more efficiently. At a bare minimum:

The SuperESOP can enforce the requirements of quality assurance to the consumer: This assurance can be provided only if the various elements of the industry collaborate with each other. Today this collaboration occurs quite rarely, and when it does it is mostly due to chance: One processor here, two fishermen there;

The SuperESOP can enforce efficiency standards for the utilization of each and every piece of hardware undreamed of by individual entrepreneurs. Unnecessary duplication of equipment and even operations would cease. For instance, boats might be treated like airplanes, they would not be waiting for the crew to rest before they would be turned around to go fishing again. And the boats might not need to be the same as those of today. They might be smaller, faster, more efficiently operated and equipped;

The SuperESOP can reach efficiency standards in purchasing supplies and equipment, borrowing money, and attending to all other financing requirements of a modern business — including purchasing insurance — that individual entrepreneurs cannot obtain;

The SuperESOP can set up maintenance schedules of all machinery and equipment in a way that individual entrepreneurs cannot achieve;

The SuperESOP can create and administer a first rate information system regarding marketing and biological data with the aim of rationalizing the capture and raising of each species as well as the timing of landings of fish, thus ensuring that temporary gluts — with their depressing effects on pricing — would no longer occur;

The SuperESOP can nurture first rate research and development laboratories. Special attention could be given especially to development, thus easing the process of technology transfer from the laboratory to the industry;

The SuperESOP can foster specialization of activities that small, independent, individual entrepreneurs cannot achieve. A boat owner, a fish farmer, or a seafood processor today has to be at least an expert in finances, engineering, and real estate. What do these operations have to do with catching fish, raising it, or processing it? With a SuperESOP, the boat owner, fish farmer, and the seafood processor would simply organize a team of people and devote all their time and expertise to catching the fish, raising it, and processing it. And all teams would preserve their independence at the same time. Whatever money the team that leases boats or fish farms or stores makes is its own money, its own reward.

This model of social and economic integration can be applied to any set of industrial or commercial enterprises. To name one specific example, one day it might be possible to organize along these lines commercial establishments on Main Street of any city or town in the United States. The first such SuperESOP might even be called "Main Street USA".

✳ ✳ ✳

NOTES

Participants in a Functional Integration management model share in three streams of income and wealth: (1) They are immediately compensated for any work that they do as independent entrepreneurs; (2) They share in the profits that are distributed once the final product is sold; and, (3) They share in any capital appreciation created by the firm as a whole.

We will have to return to this topic. For the time being, the Visitor might learn more about the rationale for this management model by either accessing any website that treats the topic of "chaordic" (Chaos & Order) forms of organization or by reading Thomas Petzinger Jr.'s *The New Pioneers: The Men and Women Who Are Transforming the Workplace and Marketplace* (1999). A good place to start might be *Chaordic Alliance — World Business Academy.*

May 12, 2001

A Plan of Urban Restoration

by Carmine Gorga

This Plan of Urban Restoration for Gloucester, MA is being developed in collaboration with a large number of political, business, and civic leaders. Most have contributed such essential elements to it that the plan is much stronger today than when its catalytic element was presented to the Gloucester City Council Ad Hoc Committee: Arts Center/Museum Complex on May 29, 1997.

While the specifics of the plan are related to our particular community, the key ideas and the goals underlying it are applicable to many other communities.

The plan is based on the reality of three deep physical wounds in our community:

One wound was left by the Super Highway Program
(Hint: The tail end — or was it the beginning — of Route 128 was dropped in the midst of our community, leaving deep scars in our landscape and ever since bleeding tourists).

The second wound was left by Urban Renewal
(Hint: Old homes were destroyed, and in their place was left a wide road, Rogers Street, vacant lots, and parking lots.)

The third wound was left by the Fisheries Management Program
(Hint: Regulations to restrict fishing came late, and they came piece-meal.)

✳ ✳ ✳

The plan contains an integration of the needs of the arts (and the tourists), the needs of commercial interests, and the needs of the fisheries. These needs are held together by possibilities in the field of financing.

The components of the plan are:

• A Tourist Information/Civic Center/Convention Site/Regional Theater on Blackburn Circle
• The building might be three or four stories high, in the form of a sea shell
• On top of the building there might be subtle wireless towers *
• A Parking Lot on Aerial Rights on Route 128 Extension
• A System of Public Transportation for Residents and Tourists alike
• The Transformation of Main Street into The Gloucester Galleria
• The Galleria can be Enclosed through a Buckminster Fuller type of contraption
• Or it Can Remain Open to the Skies
• Or it Can Have Windows that Can be Left Open Most of the Time
• The Creation of Parking all along the Galleria, through
• The Transformation of Rogers Street into an Elevated — or Depressed ** — Road
• Upon talking with John Sparks, the alternative came to mind of enveloping traffic into a tunnel so to form an external ziggurat construction
• The Creation of a Gloucester Promenade all along the Transformed Rogers Street
• The Creation of Parks on Existing Open Lots Between the Promenade and the Water Edge
• Throughout Facilitating the Meeting of Pedestrian Walking and Ships Working
• Thus reconnecting Main Street and the Downtown with the waterfront
• The Continuation of the Promenade Around the Fort Area to Meet the Boulevard ***
• A Possible Spur of the Promenade Under the Water to Create a Natural Aquarium
• A Link of Rogers Street with Blackburn Circle by Means of a Set of Staircases
• Pedestrian Walkways Linking Dogtown Common with Magnolia Woods ****
• The Rejuvenation of the Gloucester Fishing Industry
• The Creation of The Gloucester Interdependence Fund.*****

The plan, if and when implemented, will restore Gloucester to its older grandeur. It will transform the City into a Pedestrian Community. It can also implement the proposed functional integration of management and automatically bring into practice two or three key sets of economic rights and responsibilities.

Thus it will transform human relationships.

* As suggested by Janis Stelluto
** As suggested by Dr. Damon Cummings
*** As suggested by David Porper
**** As suggested by Mac Bell
***** Bob Whitmarsh provided the slogan for the Fund:
"Put your money where your heart is"
A better slogan might be: ***Do not sell Gloucester. Own it!***

These proposals are based on an integrated system of thought called Relationalism, the study of relationships between men and women in the social context.

Relationalism encompasses Concordian Economics.

Tapping, at crucial stages, the assistance of some of the best minds of this century, Dr. Carmine Gorga has developed this system of thought over more than thirty years of action and thought.

Last modified September 2, 2008

THREE SETS OF PROPOSALS FOR PEACE AND JUSTICE

A Personal Note
by
Carmine Gorga

Among other influences, I am a product of the United States Information Services (USIS) program. Soon after WW II, resources were scarce in Naples, Italy. USIS made available to me, not propaganda, but a wealth of books. I devoured them.

Preamble

We all talk peace. From the United Nations to City Halls to family parlors, we all talk peace. But, harsh as the expression might sound at first, we do not do peace. We seem to labor under the spell of The Great Rationalistic Illusion that it is enough to utter the word in order to achieve the goal. There are three actions we have to pursue, if we really want peace. We have to create three sets of teams for peace and justice — and we have to endow them with sufficient resources to be effective.

First Set
A Department of Peace

We have to stop thinking that we have to destroy the town in order to save the town; that we have to destroy the country in order to make it safe for democracy. The Department of Defense can save us from attack, but it cannot bring peace to lands where there is no peace. It is only a Department of Peace that can bring peace abroad — and in the long run it is the only instrument for mankind to win the war against terrorism.

Let us establish a Department of Peace right here in the United States. If we do that, it is reasonable to expect that England, and Germany, and France, and Italy, and perhaps even Russia and China will follow suit. Duplication of effort, redoubling of effort throughout the world should be welcomed.

Let us assist Palestinians to establish their own Department of Peace immediately thereafter. And of course, the third country that should be encouraged, persuaded, urged to establish a Department of Peace is Israel, and the fourth is Iraq, and the fifth is Sudan. We know the list.

The most important element in the chain of needs is that the Department of Peace, without resources, would be a mockery. But where do we find the resources, especially at a time of substantial deficits and budget cuts? Well, the first candidate is a voluntary — free and willing — transfer of, say, ten percent of resources from the current budget of the Department of Defense. The experts in this department will candidly tell you that it is impossible, with their means, to stop terrorism. What the voter has to see is that, given the proper means, it is possible to stop terrorism. We cannot give in to pessimism and despair.

Only a Department of Peace can plan for peace, by intimately knowing the geography, the history, and the culture of each county in which the USA is involved, by creating SWAT Teams for peace and justice for each country, then by training the people to carry out their mission of peace and justice, and finally endowing them with satisfactory intellectual and material means to achieve their goal.

Second Set
SWAT Teams for Peace

The second suggestion is for the Department of Peace to create an appropriate number of SWAT teams for peace. (Would not ten percent of the people currently within the Department of Defense give an eyetooth for the transfer of their energies toward such a function?) Call them Circles of Love. I prefer to call them Mary's Messengers of Mercy, because Mary is the only person who is highly respected in all three monotheistic religions. If we monotheists truly honor her, she will be more easily honored by other religions as well.

The Circles of Love should do precisely what their name implies: They should create circles of love around hamlets, and villages, and cities, and nations where hate prevails today. The pacification program should proceed house by house.

Depending upon the case, each team should be composed of at least three volunteers — one from each of the major faiths that prevail in the areas to be pacified. There must be no discrimination as to age or sex. The specific formation of the teams will depend on the particular needs to be addressed. Indeed, one need not even go abroad. With perhaps only minor modifications, the entire approach might also be used to help solve the problems of so many "downtown." areas in the world. In each nation there seem to be many areas in which peace does not reign.

The prerequisite should be a simple willingness to pray together with the victims of violence. The teams should implore for the shooting to stop — and for the vicious circle of revenge to stop. No sane politics issues from the barrel of a gun.

The Basic Rationale

It seems clear that the constant message of Mary is to spur us to create as much peace on earth as possible. The message is not new. What seems to be new is her insistence on the means we have to employ to achieve that aim. She seems to suggest that we create peace through prayer and love.

A More Specific Definition of Means

Governments use force trying to achieve peace. And they rarely succeed. The churches, the mosques, the synagogues, and most religions know this reality quite well. They have always preached that peace can be achieved only through love. The time perhaps has come to transform preaching into teaching and enacting.

Training of the Teams

Perhaps the most important tool to be given to each member of the team is the ability to pray together with people of a different faith — and soon after the ability to teach the blessings of such a gift to others. Each team should certainly be trained to speak the language(s) of the area they are supposed to affect. But specific tools such as leadership skills and negotiating techniques such as "getting to yes" should also be part of the curriculum. Hopefully, armies retreat and weapons are retrieved by ad hoc teams of the United Nations, perhaps; and broad political agreements are reached (why not along the lines of rotating governments as per the island of St. Martin's model?). Above all, members of the team should be familiar with the history and the culture of the place.

Eventually, the formation of these teams can take place in any part of the world, but the first efforts might need to take place at a location far away from the horrible trouble spots of the world. The teams themselves, preferably extracted from the populations that are in trouble, would experience peace, perhaps for the first time, even though only for a short while. Ideally, they might receive a greater infusion of ardor and commitment if the training were to take place at any of the world's great centers of spirituality.

Deployment of the Teams

It will depend on the number of teams available for final deployment and the specific mission to be carried out, but the basic strategy should be to start from the outermost ring of the area of trouble and proceed toward the center. The ideal is to build "circles of love" around the trouble spots of the world.

Participation of Civil Authorities

The various religions might want to start the effort on their own. But, if the formation of such teams should involve large number of trainees, financial support from various Departments of Peace might be a necessity. To a very minimum, overall support from governments might be requested from the start for a variety of purposes: for instance, to obtain current intelligence data, and at least detailed information about the geography, demographics, and economics of the area. But since the "circles of love" should be conceived as an army of love, advice as to strategic deployment of the teams should also be obtained from experts in the military of the various nations that might want to participate in the effort.

Risk to Life and Limb

Undoubtedly, there would be risk to life and limb involved in the deployment of such teams. The rationale for accepting such risk is simply stated. If the various Departments of Peace and the various religions of the world do not take the initiative to reach peace, the military sooner or later will intervene. Through the military, risk to life and limb is increased many times over.

Third Set
SWAT Teams for Justice

The third suggestion is for the Department of Peace to create SWAT teams for justice. Specifically, SWAT teams for economic justice. The visitor is thus invited to go back at the beginning of this site, where useful suggestions for the implementation of economic justice can be found.

A Summary as a Sequence of Events

This is the suggested sequence of events.

Ideas are disseminated.

Funds are obtained.

Mary's Messengers of Mercy are trained.

They pacify the area, house by house.

Negotiating teams get to "yes": armies retreat and weapons are retrieved by ad hoc teams of the United Nations, perhaps; broad political agreements are reached (why not along the lines of rotating governments as per the island of St. Martin's model?).

SWAT Teams for Economic Justice enter into action.

September 3, 2002
Last modified March 21, 2008

Toward a Common Prayer

Oh,
Allah/God/Yahweh
Oh,
One Spirit
Manifesting itself as many Gods

help me,
help my friends,
help my enemies.

Amen.

Released
on Monday, September 22, 2008
at Biarritz
after an undeclared pilgrimage
in reverse
by car
from Santiago de Compostela
to Saint-Jean-pied-de-port

physically fortified by a
ttoro, a Basque fishermen's stew
and
spiritually directed by Mary
the Immaculate Virgin
Mother of God

PART THREE

Essays Published
in Various Scholarly Journals

But follow the principle, and the knot unties itself.
Thomas Jefferson

THE IMPORTANCE OF THE U.S. FISHING INDUSTRY

SEAFOOD AMERICA
A defunct Journal of Processing and Marketing

July/August 1981, pp. 26-27, 34.

by Carmine Gorga and Louis J. Ronsivalli

Carmine Gorga is the President of Polis-tics Inc., a private economic consulting firm located at 87 Middle Street, Gloucester, Massachusetts 01930. Dr. Gorga is also an associate of Joseph Slavin and Associates. Louis J. Ronsivalli is the Director of the NEFC Gloucester Laboratory of NMFS, Emerson Avenue, Gloucester, Massachusetts 01930. The authors would like to acknowledge the technical and editorial contributions by John D. Kaylor of the same Laboratory.

Many people labor under the assumption that the U.S. fishery industry is insignificant. The reasons for this widespread belief are numerous, but perhaps the basic one is not difficult to detect. Since the fishery industry accounts for less than one percent of the gross national product (GNP) of the United States, it is assumed that the industry must be insignificant.

Through a more complete and appropriate set of measurements and comparisons we will obtain a decidedly different view of the issue. In the end, that assumption appears to be so unwarranted as to represent a myth rather than reality. We will place the U.S. fishery industry in a number of contexts, including the U.S. economy as a whole.

These measurements and comparisons reveal that the myth is, in turn, composed of a whole series of subsidiary myths.

The Bare Facts

The bare facts concerning the U.S. fishery industry are rather well known. They are summarized below. Data are the latest available and, unless otherwise indicated, they refer to the year 1980. These are all preliminary figures; that is, they might be subject to minor revisions in the future. The source is *Fisheries Statistics of the United States, 1980.*

U.S. commercial landings of fishery products were 6.5 billion lbs., for a value of $2.2 billion. Of that total, 3.7 billion lbs. were edible products valued at $2.09 billion and 2.8 billion lbs. were commercial products valued at $145 million.

Total imports were 4.9 billion lbs. Of this total, 4.4 billion lbs. were edible products, valued at $2.7 billion and .5 billion lbs. were commercial products, valued at $970 million. And, since the total value of exports was $1.0 billion, the trade deficit was $2.6 billion.

In 1979, the U.S. fishery industry gave employment to 184,000 fishermen and to 93,000 people engaged in on-shore processing and wholesaling — for a total of 277,000 employees.

The value added due to processing of both the domestic catch and imported products was a little over $7.0 billion. This is the official estimate of the contribution to the Gross National Product (GNP) offered by the U.S. fishery industry. Another aggregate figure of interest is the total consumer expenditure for domestic and imported fishery products: $12.5 billion.

What do these figures mean? In order to obtain an answer to this question we need to put these figures in a larger context. The primary source of data for this purpose as set below is the *Statistical Abstract of the United States, 1980.*

The Quantitative Importance

One measure of the importance of the U.S. fishing industry is obtained by setting it against the world fishing industry. In 1979, the U.S. landed 4.5 million metric tons of fishery products versus to 71.3 million metric tons for the world as a whole. Although the U.S. catch represented only about 5 percent of the world catch, the U.S. fishing industry was still the fifth largest in the world. In fact, the first ranking nation, Japan, landed only 14 percent of the total world catch.

Another measure is obtained by setting this industry against the U.S. economy as a whole. True, the total value added by the fishery industry — or even its total consumer expenditures — represent less than 1 percent of the U.S. GNP. However, this figure especially needs to be put in a more relevant context. It is misleading to use the GNP as a basis of comparison, because *any single industry represents always a small percentage of the GNP.* The auto industry, for instance, looms extremely large when taken in isolation. Actually, in 1979 it represented only 3.2 percent of the U.S. GNP.

Quite apart from overall national figures, it must also be recognized that the importance of the U.S. fishery industry varies from region to region. For instance, according to the final report of the Dept. of Commerce Task Force on Fisheries Development entitled "Toward a Partnership for the Development of the United States Commercial Fishing Industry" of May 23, 1979, employment related directly to fisheries in Alaska in 1973 accounted for 19 percent of the total state employment and 7 percent of the gross state product. If related to individual cities and towns, the importance of the fishery industry might indeed be found to be so preponderate as to be vital even on economic terms alone.

In addition, a more significant gauge of the importance of the U.S. fishery industry can perhaps be found in the field of foreign trade. The $2.6 billion trade deficit has already been mentioned. This figure becomes even more illuminating when it is realized not only that it is 10 percent of the total trade deficit for 1979/1980, but also that fishery products are overshadowed only by petroleum products and automobiles on the list of products accounting for the large current trade imbalance.

Before entering any deeper into the forest of specific facts and figures, it must be pointed out that there is a general line of defense in favor of the fishery industry which ought to be continuously borne in mind. Dollar values are an indiscriminate standard. They cannot distinguish among real values.

The perceived large automobile industry, for instance, is undoubtedly important to society, but is it as important as food? Besides, there are assets whose importance cannot even be measured in dollar values. Air or water, for instance, do not have much economic value, but life is not conceivable without them. Seafoods cannot be ranked that high. Yet, seen as a unique source of proteins, they are vital to survival. The body is unable to synthesize such proteins. More specifically still, they have peculiar therapeutic and dietary properties of inestimable value. Suffice it to say that recent laboratory studies indicate that fish oils seem to counterbalance the adverse effects of cholesterol and triglyceride in the bloodstream, thus reducing the danger of coronary disease.

This much needed to be said. It ought to give more weight not only to the figures presented above but also to the remaining set of figures. Some of the most meaningful values are obtained when the U.S. fishery industry is compared with the meat and poultry industry, the other major sources of proteins.

The fishery industry seems to occupy a second place in relation to these industries. But how far behind does it lie? In 1977, the figures for value added *at the processing level alone* were $7.4 billion for the meat and poultry industry vs. $1.1 billion for fishery products, or about seven times as large. Is not the much vaunted importance of meat and poultry products compared to fishery products still largely another myth?

But how is this myth reconciled with the apparent reality of the huge discrepancy between the often repeated figures concerning per capita consumption of the relative products? The figures for 1979 were: 181 lbs. of meat products and 60 lbs. of poultry products, vs. 13 lbs. of fishery products. This "reality" is another myth. Much of the discrepancy, it turns out, is due to the different methods of reporting the figures. Meat and poultry products are given in *carcass weight,* but fishery products are reported in *edible weight*! Thus raw figures for fishery products have to be multiplied at least by three, or meat and poultry products have to be divided at least by three or perhaps better by four. (Fat is almost nonexistent in fish, and bones are much heavier in meat products.) The remaining discrepancy, rather than being taken as an unalterable given, ought to be taken as a potential to exploit. Just like the considerable foreign trade deficit accounted for by fishery products, the discrepancy in per capita consumption between fishery and meat products is an indication of what can be achieved by the U.S. fishery industry. Stated very briefly, when the distribution of fishery products which is largely confined to coastal areas becomes as capillary as it is for meat products — and when the quality of the two products is equally comparable — then the per capita consumption of fishery products will increase and imports might even decrease.

A final set of figures is given by a leading trade journal, *Quick Frozen Foods.* According to the November 1980 issue of this publication, in 1979 the value of frozen food sales climbed to almost $24 billion, with frozen fish sales for the first time surpassing $7 billion, thus representing 29 percent of this total. Although the increase in the value of frozen fish from the previous year was reported to be *"entirely* due to higher prices," the gain was nonetheless "so great that the category became the largest in dollar volume of them all, even exceeding prepared foods."

The Quantifiable Importance

The above figures relate to direct, already measured effects of the U.S. fishery industry. And a note of great importance needs soon to be added. Those figures relate to commercial fishing. If figures concerning sportsfishing, both inland and on sealanes, were to be added, according to official estimates provided by *Fisheries of the United States, 1979*, many of those figures would have to be doubled. The entire exercise might not be valid, but one figure can certainly be doubled: the figure concerning per capita consumption of fishery products. Thus from 13 lbs. per capita we automatically pass to about 26 lbs. per capita. And when the figure for meat and poultry products is actually divided by three or four we reach a 45 to 60 lbs. per capita consumption of meat products and 15 to 20 lbs. per capita consumption of poultry products. (The "softness" of this estimate might also take into account the additional meat products derived from hunting, about which there seems to be no official estimates. What is known is only that hunters are one third as numerous as sportsfishermen, or 33 vs. 91 million people.) The often lamented gap between consumption of meat and fishery products is considerably narrower than it is so frequently assumed to be.

There are also innumerable *indirect* effects, however, which ought to be measured in order to have a more precise understanding of the true importance of this industry. This measurement goes beyond the scope of this article, but a mere — even though partial — list of those indirect effects is well within its scope. Three categories of such effects are of direct interest here: efficiency, employment and income.

If the goal is to make proteins available to the consumer, fishery products are certainly the most efficient. Conversion factors to produce a pound of beef from other food (especially grains) is in the order of about 10:1; for chickens, the ratio is 2.4:1. For fish farming (carp), the ratio is 1.6:1. For fish growing in the natural environment, of course, the ratio is 0:1. (This point does not imply that costs for harvesting fish are zero.)

If precise calculations were made, how many jobs and incomes does the fishery industry — either in part or wholly — generate for rope and twine men, carpenters and boat-yard people, real estate, insurance and banking people? And what are the relative figures for lawyers, public officials and consultants?

No such list would be complete without finally mentioning the by-products of the fishing industry, from medicinals to cosmetics, from chicken feed to fish flour.

The Qualitative Importance of the Fishery Industry

Computers cannot, but the human mind can integrate qualitative elements. No analysis would therefore be complete without mentioning some of the qualitative elements that are such an integral part of the fishery industry. These elements can be grouped under at least the following three categories: tradition, aesthetics and the way of life.

Does not tradition contribute to the enrichment of every human being? The U.S. tradition both literary and historical, is heavily tied to the fishing industry.

What is the value of looking at fishing vessels along the coastline of innumerable cities and towns? What is the value to the tourist industry of the view offered by such vessels on the horizon? Indeed, what would become of the appeal of such cities and towns if the fishing industry were to disappear?

The life of a fisherman. To utter these words is to reduce such abstractions as "ancient tradition" and "aesthetics" to a living reality — a reality which includes hardship as an integral component.

How "important" is the U.S. fishery industry? As the above findings demonstrate, the fishery industry is a complex entity. As such, it is subject to differing interpretations. Ultimately, judgments are formulated on the basis of one's own perspective and even one's own function in society.

So far we have tried to adhere to the facts and, in this same vein, we are not now going to impose upon the reader our own subjective evaluation of the importance of this industry. We will be satisfied if the myth of the insignificance of this industry is dispelled once and for all.

When the facts are brought into their proper context, it seems impossible to reach any other conclusion. The U.S. fishery industry is *not* insignificant.

The Revised Keynes' Model* (an Abstract)

Atlantic Economic Journal, Sept. 1982, 10 (3) 52.
The original publication is available at www.springerlink.com

Carmine Gorga

The current crisis in economic affairs must be due to many factors. But in a fundamental sense it is due to structural and conceptual weaknesses contained in Keynes' model of the economic system.

The proposition that S = I is not an equivalence, as it must for it to be formally valid.** The terms are neither reflexive nor symmetric nor transitive.

Saving has the potential of assuming 100,000 meanings. And, by necessity, so does Investment. Consumption means spending; but in contemporary economics this meaning is arbitrarily cut off at spending on consumer goods.

Keynes' model must be revised.

Manipulating the original model, one obtains:

$$\text{Income} = \text{Saving} + \text{Consumption} \quad (1)$$
$$\text{Investment} = \text{Income} - \text{Saving} \quad (2)$$
$$\text{Investment} = \text{Consumption.} \quad (3)$$

The meaning of terms is different in this model. SAVING means all non-productive wealth. This term becomes clearer if it is substituted with the word "Hoarding."*** INVESTMENT means all productive wealth. And CONSUMPTION means any expenditure of money (or other wealth).

The relationship between Saving (or better, Hoarding) and Investment is changed from equality to complementarity (originally erroneously identified as inverse proportionality).

Equation (3) becomes a formally valid equivalence by inserting in it the theory of Distribution, and substituting the word Investment with its old meaning of Production. One thus obtains:

Production = Distribution = Consumption. ****

NOTES (Not in original publication)

* Copyrighted 1979, 2002

** Using the looking glass of S = I, unable to distinguish saving from investment, the economics profession has fallen through the rabbit hole of "Adam Smith's Fallacy." This is the assumption that private greed turns out to be public good. This is a world in which—as today's events confirm and Keynes pointed out—"nothing is clear and everything is possible."

*** Through the looking glass of hoarding, the world looks totally different. Strangely, later, to my unending surprise I had to discover that that is the lens constantly used from Moses, through Jesus of the Parable of the Talents, to Locke. Adam Smith offered a discontinuity in this millennial tradition.

**** In new notation, this equivalence reads:

Production ◄─► Distribution ◄─► Consumption.

Graphically, this equivalence can be represented as:

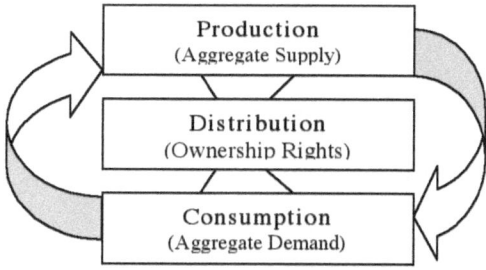

The Economic Process

For detailed analyses, see *The Economic Process: An Instantaneous Non-Newtonian Picture* (University Press of America, 2002) and *The Economics of Jubilation: Blinking Adam's Fallacy Away* (forthcoming).

The Productivity Standard: A True Golden Standard

in Dawn M. Kurland (ed.), Every Worker An Owner: *A Revolutionary Free Enterprise Challenge to Marxism,* Washington, D.C.: Center for Economic and Social Justice, 1987, pp. 83-86.

by
Carmine Gorga and Norman G. Kurland *

* Dr. Gorga is President of Polis-tics Inc., Gloucester, MA 01930. Norman G. Kurland is president of the Center for Economic and Social Justice, Washington, DC.

Fiscal policy is nearly all played out, and traditional monetary policy is effectively neutralized. It cannot be any tighter without causing a severe recession and it cannot be any looser without fanning again the flames of inflation. In the meantime interest rates remain stubbornly high.

The era of "fine tuning" has come to an end.

The discussion is back to fundamentals, as evidenced by the alternative with which we are presented: either add some technical adjustments to the existing Paper Standard or restore the Gold Standard.

The Paper Standard promises us flexibility; the Gold Standard stability. Flexibility to deal with the great unknowns of the next few years; stability which comes from the confidence that the government is not free to debauch the currency: therefore, psychological stability first and stability of the money supply thereafter.

The limitations of the Paper Standard are numerous; but the Gold Standard is not perfect either. As Mr. Lewis E. Lehrman has frankly admitted, "The gold standard, being a human institution, is imperfect."

Yet, notwithstanding well-known weaknesses in both systems, positions are becoming so polarized as to add evidence to Professor Paul W. McCracken's statement that "there are so few helpful ideas around to deal with the most vexing problems of economic policy in the industrial world today."

In order to break the impasse, we need a new set of ideas. Urgently, we especially need a standard that will give us both flexibility and stability. This possibility is technically and politically within our reach, provided we give serious thought to it. The institution capable of bringing about this historic compromise might be called the Productivity Standard, a standard which shares with the real bills doctrine historical roots and aspirations, but nothing else. The mechanics of the two are completely different.

The Productivity Standard can be carefully constructed restricting some and enlarging other key elements of the monetary system as it exists at present. The foundation of the new structure needs to be limited. It needs to be restricted to all productive — or reproductive — wealth, "real" wealth from which a direct income stream is produced: active machinery, equipment, supplies and the like. (The Productivity Standard says what it means: it is not meant to cover inventories alone, as the real bills doctrine does; and in certain cases it would not cover inventories at all.)

Using all productive wealth as the foundation of the new standard is to follow the middle road. It is to follow the Golden Mean between the extreme of the Gold Standard: gold alone; and the extreme of the Paper Standard: all wealth, as the basis upon which to tie the value of the currency.

Upon such a restricted foundation, the structure of the Productivity Standard can thereafter be built anew. We would then obtain a true Golden Standard. In this endeavor, we should be guided by three cardinal principles. First, federal credit should be extended to discount only eligible industrial, commercial, and agricultural paper — for whatever length of time it requires to repay the loan, and not 3-month loans, as in the real bills doctrine.

The legislative power for these operations is already embodied in Paragraph 2, Section 13 of the Federal Reserve Act of 1913. In the light of the Productivity Standard, however, this power has either not been used or it has been used improperly. In various recent or past "rescue" operations the "discount window" should have not been put into effect at all. In others, the discount factor should have been much lower.

One reason this power has not been properly used is that by itself, economists say, the discount window does not insure the control of the money supply. What institution can ever do that by itself? A deeper reason can be found in the fact that the Federal Reserve System has not been given by the Congress — and by economists — clear directions on how to distinguish eligible paper from paper transactions involving the transfer of public and private securities, consumer credit, speculative credit and government credit. Speculative loans in particular would have to be strictly defined as loans that cover transactions involving existing, nonproductive wealth which is scheduled to remain non-productive for the near future. Hence, inventories that are not an integral, functional part of the operation would not be eligible for federal credit. On the other hand, loans to cover the creation of new wealth, no matter how risky, cannot — from a strict economic point of view — be called speculative loans.

Once these issues of definition are settled we can either empower the Federal Reserve System to operate a discrimination between (loans for) productive and nonproductive resources or, perhaps preferably, we can create a new organization with such a power. This organization might be called New Federal Credit (NFC) Agency. "New" for "Not Elsewhere Warranted" federal credit, or simply federal credit for new productive activities that are carried out by new or established enterprises — enterprises involved in the creation of marketable goods and services. Federal credit is by definition new credit. It ought to be extended only for new productive activities, if we ever want to strengthen the basis for an automatic control of the money supply. It is in fact relatively easy to model, forecast and eventually achieve an automatic control over credit for productive activities; as the experience of recent years has amply demonstrated, it is instead impossible to regulate other forms of credit such as consumer credit and especially speculative credit.

Two points must be clarified. Federal credit does not imply borrowing from the taxpayer. It implies the creation of new money — new money that is automatically taken out of circulation as soon as the original loan is repaid, i.e., as soon as the money has performed its function. In addition, the creation of new money need not become part of the political process because the New Federal Credit Agency would have no power to initiate the allocation of credit. It should simply and automatically satisfy the demand for credit after individual banks have approved the loan for the specified purposes. Thus, while still creating new money, the danger of fiat government money would be automatically eliminated.

The second crucial principle of the Productivity Standard is that federal credit should be extended at cost and not at an arbitrary rediscount factor, as in the real bills doctrine — a cost to the final borrower not exceeding perhaps a 2% or 3% interest rate, in addition to a variable insurance premium to cover default risks. The insurance company, or companies, should be expected to be private, so that the new frontiers of capital formation insurance would be opened to this industry.

If the creation of new enterprises and the preservation of old ones is vital to the welfare of the nation, then it is counterproductive for the federal government to make a profit on such transactions. Besides, federal credit ought to be extended at cost if we ever want to eliminate some of the exogenous causes of price inflation. Thus we would immediately bring down the most significant interest rates.

The third indispensable principle of the Productivity Standard is that if federal credit has to be extended at all, and if it will be extended at cost, then in theory it should be extended to all. (The real bills doctrine never paid any attention to this crucial area.)

In practice, not everyone will qualify or would want to qualify. Eligible industrial, commercial and agricultural paper — provided there is an automatic distribution of wealth — is indeed "self-liquidating." It essentially represents sound enterprises with feasible plans which can reasonably be expected to repay the loan, for the most part, in three to seven years. Extending federal credit to all only means that the ownership of future wealth, the wealth produced with the use of national credit, must become as widespread as possible.

We have been so very clever in extending consumer credit nearly to all. We can be equally inventive in extending capital credit. In fact, even though we are at the very infancy of the field, there is already an array of financial mechanisms to achieve this aim. Some of them are inscribed in the very tax code of the land. The most important is the leveraged employee stock ownership plan or ESOP. Through this and other potentially more effective mechanisms, the third essential pillar of the new system can immediately be made to sustain the Productivity Standard.

The use of these mechanisms would have to be made such an integral part of the system as to be mandatory, because the widespread ownership of future wealth, first, would properly have to belong to those who create it. Second, the need for alternative policies aimed at redistribution of wealth would gradually be undercut, thus leaving owners of wealth in peace. Third, and more important, the widespread distribution of future wealth would begin to build not only a very sturdy constituency for the free market system but a very sturdy economy as well. Those who should object to such an imposition would be free to obtain credit on the open market, as against federal credit extended at cost.

The thorough application of these three principles would give us the stability of the Gold Standard, because they would gradually transform the Paper Standard into a full-fledged Golden Standard — and would still preserve much of the flexibility of the Paper Standard.

The transition envisaged here can be achieved without much trauma in the economic body because the Federal Reserve System would still continue to borrow and lend money. Given its initial endowment of assets, it might even continue to buy and sell government obligations, thus contributing to the regulation of the money supply; but its ultimate source of funds would no longer be the national credit. Its sole source of funds would be banks and other financial institutions from which it would borrow and to which it would lend. The interest rate for these funds would be the going market rate. And these funds, conceivably at rates even higher than the current ones, would be primarily available for paper transactions, consumer loans — including home mortgages — loans to the government whenever it incurs deficit spending, and speculative loans. These activities would obviously be discouraged by the high interest rates until everyone — government included — would be put on a balanced budget basis. (These measures would be worth ten Constitutional Amendments to achieve a balanced federal budget.)

During the transition, and there is no reason to demand that the transition should not last forever, we would in essence have a two-tier — or, more accurately, a multi tier — interest rate structure. In accordance with the risk involved, there would be (lower) variable rates for loans covering productive activities as well as (higher) variable rates for all other activities. Both sets of rates would ultimately be determined by the market.

Thus the Productivity Standard would give us great flexibility: it would automatically respond to various market conditions. And it would give us stability as well, or at least as much stability as the market needs and wants. The government would lose the power to arbitrarily create new money, but not the power to contribute to the control of the money supply. Finally, society would regain the power that it so desperately needs now: the power over the federal discount rate through which alone it can hope to bring down the most significant interest rates, the interest rates that are the wellspring of economic progress.

Bold New Directions in Politics and Economics

The (Defunct) Human Economy Newsletter, March 1991, 12 (1) 3-6, 12.

by
Carmine Gorga *

Editors Corner:

This Newsletter is dedicated to the proposition that the economy exists for the benefit of humans rather than vice-versa. For that to be true it is necessary for the economy to be both humane and sustainable. We invite contributions to this effort.... We are also extremely grateful to Dr. Carmine Gorga for allowing us to print his essay on *Bold New Directions in Politics and Economics* which begins on the next page. We think that this essay is remarkable in breaking new ground and would appreciate any feedback to it.

Editorial Staff: Mark Friedman, Steven Hickerson, Jason Kesler, E. Dale Peterson, Donald Renner, Richard Schiming, Robert Simonson, Gerald Alonzo Smith, Economics Department, Mankato State University.

ABSTRACT

Clearly the times call for bold new directions in politics and economics. There is a crisis in our thought processes first and in our actions thereafter. This paper contains the broad outline of a long-considered response to this long-standing crisis. It is a three-pronged response: In politics, we must go beyond both Individualism and Collectivism. In economic policy, we must go beyond (a) prevailing practices of taxation on land and natural resources; (b) concentration of ownership of income and wealth; (c) top-down management of the money supply; and (d) certain forms of organization of industrial and financial assets. In economic theory, we must go beyond the confines of Keynes' model of the economic system.

Introduction

This paper is divided into three sections. The first treats issues of political science. The second, issues of economic policy. The third, issues of economic theory. A few concluding comments attempt to address more directly the concerns of the members of The Society for a Human Economy.

The work outlined below is the result of over thirty years of research that, at its major junctures, has been carried forward with the assistance of some of the best minds of this century — notably, Professors Vittorio de Caprariis, Robert A. Mundell, M. L. Burstein, and Franco Modigliani.

The title of this paper is suggested not only by the motto of The Human Economy Newsletter, namely "New Directions in Economic Thought and Action," but also by a personal communication to this writer from Professor William J. Baumol. Upon reviewing a paper entitled "The Dynamics of the Economic Process," Professor Baumol has written: "You are certainly striking out boldly in new directions and your work promises to yield new insights and results." This is not a singular assessment. Professor Michele Boldrin has remarked: "I find admirable your effort to combine insights from so varied and different areas of research into a new and fascinating picture." This work is available as one of the Human Economy Papers and is listed in this Newsletter, Volume 11: Number 1 (March 1990).

Beyond Individualism and Collectivism

Both Individualism and Collectivism foster the "I vs.Thou" (I-T) pattern of thinking and action: one promotes the individual at the expense of society, the other promotes society at the expense of the individual. Both systems are faulty because they are based on abstract entities. The individual, as pinpointed by Professor Alasdair MacIntyre, is a creation of the last four or five hundred years of political theory. It is an abstraction. And a greater abstraction is society by itself.

As society clearly does not exist without the individual, so the individual — the isolated, the lone individual — does not exist without society. Does a fish live out of water? Can an individual human being live without tradition, the gift of companionship, the hope of the future? The reality is composed of an individual human being placed within the social context.

From the I-T model of political science we must pass to the I-R-T model, the I in relation with the Thou. Synthetically, this model suggests that the social and political reality is enclosed in the Social Man, the Civilized Person. (Should we reduce the expression "the Social Man" to Somism? Or should we prefer Sopism for "the Social Person"? Personalism will not do: legally, the person is a creation of the state; conceptually, the person — unless civilized — remains isolated from its context). Analytically, in this model there are three entities to analyze: the I, the Thou, and the Relation linking the two.

Notwithstanding Descartes, whose formula "I think, therefore I am" had the unfortunate result of reducing the human being to a thinking machine, the I is composed of body, feelings, and mind. These elements are like organs that operate, freely rather than compulsorily, within an organism. They can go their own merry way toward a destructive end or they can be fused together into the dignity of the individual human being. Through this spiritual integration man and woman, the animal, a meager companion for social and intellectual intercourse, is transformed into a potentially civilized person.

To realize this potential takes an act of volition enclosed in the concerted effort of all human virtues. It is they that empower men and women, because, as St. Thomas Aquinas said, "virtue is the peak of power".

Since it adds external strength to inner strength, most empowering of all is a procedural virtue that, as Fr. William Ferree, S. M., points out, has been defined only during this century by Pope Pius XI: social justice. Its definition is an attempt to return to the concrete Aristotelian conception of justice as justice in action, with the social dimension explicitly added to it. Social justice is organizing for the discovery and implementation of the just: namely, the common good, the good of the I and the Thou. In progression, with Paul Tillich, we can then say: "So we shall speak first of justice, love and power in human relations, then of power, justice and love in social institutions, then of love, power and justice in relation to the holy."

The mountain of social order can also be scaled through the path of solidarity: the commonality of interests is approached directly and the range of convergence of rights is left behind. The path is less rough and threatening, and makes social organization a little easier to achieve. The goal is the same. As Pope John Paul II specifies, solidarity "is not a feeling of vague compassion or shallow distress at the misfortune of so many people, both near and far. On the contrary, it is a firm and persevering determination to commit oneself to the common good; that is to say, to the good of all and of each individual because we are all really responsible for all."

Is the existence of the common good — both as end and means — a pure esoteric matter? Is it a matter that can be easily dismissed with a grain of cynicism? Yes, it can; but at one's own risk and peril. As all other self-fulfilling prophecies, cynicism — no less than realism — gathers what it sows. This conclusion is, quite surprisingly, reached by both the best religious tradition and the best economic theory, and is offered as a matter of fact as well as deep theory. As fact, while Professor Milton Friedman speaks of international interconnections that produce a pencil, Pope John Paul II speaks of interdependence "sensed as a system determining relationships in the contemporary world in its economic, cultural, political and religious elements, and accepted as a moral category." As theory, one field speaks of "general economic equilibrium," "competitive equilibrium, "social welfare"; the other speaks of the "common good." Economic theory, in the rich tradition epitomized by Professors Kenneth J. Arrow and Gerard Debreu, proves the existence of a social optimum with the help of the logic and mysticism of mathematics; theology proves the existence of the common good with the help of the logic and mysticism of morality. (Both disciplines list a set of specific conditions to be met for many independent decisions to create an optimum social order rather than chaos; and if those conditions are not respected, in the end, it is neither the fault of theology nor of economic theory.) While the teleology of economic theory is profit maximization, the teleology of theology is dignity maximization. The equilibrium of supply and demand creates the market; the equilibrium of rights and duties creates the just. Both economic theory and theology finally agree that it is the just that creates social order, the only milieu in which the market thrives and men and women can fulfil their human and divine destiny.

But how do we determine what is just? Procedurally, in the peace of our soul we tentatively ascertain what is just; only then can we try to convince others of the validity of our definition — all the while being open to be convinced by others of the validity of their definition. Thus we discover the just.

And we do something else as well. It is at this precise moment of common agreement that we start getting organized for the implementation of the just; it is at this precise moment that we enter into a pact of solidarity with others, a pact of love, a pact of respect for each other's needs. While following this procedure we not only empower the I, we also empower the Thou. Thus we establish a relation of true equality between the two entities. This procedure for the discovery and implementation of the just creates the moral support on which political democracy can be built at every level of human association.

Substantively, since the just calls for a defense of what belongs to us, the dictates of solidarity and social justice demand that we be very certain about the definition of the just.

Historically in Western culture the majority of existing "sacred and inviolable" rights, rights that can be protected in a court of law, have centered around the rights of property. The radius of these rights is still largely determined by the Lockean definition of property as direct possession of real and financial property.

Three major developments have occurred since Locke's time: taxation has become a widespread burden and correspondingly tax evasion an endemic phenomenon; the corporation has become the dominant envelope in which business is conducted; and much business is conducted through the use of credit, especially national credit. Of these phenomena, national credit seems to deserve a word of explanation. Looked at in the present, national credit is the power to create new money; looked at prospectively, it is the fountainhead of economic energy and vitality of the nation; looked at retrospectively, it represents the value of congealed toil of every citizen.

These new realities have created new rights, some of which still lack definition. Among these, the property rights that most need to be explored can generally be described as: 1) The right of every citizen to directly enforce the obligation that all other citizens pay their justly apportioned share of taxes, because if one does not pay taxes others have to pay them — the presupposition is that the tax burden is not lopsided; 2) The right of employees to share in the ownership of the products of the corporation, because wealth (which includes new capital) is created by the combination of labor and capital; 3) The right of every citizen to share in the benefits that the use of national credit can bestow, because all citizens contribute to the creation of the specific values embodied in national credit; and, 4) The right of "stakeholders" — namely, bondholders, suppliers, customers, and employees — to the preservation of the integrity of the corporation against external capricious and arbitrary forces, because the corporation is an indirect creation of stakeholders; without stakeholders, the corporation collapses.

Since taxes unpaid by someone else affect my property, they might be defined as my negative property (debt). Such a definition attempts to cover the reality that tax evasion does not deprive often fumbling government officials of the means to perpetrate additional mischief; these excuses are separate political issues; tax evasion, primarily and directly, defrauds other citizens of their property. Since — as Pope Leo XIII was one of the first to recognize — one is barren without the other, new products might be defined as joint property of their creators, the owners of capital and labor.

Since everyone contributes to its creation, national credit might be defined as common property. And, finally, since — as Max DePree, among others, has suggested — stakeholders have legitimate interests in the operation of the corporation, the corporation itself might be defined as complex property. The corporation produces a bundle of benefits: shareholders have a direct and primary interest in these benefits; stakeholders have an indirect and residual interest in them. The residual rights of stakeholders can be claimed, not against shareholders, but against offending members of the community at large. As is traditional in the birth of new rights, the differential rights that issue from these definitions are likely to be measured and affirmed first in the political realm rather than a court of law.

It remains to analyze (a) why these specific rights are selected, (b) what are the limits within which these rights can be enforced, and (c) what are some of the likely effects of either their enforcement or non-enforcement. These are questions of political economy that are treated next.

Four Conditions for Free Markets

Because of the widely recognized failure of past attempts at regulation, there is a great demand today for the creation of free markets — both in the West and in the East. But unregulated markets, as Professor Paul A. Samuelson has put it, create Charles Dickens capitalism. How to escape this dilemma?

The traditional escape route is to have recourse to the definition of the just. Once a society reaches a fundamental agreement on what is just, or with Aristotle what is due (or, actively, what belongs) to each one of us, the foundation is laid for lasting and peaceable solutions to human problems.

In this decade, we need to reach agreement that the four new property rights mentioned above are indeed just: 1) The right of a private citizen (not simply the government) that another pay his justly apportioned share of taxes; 2) The right of employees to share in the ownership of the products created jointly with capital, products that include new capital; 3) The right of every citizen to obtain access to the use of national credit; and, 4) The right of stakeholders to the preservation of the integrity of the corporation against external capricious and arbitrary forces.

Once these differential property rights are agreed upon as defining most of the current particular "just," the specifics of the translation of these definitions into rights enforceable in a court of law will be easily obtained.

The reason for the selection of these four rights is that, as one goes beyond the rhetoric of current fiscal and monetary macroeconomic policies, one discovers that from the lack of affirmation of those rights stem four policies that have long been dominant in the West — no less than, mutatis mutandis, in the East: (1) Near tax-free status of land and natural resources; (2) Concentration of ownership of income and wealth; (3) Top-down management of money supply; and, (4) Concentration of organization and management of industrial and financial assets.

These four policies little by little, surreptitiously, create Charles Dickens capitalism — or the Gulag. This result occurs without malice or forethought. But intentions are, literally, immaterial: they are otherworldly. It is concrete actions that we are concerned about. And here a subtle distinction needs to be kept firmly in mind: Policies do not create actions; people do, people act. They act, first of all, by accepting or rejecting, improving or corrupting the social fabric they inherit from previous generations. What economic policies achieve, assisted by a myriad of other cultural factors, is to set limits to actions: limits to the amount of good as well as evil that human beings can accomplish. Policies, as all other visible and invisible forms of organization of human effort, represent the framework within which human beings act, so much so that most of those who live outside it are by definition the heroes, the martyrs, or the saints.

With these caveats, it is important to realize that those four policies operate in concert and permit actions that turn to the detriment of everyone. The poor most of all. But do not the rich also suffer from inflation and deflation, pollution, exploitation, and conflict that are fostered by those policies?

And what of fear? What of conflict across national borders?

Still more important is to become aware of the chain of causation that leads to the following dichotomy: enforce those rights, and you create and preserve free markets; do not enforce them, and you foster a phenomenon that used to be called monopoly and, more precisely, can be defined as hoarding of wealth (a) beyond one's needs, (b) to the sacrifice of the satisfaction of other peoples' needs, and (c) holding it in a non-productive state. This last characteristic of hoarding is the most important from an economic point of view; has been missed by economic analysis; and is still missing from economic theory.

The non-payment of taxes, in addition to shifting the financial burden onto other people, leads directly to hoarding of land and natural resources thanks to the dynamics of two factors: through resulting higher asking prices, barriers to new entry are raised; and through lower maintenance costs, the protection of previous hoards is reinforced. But hoarding is also fostered by the illegitimate appropriation of other peoples' (i.e., workers' and even, in some ways, capitalists') wealth: at one time more than another, many industrial products sit unused in factories as well as in private homes (i.e., are hoarded). Much national credit is also either not used (i.e., is hoarded) or is misused to hoard real wealth. Finally, many resources are hoarded during takeovers, mergers, and acquisitions: at one stage of the business cycle more than another, factories are boarded up, supplies are unnecessarily stockpiled, and managers and workers are laid off — and are thus, temporarily if not permanently, forced to hoard their skills and abilities.

Four marginal changes, if gradually but relentlessly implemented, would transform negative effects into positive ones. By a ten percent yearly increment over a decade: (1') Shift the burden of taxation from man-made improvements onto God-given land and natural resources; (2') Expand capital ownership not only through Employee Stock Ownership Plans (ESOPs) and cooperatives, but especially through a non-inflationary and non-deflationary macroeconomic national incomes policy — or, more specifically, shift the on-again off-again call for a "social contract" to the steady call for a legal contract; (3') Institute a system of bottom-up management of money creation (a) for capital expansion only, (b) at cost, and (c) to benefit all; and, (4') Leave corporations absolutely free to grow or decay through internal development, but starting a pilot project with some of the largest ones prohibit them from buying or being bought by other corporations; stop the procedure at the level of corporations doing only intrastate business or some other objectively defined level. Internal growth, yes; external acquisition, no. We are concerned with methods of growth, not limits to internal growth.

If these four policies are instituted, free markets are not only created but preserved. Access to the ownership of land and natural resources is made freer for rich and for poor, for present and for future generations. The right of access to public financial capital is preserved for all. Private capital —
both physical and financial — is protected from external piranhas. Labor is gradually rewarded more through profits than through wages. Labor unions benefit from these processes, if they aid in their development.

Hoarding in Economic Theory

The prohibition against hoarding exists in every religion, from Judaism to Hinduism. It became a firm and elaborate tenet of canonic law in the Catholic Church during the Middle Ages. It is in vigor in Islamic law. In each context, the prohibition against hoarding is supported by the best economic thinking prevalent in the specific culture.

Yet hoarding has received scanty attention from Western economists during the last four to five hundred years.

The essential reason for this neglect is that, especially with the Reformation, hoarding came to be confused with a similar-looking, but completely different, phenomenon: "accumulation." When wealth beyond the satisfaction of one's needs legally belonged to the poor, hoarding was morally prohibited; when the accumulation of wealth (rather than work) became a calling sanctified by God, the prohibition against hoarding was rendered ineffective. Indeed, with Adam Smith, accumulation became identified with what we call investment and was justified as a means to increase the wealth and presumably the welfare of nations. In addition, during the last fifty years — as D. H. Robertson feared — hoarding has to all intents and purposes been eliminated from the vocabulary of economists because the economic system is being analyzed through the lenses of a formal model which does not include hoarding as one of its component parts. This is Keynes' model of the economic system. Any elaboration of that model suffers from the same limitation.

This inability to take hoarding into account is one of the reasons why that model must be revised. There are many other independent reasons that lead to the same conclusion.

Once that model is revised, vast new vistas open up to economic analysis. A fundamental restructure of Keynes' model leads to a system composed of three modules: real wealth, ownership rights over wealth, and monetary wealth. This transformation is effected through two mental operations: first, for analytical purposes, the world of real wealth is separated from the world of financial wealth; second, the world of ownership of wealth is re-inserted into the economic system — where it stood at the dawn of economic analysis. This operation places again the world of morality, politics, and the law at the very core of the economic system — not as an external given, but as one of its internal, integral components. At the same time, no discipline loses its autonomy.

The three worlds of the real, the legal, and the monetary sub-systems provide a complementary and mutually enriching understanding of the economic reality. In the new framework of analysis, there is one distinct mathematical model for each perspective from which the economic system can and ought to be studied. The economic language is precise and unchangeable throughout the discourse, hence it can be safely translated into mathematical terms. And the language, respecting throughout basic principles of logic, bridges the gap that exists today between technical economic language and common language.

As the new framework integrates the work of various mental disciplines, so it closes the gap that exists within economics: the gap between macro and micro economics. The new framework describes — in turn — the economic system of the individual person, the corporation, the city, the state, and the world. The differences among these entities are reduced to differences of quantity, not quality. As William A. Schirra stresses, "The quality of justice permeates the economic system for all."

This organic description of the economic system as a whole is no longer static, but inherently dynamic. In fact, the description of the dynamics of the three basic modules is greatly assisted by recent developments in nonlinear mathematics and fractal geometry. The system as a whole can thus be studied as three solids moving — singly and jointly (one into the other) — in space.

And the entire construction is anchored to this reality. Analysis reveals that the system is primarily driven not by government actions and investment decisions taken by groups of people but by individual private decisions concerning the type, the amount, and the timing of hoarding. Personal responsibility thus becomes the touchstone of the entire economic reality.

More. Since it is only goods hoarded that become scarce, it is evident that hoarding causes scarcity — and thus inefficiency. Implicit in this analysis is an ultimate realization: moral actions are efficient actions. The gap between morality and efficiency that has plagued our minds for four to five hundred years is closed. Morality and efficiency go hand in hand.

The validity of these statements can henceforth be measured through computer modeling and econometric analysis.

In this paper we have covered an enormous amount of ground rather breathlessly. It is now time to take a deep breath and start filling in the many gaps that need to be filled. The collaboration of the reader is more indispensable than ever.

Concluding Comments

How does this new framework of thought and action address the concerns of the members of The Society for a Human Economy? It is obviously impossible to reduce the concerns of each and every member to a homogeneous formulation, but the common concern seems to range from the ability of natural resources to sustain our consumerist habits to the set of human relations that are thwarted by the prevailing methods of organizing human effort.

After stating the obvious that no reader is looking for magic formulas and this writer is certainly not providing one, the new framework of thought — if carried out into daily practice — would meet many of those concerns because it is based on personal responsibility: responsibility toward oneself, other human beings, and the planet earth as the center of our universe. (Since the universe seems to be infinite, each point in it stands at its center.) The new framework is based on responsibility and the accompanying freedom provided by economic security. Both characteristics will do wonders to protect our natural resources.

If everyone pays his share of taxes on land and natural resources, these resources begin to be more appreciated for their intrinsic values and therefore they begin to be better used. (Taxes should be raised upstream to avoid pollution, and not downstream as payment for pollution.) Also, once these resources are no longer hoarded, more people are free to have access to them — and, provided all other measures called for above are implemented, they will have the financial and cultural means to use them wisely.

In addition, the resources to be opened up are those that radiate from the downtown of our metropolitan areas: fewer parking lots, fewer lots filled with weeds and rubbish, and fewer abandoned buildings — as well as less forcibly punctuated superdevelopment — at the very core of those areas. Neither would the next band of land be overcrowded, nor would the band next to it be underdeveloped, i.e., hoarded by the few for the benefit of the few, hence necessitating a leapfrog over to the next band. Nor would the wilderness that extends beyond be punctured by unsightly and costly developments. Just think of the financial costs and the frayed nerves that are expended due to overstretched lines of commuting to work and pleasure, lines of communication, lines of police and fire protection, lines of sewer and garbage collection. Are not these lines overstretched because many plots of land in between are hoarded expecting their price to become higher and higher — or, in recessions and depressions, to fall less steeply than other prices?

To develop lands wisely from the core cities outward is to practice conservation. That would be the ultimate effect of a progressively higher tax burden on land values, provided it never reached confiscatory levels. And a similar effect would result from higher taxes on natural resources. Would not all non-renewable energy sources be treated with greater respect if they were taxed for the benefit of all? Indeed, by raising their development cost, would not the gap with the production cost of such renewable energy sources as solar cells become smaller?

Surely consumerism is the malady of the age. But to consider it the cause, rather than the effect, of our problems is misguided. Consumer goods are mostly stolen away from their rightful owners, the people who directly or indirectly produce them. That alone creates a guilty conscience that contributes to their destruction. But there are many other causes that produce the same effect: if one is dissatisfied with one's inner world — namely, the world of work, the world of self-expression — then one searches for satisfaction in the external world. Hence goods are sought after as an expression of one's power. And then, if one acquires them on credit, one hates them before, during, and after the act of consumption as they become an expression of self-enslavement. Thus not only are those goods destroyed at that stage, but more trees, more fauna, more landscapes are destroyed to generate income to pay for goods already destroyed.

Switch the reality of work from a wage to a profit paradigm by enabling employees to become owners of corporations in which they work, and you put men and women in charge of their destiny; in charge of relations with fellow workers; in charge of waste.

Let everyone benefit from the blessings of capital formation through a switch from a private saving to a national credit paradigm, and you undermine the classic rationale for hard-heartedness and selfishness: "I got mine the hard way; get yours the same way (if you can)."

Let entrepreneurs develop corporations in the old-fashioned way rather than by steal and stealth, and all beneficiaries will feel secure in their income stream.

What can be expected as the combined result of these four marginal policy changes? Perhaps one effect will be of overwhelming importance: The aim of economic life will be the enhancement of one's dignity rather than one's cash balances. Work for money will become again work for production of valuable goods and services. From service exclusively to oneself and, often, to evil we will pass to service to oneself to others and to God.

* Dr. Gorga is a Fulbright scholar. A lecturer and author of numerous publications in economic policy and fisheries development, he is president of
Polis-tics Inc., an economic consulting firm in Gloucester, MA. He is currently working on a book entitled "A CIVILIZATION RENEWAL: Through
Personal Responsibility and Economic Security."

Reprinted with permission from
Social Justice Review, January/February 1994, 85 (1-2) 3-6.

Four Economic Rights
Social Renewal Through
Economic Justice for All

Carmine Gorga, Ph.D.

To realize the importance of the four economic rights examined below, one has to place them in the context of the forces they have to oppose in order to assert themselves. The opponents of rights are not some vague and unidentifiable forces. The opponents of rights are the active forces of privilege.[1] The essential differentiation between rights and privileges is this. Rights unite; privileges divide.

A NATION DIVIDED BY PRIVILEGES

The dynamics of privilege become apparent in nearly every morning newspaper. We know the headlines by rote: this group wants a tax reduction; that group wants an increase in services. The dynamics are all there. Privileges, since they are not due to us, are always acquired to the detriment of other people. Hence the recurring struggle of wills. No issue is ever settled. No one is ever secure about anything.

Based upon such quicksand, there are never enough resources to satisfy the grab for privileges.

Hence, it takes force to extract privileges. But once the privilege is obtained, its use fosters passivity: there is nothing to do but to enjoy the privilege until the next challenger comes around. By then the will and the strength of the user of privilege has generally been so enfeebled that surrender is near. Yet the newly dispossessed will rise again.

A NATION UNITED BY RIGHTS

Rights unite us all. They make us all equal.[2] The magic of rights is this. Once a right is asserted in one particular case, it is asserted for all. (It is the extension of the application of rights that often is a horrendously slow process.)

The opposing political will must be broken. The opposing will is more easily broken if the request is advanced in a reasonable fashion, hence the success of nonviolent political movements and if the request makes it absolutely clear that the privileged group is not going to be denied the exercise of the right that is proposed. The right must be universal.

Once the opposing will is broken the right is exercised by all and it is exercised actively. As opposed to privileges it takes a continuous act of the will to exercise that right. The right then implies a duty.

FOUR ECONOMIC RIGHTS

As there are four factors of production, namely, land, financial capital, labor and physical capital, so there must be four specific rights of access to those factors otherwise, instead of being productive, as Pope John Paul II points out, we will be marginalized.[3] Rooted in the natural law, these rights can be formulated as follows:

- the right to share in the bounties of nature,
- the right to share in the bounties of national credit,
- the right to own the fruits of one's creation,
- the right to protect the fruits of one's creation.

These four rights, once exercised in full, will renew the very roots of our culture and our civilization. They will work from within existing structures and might allow us to transform the provision of goods and services from the brutal exercise it has lately become into a very spiritual enterprise, as it inherently is.[4]

THE RESOURCES OF THE NATION ARE POTENTIALLY INFINITE

The resources of the nation are potentially infinite. The evidence that this statement is true is overwhelming.[5] The issue therefore is not scarcity, but greed justified by social disorganization. No one knows today what is enough. Consequently one is compelled to accumulate more than one needs. When one does that, one deprives other people of their due because at any one moment resources are finite.

If the social organization is right, everyone knows what is enough. What is enough is what one needs today. If the social organization is right, one can assuredly implement the Gospel's injunction: "Look at the birds of the air... Consider the lilies of the field... O men of little faith..."

The issue then is one of social organization. If the resources of the nation are potentially infinite, everyone has the right of access to them. They are a common good.

But how can society enforce such a right? The issue is not only one of will but also one of reality. Some solutions work, some do not. Some solutions work in one society, at one time; some do not.[6] The solution that seems to be best applicable to the needs of the modern world lies in the use of taxes on land and natural resources. They have to be generally higher than they are today and taxes on buildings and other human activities have to be correspondingly lower.

Owners who do not want to, or think they cannot afford to, pay justly and fairly apportioned taxes on land and natural resources will not be dispossessed; they will simply sell their property and enjoy the fruits of interest on the money obtained in exchange for the transfer of their right of ownership to more capable hands who will make, for instance, the weeds and rubbish filled lots, in too many downtown areas today, bloom. These taxes are effective because they tend to eliminate hoarding, thus opening access to unused resources that ought to be used.

Let us briefly put the issue another way. We all have the duty to pay taxes on our property of land and natural resources. We all have this duty because most of the value of our land and natural resources comes first from God or Nature, if you will and from the community thereafter. A rock in Arizona is worth a pittance; a rock in Manhattan is worth lot. The difference lies in what the community brings to the rock: sewer lines and telephones lines, and on and on.

Correspondingly, we all have a right in this matter. We all have the right to enforce the payment by all of a fair assessment of taxes on land and natural resources because, if one does not pay his fair share of such taxes, all others will have to make up the balance.

THE RIGHT OF ACCESS TO NATIONAL CREDIT

Either in a positive or negative way, we all contribute to the value of national credit. Therefore, national credit is a common good *par excellence*. It belongs to all of us.

National credit is a precious resource. From certain points of view it is more precious than natural resources: misuse of natural resources reduces their availability and increases their price. Misuse of national credit reduces the availability and in creases the price of all goods and services. National credit is mostly an untapped resource: what central banks tap is mostly bank credit. Bank credit is created by the savings of a limited number of people; national credit is created by us all.

The use of national credit constitutes one last frontier. We must not mishandle it as we have mishandled so many other frontiers in the past. Properly handled, the use of national credit will function like manna from heaven. It will fuel our creative engines to make us satisfy our immediate as well as our future needs. Properly used it will be just sufficient to our needs. We will always have enough of it.

In-depth consideration of the potential use of national credit leads to the formulation of three essential criteria for its proper use: 1) national credit must be used only to issue loans that are necessary for the creation of new wealth; 2) it must be issued at cost; 3) it must be issued to the benefit of all.

The rationale for the first criterion is best seen in the negative. National credit cannot be used to finance the purchase of consumer goods because these goods do not generate the income necessary to repay the loan. National credit cannot be used to finance the purchase of goods that are to be hoarded. National credit cannot be used to finance the purchase of government debt unless the debt is issued to create new wealth.

The rationale for the second criterion is easily specified. Interest rates for credit to create new wealth must cover only the cost of administration of the loan instruments and insurance of default risks.

The rationale for the third criterion is more complex. Some people are inept at creating wealth; some do not care about it. We must all pursue our destinies. And we must not become slaves of the creators of wealth in the process. The application of this criterion, rather than a limitation, presents us with a tremendous opportunity. It means that entrepreneurs have to share the ownership of the wealth they create with all those who help them create it: Employee Stock Ownership Plans (ESOPs) and cooperatives are some of the ideal legal instruments that serve to achieve this aim.[7]

THE RIGHT TO OWN THE WEALTH ONE CREATES

If men and women have an indisputable right to own common goods as land and national credit, how much stronger is the right to own the wealth one creates? That is the fundamental premise on which ESOPs and cooperatives rest. They are legal instruments that allow a fair apportionment of the right of ownership over the wealth that employees create in cooperation, of course, with the owners of capital.

Employees are outside contractors. They offer their labor and receive wages. They have no right to the wealth created by the corporation wealth which includes consumer goods, goods to be hoarded and capital goods.

ESOPs and cooperatives change all that. Following an established set of rules and regulations, they transform employees from contractors into stockholders. From outsiders employees become insiders. Employees then become much more efficient workers. Provided ESOPs and cooperatives are not simply window dressing, legal arrangements to cajole the taxman, but in fact do respect the whole person of the employee, they are mostly successful. ESOPs multiplied during the Eighties.

The question is how can ESOPs and cooperatives be made tools of national policy? The answer lies in seeing them not as concessions from existing owners and managers to employees, but as means to give life to universal rights. Three procedures might speed up the tempo of the assertion of this right.

First, when the use of national credit is called upon to assist in the creation of new wealth, the use of ESOPs and cooperatives must be made mandatory. There will still be no compulsion in this practice because those who did not want to extend the right of ownership to their employees would be free to recur to existing, although more expensive, credit channels.

The second procedure for a speedy assertion of this right is to link any grant of public money to the expansion of ownership of the resulting wealth to all employees of corporations creating that wealth.

The third procedure is to link the vicissitudes of inflation and deflation to the exercise of this right. We all more or less agree that during inflationary periods asking for higher wages adds to the flames of inflation just as during periods of deflation imposing lower wages adds to the ravages of deflation. These negative spirals must be broken. They are generally broken through the exercise of force or the (generally vain) promise of future advantages. How much more reasonable is it to prevent the problems by the use of fundamental rights?

THE RIGHT TO PROTECT WHAT ONE OWNS

Included in the right of ownership of wealth is the right to protect it from outside incursions into its uses and enjoyment. As Pope Leo XIII maintained, the right of property is "sacred and inviolable."[8] The consequences of this right have been mostly feared and resented by governments and reformers alike. But it is proper and unavoidable. All justification for that fear and resentment will be annihilated once the ownership of wealth becomes not a privilege reserved for the few but a common right for all.

To this right corresponds a duty, the duty to respect other people's property. This set of rights and duties can assume a hundred different manifestations, from trivial to momentous. Perhaps the application that is of utmost importance today regards the buying corporations as if they were "things" and not entities deeply affecting the lives of the people within and without their direct area of influence. This practice produces uncountable horrors.

The practice of corporate aggrandizement has deep roots in human nature. An old example is how hermits became monks and monks created institutions too large for their own good. So new religious orders were created. And the process started anew again and again. We have had more than a century of intense experience to prove that this practice creates havoc in the economic realm. It must be stopped.

Only if we put a stop to this practice, will we protect our civilization from the quick and the cunning. Thousands of years ago, we made a huge stride forward when we decided that the murder of another person was not a private affair. We will make a huge stride forward when we will realize that the buying and selling of corporations is akin to industrial murder. This practice cannot be tolerated. Captains of industry should not operate in a business environment in which the fruits of the labor of many can be gobbled up at the whim of any operator who, with the promise of quick results, gains command of untold financial resources. Our time horizon has to widen beyond the next accounting period; our horizon of concerns has to expand beyond the production of goods and services. What we affect, in the final analysis, is always the life of particular men and women.

Since the practice of buying and selling corporations is so ingrained, we cannot hope to put an abrupt stop to it just as we cannot abruptly increase taxes on land and natural resources to the desired level.[9] We must start by imposing this prohibition on a limited number of the largest corporations and gradually extend it to the smaller ones until it reaches a level of reasonableness that is satisfactory to everyone, including lawyers and investment bankers. But industrial murder must be stopped.

AN ORGANIC POLICY

These four rights form the backbone of an organic economic policy that will gradually produce self-reinforcing benefits. The dissolution of the power of privilege that ensues will, of course, require constant vigilance, but it will proceed by its own internal dynamics and thus will direct the whole gamut of problems affecting our world today on the way to a proper solution. There are many ways of demonstrating the validity of this position. The simplest is to expand upon the set of distinctions between rights and privileges outlined at the outset of this discussion.

THE LARGER CONTEXT

In the beginning an attempt was made to place this discussion within the historico-political context. These issues can also be studied from the sociological, teleological and theological viewpoint. It is on this vast ground that we will find the ultimate justification for the suggested policy.

Privileges are based on envy, use greed as the engine to set the social dynamics in motion, are extracted through violence or the threat of violence and foster sloth.

Rights are based on self-sufficiency, use self-reliance as the engine to set the social dynamics in motion, are exercised through mutual respect and foster the dignity of the person.

What did God — or Nature, or at the limit, our own will — put us on this earth for?

NOTES

1. The early colonists and those who freely followed them in an ever widening procession from every corner of the world were propelled upon these shores by the same desire: to escape from he iron clasp of privilege.

2. To be equal does not mean to be identical. To be equal means that no one has privileges. To be equal means that everyone has the same rights.

3. See, e.g., Pope John Paul II, Encyclical *Centesimus Annus* (1991) 33. The Welfare State is blind to this reality. Hence, it goes after the symptoms of poverty and compounds the difficulties by trying to establish rights via entitlements. All that is wrong with this shortcut becomes evident only if it is realized that entitlements are not rights. They are privileges masquerading under the cloak of rights.

4. Is not growing wheat a glorious spiritual exercise? Is not making bread a glorious spiritual exercise? Is not sharing information a glorious spiritual exercise? No. Michelangelo, Rembrandt and Van Gough were not the only human beings blessed with the ability to give so much to all of us. The old lady who sweeps the floor gives us just as much every day. Without her services we would either be compelled to sweep the floor ourselves — God forbid — and so deprive ourselves of the enjoyment of Michelangelo, Rembrandt and Van Gough. Or we would be living in a pile of dirt.

5. Not only is Einstein's formula for the conversion of mass into energy assuring us that a grain of sand does indeed contain all he energy that we will ever need. Not only is the sun's energy falling on a small patch of the Sahara desert capable of producing all the energy that we will ever need. Both Israel and Saudi Arabia, as the few positive headlines of this exasperating century shout, are making the desert bloom. Saudi Arabia has become a net exporter of wheat!

6. In ancient Israel, the solutions that gave access to natural resources to all were essentially two. For

the short run, all the uncollected staples belonged to the poor. They had free access to them. For the long run, the institution of the Jubilee was supposed to take care of the fundamental issues: Ownership of the land was to be relinquished every 49 or 50 years and returned to the original owner. During the Middle Ages, the Catholic Church mostly enforced the rule that all "surplus" wealth *legally* belonged to the poor. Islamic banking institutions are still fighting against usury, in the face of enervating snickering from the international financial community. Modernity, the Age of Entitlements, has desperately and disastrously tried to enforce a different rule: redistribution of wealth. Some applications of this rule have assumed the form of "land reform"; as if that policy were not unfortunate enough, most have assumed the myriad forms of forced transfers.

7. For those who are outside the work force and are not yet independently wealthy, traditional and nontraditional channels of charity must be used to achieve the substance — although not the form — of economic justice. This is not to say that the form and substance of economic justice cannot eventually be united in nontraditional policies that will eliminate the need for charily altogether.

8. Pope Leo III, Encyclical *Rerum Novarum* (1891) 35.

9. The use of national credit and the expansion of ESOPs and cooperatives are inherently gradual processes, simply because the creation of new wealth is unavoidably a gradual process.

----

*Carmine Gorga, lecturer and author of numerous publications, is president of Polis-tics, Inc., a consulting firm in Gloucester, MA, and is currently working on a book entitled *A New Monetary Order: Based on Rights, not Privilege.*

Fisheries Renewal
A Renewal of the Soul of Business

Reprinted with permission from
The Catholic Social Science Review, Volume II (1997) 145-161.

by Carmine Gorga, President of Polis-tics Inc., Gloucester, Massachusetts, and Stuart B. Weeks, Center for American Studies, Concord, Massachusetts

"Boats Buy Houses. Houses Do not Buy Boats."
Lena Novello,
First President of the Gloucester Fishermen's Wives Association

If you go down to the Gloucester waterfront today, you can plainly see that the seafood industry is in a state of disorganization and despair. You see few fishing boats hailing out to sea to fish for cod, haddock, and flounder, the mainstay of the fleet, because, with the aim of increasing their stocks in the long run, fishing for these species is being drastically curtailed by the Federal Government. You see seafood plants that, due to the decreased catch, have been forced to close their gates. Upon consideration, you will quickly realize that wharf space left idle for a number of years naturally invites aspirations in the soul of the service industries to fill it with condominiums, motels, and retail outlets. Very few will disagree that if these aspirations become a reality, the soul of Gloucester — a 370 year old fishing port, the oldest fishing port in the United States — will be inalterably changed.

What will you see thirty years from now? Even though they are combined now and will undoubtedly continue to be combined in the future, we would suggest that for clarity of perception we contrast two distinct visions of reality: (1) A dispirited people, paid low wages, hurriedly going about *serving* tourists in motels and retail outlets; (2) Or proud people, paid a living wage, *working together* with other people in modern ships and plants, producing valuable products, from seafood to biochemical products. Reduced to its bare essentials, the issue is whether we ought to create institutions that foster dependence and control over other people's lives or institutions that foster interdependence among self-reliant people.

Assuming the latter is our choice, how do we go about realizing this vision? Technically, the need is to find resources, natural and financial, in such quantity and of such quality as to allow this community to be in charge of its own destiny. The complexities of the situation stem from the intricacies and interrelationships among three topics that are indispensable for fisheries development: Conservation, Financing, and Organization.

Beyond all technical features, the main point of this article is the realization that to have true renewal of the fisheries, as distinguished from one or another specific development project within the fisheries, we need to have a thorough renewal of our economic policies and practices. As the discussion progresses, it will become apparent that the obstacles to economic growth are within ourselves. We will see that the need to find natural and financial resources is ultimately transformed into the challenge, simply expressed, to become more virtuous as citizens and to create institutions that help rather than hinder us in the practice of all our virtues. In sort, we are challenged to become "fishers of men," before we symbolically, and fishermen in reality, can once again become fishers of fish.

✳ ✳ ✳

Let us explore the political environment first. You probably expect fishermen and fish processors to be the most prominent players in fisheries development today. And they are. But if they open their hearts to you, they will reveal that at the bottom of their trials lies the feeling that they are being led by strings that are not in their own hands. The strings, in fact, today are in the hands of environmentalists, whether or not armed with government regulations, and in the hands of national fiscal and monetary planners. This is a new political reality.

Traditionally, fishermen and fish processors in this country would have relied on engineers and accountants to have their business plans approved by the local bank and accepted by the community at large. No longer. Today, they will not go far unless they find ways to embrace the essential concerns of environmentalists and to adapt to the goals of national monetary planners. It is a relatively new story, a story common to nearly all economic development projects; and a relatively well-known story. During the last thirty to forty years, often at risk and peril to their own safety and fortune, environmentalists have saved us from environmental disaster, and financiers have saved us in trying moments from financial ruin. The environmental disasters that have been skirted are too well known to be recounted here. Who can forget Love Canal? How many such dangers have we avoided? The chief financial disaster that was averted as recently as the late 80s is the danger of galloping inflation. The decisive actions of the Federal Reserve System put a stop to that. In brief, environmentalists and financiers have gained their present place in the sun because there were excesses in the past: Forests were — and still are — destroyed; financial resources that perhaps ought to have been more sparingly used were — and still are — unnecessarily squandered.

However, the pendulum now seems to have reached the end of its arc. A growing number of people no longer unquestionably accept the assumptions of environmentalists and financiers. Rather, they see those assumptions as creating, unwittingly perhaps, the *first set* of obstacles in the path of economic growth. The new concern, to be precise, is with environmental *alarmists* and *apologists* of the financial status quo. Largely because of opposition from these two groups, the country is littered with development projects that cannot take off. Right here in Gloucester, two major — indeed pivotal — projects have been blocked for years: A protein recovery plant and a fish farm out at sea. So many other projects hinge upon the existence of these two entities that both can now be considered as essential parts of a viable seafood industry infrastructure.

This political reality is not without consequences. Environmental alarmists are in danger of making us a nation of impotents, powerless to create the structures that we need. They are reducing many of us to automatons capable only of uttering such expressions as: *No, No, Not In My Backyard (NIMBY)*. Apologists of the financial status quo are in danger of making us a nation of beggars, powerless to create the financial resources that we need. They are reducing us to automatons capable only of uttering such expressions as: *Give Me Grants, Give me services, Lower my tax Burden*. Does not the combined result of such actions produce a vacuum in our lives? Is not this vacuum necessarily filled with the growth of government intervention in human affairs beyond any tolerable bounds, and certainly beyond the imagination of the Founding Fathers? In short, are not these policies leading to social disintegration? Passivity reigns, until resignation prevails. In the meantime, anger accumulates.

Before catastrophe befalls us, let us be clear about the nature of the concerns of financial apologists and environmental alarmists. Their thought processes, interestingly enough, appear to be tightly joined at three key nodes: One is their apparent disregard for vital lessons of history, the second is their intolerance for risk, the third is their notion of scarcity of resources. These are issues too large to be adequately treated here. For the moment, it is sufficient to ask three questions: How many financial and environmental catastrophes predicted in the past have, in fact, occurred? Is it ever possible to build a risk-free society? Is it true that there is a constant scarcity of natural and financial resources?

We shall concentrate our attention on the last question. The reason is obvious. Who can get excited about economic growth, with its attendant grave questions of justice, if there are no physical resources? Who can get excited about "abstract" issues of justice, if there are no financial resources?

∗ ∗ ∗

Is there scarcity of natural resources? To accomplish their goals, environmental extremists often use alarm to frighten us and, unwittingly, to render us powerless. Specifically, in the fisheries, they paint ghastly pictures concerning potential irremediable damage to the stocks of wild fish, even their total extinction. And, since traditional fish stocks are indeed depleted, they conclude that there is nothing we can do but shut the fisheries down. Currently, that is the aim of some of the most talked about policies: Closure of fishing grounds, boat buyback arrangements, limited-entry programs, individual transferable quotas (ITQs). All is sugar-coated with the promise of rather massive federal aid — as if federal aid meant something other than a transfer of money from taxpayer pockets. Curtly expressed, this is a defeatist program.

Our effort is to show that there is plenty we can do, and indeed must do, to keep the fisheries alive and vibrant — at *no* cost to the taxpayer. The solutions start by meeting head on a problem of definition, proceed along the path of understanding the dynamics of fish stocks, and branch out into questions of financing and organization.

When we think of fish, we tend to think of individual species. But that, it turns out, is not a pragmatically viable definition. Fish do not exist as individual species separated from one another; rather they are part of the total marine biomass. And it is with the total marine biomass that we ought to be primarily concerned. To tackle the problems of any one species, in other words, we need a *multi-species management plan.*

Of course, there is plenty that we must do for each species of fish as well. First of all, we need reasonable conservation measures; then, depending on the specific species and the specific environment, we can think of reseeding the oceans with the assistance of hatcheries or removing obstacles in salmon runs. Yet, the pay-off lies in concentrating our efforts on the total biomass.

Anecdotal information yields always the same result. In periods of crisis, there is not a fish to be had. But is this condition permanent? Is one entitled to extrapolate future trends from this type of "research?" Long historical — as distinguished from anecdotal — statistical series, mathematical models, and biological theories clearly show that in nature we are faced not with stasis, but with dynamics.[1] The dynamics of fish stocks is uniquely grasped with the assistance of a Predator-Prey Model developed in 1925 by Lotka and Volterra, respectively a mathematician and a biologist. Through this model, they explained the ebbs and flows of the sardine fishery in the Adriatic sea. The model is sketched, in simplified fashion, in Figure 1. The simplification consists in the elimination of the cycles in which both predators and prey either fall or rise together.

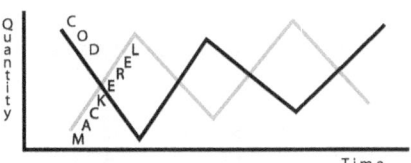

A Simplified Fish Predator-Prey Model
Figure 1

When overfishing of traditional species occurs, this model leads to the question: Who does the overfishing? Could it be that natural predators — rather than, more than, fishermen — do the overfishing? Whatever the specific answer to this question, it is evident that, while at present such traditional species as cod and haddock are depleted, the ocean is teeming with their natural predators: Dogfish, menhaden, mackerel, herring. We ought to focus our attention on these species. Once we do that, we switch our frame of reference from the relative scarcity of any one species to a frame-

work of plenty — or at least to the framework of "The Feast of the Enough."
Within this mental framework, we say good riddance to powerlessness.
Good riddance to retrenchment. Good riddance to the miasma of boat buy-
back programs, through which, as Ed Lima, the executive director of the
Cape Ann Fishermen's Cooperative Association, says, "The owners go to
Florida, and the crew goes to hell." If de-industrialization is not working
within the rest of society, why would it work in the fisheries?

Powerlessness can be replaced with activity and with self-reliance.[2]
Under the leadership of Angela Sanfilippo, the current president of the
Gloucester Fishermen's Wives Association, we will develop a 2020 Vision,
a Vision for the year 2020 for the Port of Gloucester and gradually we will
cooperate with the rest of New England. Then we will resolve the issue of
sustainability for each species. Once the "maximum sustainable yield" is
set and accepted by all participants in the process of fisheries management,
we will focus on the marketability of abundant underutilized species.

There is much that can be done in the way of systematic effort to bring
these species to market. New ways of advertising for them and preparing
them for the table will be developed. School lunch programs will help introduce fresh underutilized species into the diet, and so will army lunch
programs. But what else can be done to speed up the necessarily slow
tempo of their market penetration? What else if not their indirect utilization? The indirect utilization of these renewable resources will be the result of two factors. One is technology; the other is financial resources. We
will not insist on the technological issues, except to remark that our scientists and engineers are exposing us to an embarrassment of riches. We
have many choices. Underutilized species can be transformed into such
marketable products as surimi, fish oils, fish flour, fish food pellets, leather,
biochemicals, and on and on. The bottleneck is not in the inventiveness of
our scientists but in the obstacles unwittingly placed in the implementation of those ideas by over diligent environmentalists. By prolonging the
process for obtaining all necessary permits, these environmentalists have
a major impact on financing. Some projects, in periods of escalating costs,
are dangerously delayed; others become so uncertain that start-up financial resources vanish.

Given the implementation of the two pivotal projects we have singled
out earlier, namely a protein recovery plant and a fish farm out at sea, it is
easy to sketch the overall picture. Underutilized species are reduced to fish
food pellets which are fed to salmon raised in fish farms. Underutilized

species are thus brought to market *via salmon*. The entire fish is utilized by producing biochemical by-products. No waste is tolerated.

We have never advocated nor are we advocating here a protein recovery plant or a fish farm *at any cost*. These and any other endeavor have to be environmentally sound. But the standard ought to be science, not ideology; knowledge, not hearsay; present possibilities, not memory of technologies that failed in the past. The old fish dehydration plant, for instance, was so malodorous at times as to be not only a public nuisance (many nostrils still remember those choice summer nights); it was even a health hazard. Its existence was tolerated for too long; eventually, it was shut down. It should have been shut down much earlier.

The point is that the pendulum has swung far on the other side. Environmentalism has to be taken into due consideration, but it cannot be made so dominant as to be the exclusive concern. We need to reach a new sense of balance. Two of the most important considerations to enter this balance can be easily pointed out. *First*, since fish is a quasi-vital food, the demand for fish is destined to grow. Seafood will either be produced nationally or it will be imported. Fish, in fact, has consistently been one of the top ten on the list of imported items for the last few decades. *Second*, the harsh reality is that, in August 1994, the unemployment rate in Gloucester was 10.5%. In August, mind you, not January, about 1,500 people were in vain searching for work. Multiplying this figure by an average number of dependents, the harsh reality is that 4,500 people were in rather tough straits. How is our community going to satisfy those needs? How are we going to create 1,500 jobs? Where are the opportunities for Gloucester, if not within the broad range of maritime industries? Which other activity has the same potential for growth? Are not tourism and the service industries in our city, ultimately the two most talked about alternatives to the renewal of the fisheries, dependent upon the attraction of the fishing fleet? For sure, change is inevitable. But change for the worse ought not to be easily grasped.

If tourism and the service industry win the day, the traditional character of Gloucester is lost. "In the middle of the night," says Josephine Russo, a fishing captain's wife who, still relying on a thread of hope, recently joined with other women to form the Cape Ann Fishermen's Cooperative Association, "you used to wake up your men and prod them to go to work. Today, there is no future in fishing. What will my son do?"

The essence of the many issues involved here is pithily expressed by

Lena Novello, the first president of the Gloucester Fishermen's Wives Association. She proudly quotes her father saying that *"Boats build houses. Houses do not build boats."* This quote can be rephrased in many different ways: *Boats produce income with which to buy houses, houses do not produce income with which to buy boats; or, capital goods pay for consumer goods, consumer goods do not pay for capital goods; or, save first, spend later; or, produce first, consume later; or, work now, play later.* The essence of the issues can also be put in these terms: Do we want to be a nation of producers or a nation of consumers? Do we want to utilize our resources fully, or do we want to exploit other people's resources? How long will other people have patience with us?

At a point, the soul of America will be lost. The process of de-industrialization can go just so far. If the work ethic goes, the attempt will be made to replace it with empire building, with the exploitation of other people — both within the United States and abroad. Then the American dream recoils into a nightmare. Alexis de Tocqueville, the famous French observer of our society during the last century, expressed this vision quite precisely and eloquently. He said: *"America is great, because America is good. And if America ever ceases to be good, she will cease to be great."*

The issues are that important. They clearly affect more than one fishing community. Indeed, they affect the status of economic growth as a whole — in this country as well as in many other countries of the world. These are not abstract issues. They affect the quality of community life. They affect the life of each one of us.[3]

* * *

Is there scarcity of financial resources? Where are the financial resources to create schools in which consumers are educated by the industry as to the essential characteristics of each species of fish, how to treat that fish from store to skillet, how to best prepare for the table each portion of each species of fish, and schools in turn to educate the industry as to consumer preferences, consumer limits of patience with the requirements of each species of fish as well as consumer financial preferences? Where are the financial resources to retrofit existing vessels so they are able to catch underutilized species? (While groundfish, as the word implies, is caught at the bottom of the ocean, most underutilized species are caught in the middle of the water column.) Where are the financial resources to create hatcheries, to build fish ponds and fish farms, to build protein recovery plants, to introduce new technologies in existing processing plants, to build entirely new plants for the creation of biochemical products, to build laboratories in which alternative futures are tested? Are not financial resources scarce? This is a nation that is supposed to save little (and, certainly less than Japan, for instance).

Let us pause for a moment to consider some of the consequences of this widespread notion. The notion of the scarcity of money has made a beggar not only of the general public but even of a great many captains of industry. Is not the corporate agenda today increasingly occupied by the constant search for grants, subsidies, and tax deductions?

The habit of searching for grants, subsidies, and tax deductions pits us one against the other. And engulfs us in a bottomless abyss. Grants, subsidies, and tax deductions have never been and never will be sufficient to meet our needs. East Coast fishermen are in the process of receiving $4.5 million in grants from the Federal Government; but they have already presented formal requests totalling $54 million. Pity us all: The administrators of the grants, the grantees, and those who will be losers at the grantsmanship game. A thought process that starts with scarcity is unavoidably led through a tortuous route back to scarcity. In the meantime, taxpayers, who by definition have scarce resources, are forced to foot the bill left behind by the pursuit of grants, subsidies, and tax deductions. Are these not the forces that lead to disintegration within our communities? Are these the proper principles with which to organize society?

The financial reality is diametrically opposed to what is generally believed. Just as there is no scarcity of natural resources, so there is no scarcity of money. Those who believe in the scarcity of money see only one source of money. In fact, there are two. Financial resources exist not only with savers, but also with the ultimate (modern) creators of those resources: The Central Banks; here in the United States, the Federal Reserve System. Figure 2 suggests that entrepreneurs — to obtain their *loans; loans*, not grants; *loans*, not subsidies; *loans*, not tax deductions — have the choice to ask their banks to go, not laterally to private investors for their savings, but vertically to the Federal Reserve System for newly created money. Government agencies with taxing power also ought to use this avenue to satisfy their financing needs in the process of creating and modernizing our crumbling public works infrastructure.

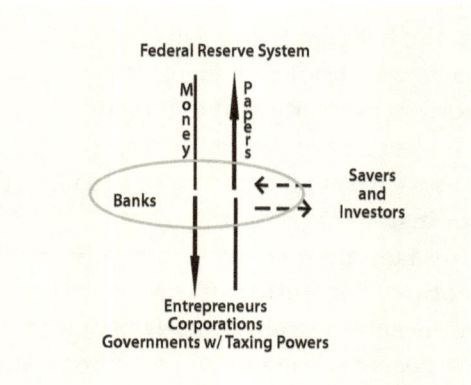

Alternative Money Flows
Figure 2

Technically, this proposal calls for the use of the Discount Window as the first, rather than last, resort. This proposal is in keeping with the original spirit of the Federal Reserve Act, a spirit expressed especially in Section 13 of the Act of 1913, a spirit uniquely infused into it by the then Senator John W. Weeks, who, as a member of the Senate Banking and Currency Committee, was responsible for over four hundred amendments to the original bill. That spirit was not destined to bear full fruit because it was guided by a flawed economic theory, the Real Bills Doctrine. Yet, an echo of that spirit still resounds in today's policies that permit the use of the Discount Window as a means of "last resort." The Discount Window is used for overnight loans to banks and for exceptional rescue mission. In times of crisis, its gates are flung wide open to avoid financial panics. The question is: Why wait for strictures and panics to make full use of this resource? If the Discount Window can produce so much good in abnormal conditions, how much more good would it produce were it used everyday under *normal* conditions? Of course, as specified below, proper guidelines would have to be followed.

The flawed Real Bills Doctrine was allowed to die, to be replaced by two equally flawed theories, the Gold Standard and the Fiat Standard, according to which money is created either on the basis of the amount of gold in the nation or on the basis of a fiat, an autonomous decision of the central bank. The authors, and other people across the country, are advocating the adoption of a different standard, the Productivity Standard. This standard assumes that the money supply is created on the basis of national credit, that national credit is uniquely related to the productive capacity of the country, and that national credit has to be administered by a central bank, like our Federal Reserve System. From these propositions it follows that people, provided they use it responsibly, have an unquestionable right of access to national credit.

Procedurally, this doctrine inspires a monetary policy in which We, the People, decide how much, when, and why we need to use the specified amount of national credit. Provided the request is legitimate, the Fed and the financial system as a whole simply validate those decisions. Then "papers," namely all necessary documentation — just as in today's system — are presented to the Fed via the financial system, and money comes down to individual entrepreneurs, corporations, and government agencies with taxing power.

Substantively, the essential provisos of this doctrine are that newly created money be issued: (a) at cost; (b) to benefit all citizens through individual ownership, ESOPs, or cooperatives; and (c) only to create *real* wealth — *not to cover operating costs nor to purchase consumer goods, goods to be hoarded, or financial paper of any sort.* Without exploring all the techniques that ought to be deployed, with the strict adherence to these basic requirements, it becomes self-evident that, if real wealth is created, the Federal Reserve System can literally create as much money as necessary without sowing the seeds of inflation at the same time. If this policy is followed, it is also self-evident that there are and there will always be enough financial resources to match real wealth with real needs. Real needs have to be distinguished from fanciful desires; real needs are those that try to make full and wise use of existing resources.

Where is the scarcity of financial resources, then? There is no scarcity of financial resources. This is not to deny the institutional limits of the past or those of the present. This lament is real; but only as a consequence of the bewitching power of negativism to become a self-fulfilling prophecy. Assuming that the financial resources of the nation are scarce, apologists of the financial status quo quite naturally conclude that it is better for the few to appropriate the largest possible share of those resources. "The devil take the hindmost," it used to be said. Woe to the rest of society! Financial apologists maintain that the money newly created by the Fed ought to be exclusively put at the disposal of the owners of existing savings. Open Market Operations are ideally suited to this type of monetary policy.

Financial apologists also have a *prima facie* justification for their claims. They say that, in case of default, savers alone have the resources to repay the loan out of their savings. In most cases, this is entirely true. In fact, this objection cannot be overcome by recalling the infinite subtleties of financial shenanigans. This objection must be met on its own ground; it must be covered from a substantive point of view. The resolution of this issue is this: There is not one specific way in which the newly created money can be borrowed by people who have no previous savings, and still the Federal Reserve System is given all the necessary assurances for the repayment of the loans; there are five such potential solutions. They are as follows:

Solution # One. As a stopgap and a means of pointing the way toward permanent solutions, the first approach is to use the money that comes down the pike in the form of grants from Federal and State governments as *premium payments* to insure the loans.

Solution # Two. The second solution is the use of ESOPs — and, as we will suggest in a moment, SuperESOPs. This is a generally successful financing technique that achieves many goals, including that of using the assets of existing corporations to let employees — by definition, mostly people without savings — attain access to capital credit and repay the loans out of future profits. Apart from a full understanding of its rationale, the ESOP Movement is a "revolution" that has already largely taken place in the United States. More than ten million people are benefiting to one extent or another from the blessings of this financial technique.

Solution # Three. The third solution is the traditional, old-fashioned one. Let private investors pay for those premiums. And let them gain the benefits of ownership afterwards. Here the "revolution" is all to come. While we make *consumer* credit abundantly available to nearly everyone, *capital* credit is kept under strict wraps. And yet, while consumer credit enslaves, capital credit makes us free. Recall Lena Novello's statement of the economic relationship between boats and houses. As Louis O. Kelso, the father of ESOPs, long but not always consistently advocated, to make capital credit available to the many, *private* insurance must cover the risks of default. This is a whole new field of enterprise that will become a reality as soon as our financial wizards open their imagination to it.

Solution # Four. The fourth solution is to have a community-wide subscription to raise the funds — for eventual profits — needed to insure those loans. Is this approach a "revolution on top of a revolution"? Not necessarily. Community-wide appeals have a long tradition, especially in periods of crisis such as the one currently enveloping the fishing industry; but the details of implementation of this fourth solution are undoubtedly daunting. Computers will help.

Solution # Five. Let private charity and foundations fill the gap. If private charity is looking for ways to restrict its field of concern and power, no better opportunity might ever come along. The goal is — and ought to be — to restrict the field of charity and enlarge that of justice.

To summarize the benefits of the use of the discount window as a means of first resort for access to national credit:

There are always enough financial resources to fund the process of creation of real wealth;

The money can be issued at cost; and,

The ownership of this money is directly or indirectly apportioned to benefit all the people.

Are not all the inhabitants of a country creating, through their own sweat and tears, the specific value embodied in its national credit? It is not the loan, by and of itself, that creates new wealth. Rather, it is human labor that ultimately creates real wealth and makes the repayment of the loan possible. Should access to national credit, therefore, be reserved to the few? Or should it be granted to all inhabitants of a country as an essential economic right?

* * *

The natural resources are there. The financial resources are there. Are these convictions putting us in danger of going overboard and letting us fall into a presumed Age of Plenty? Between the scourge of scarcity and the corruption of abundance, enough is a feast. This issue deserves a moment of our attention. It is the ambitious subtext of this article to convert the reader to a mentality in which, in Stuart's felicitous phrase, "Enough is A Feast." Between abundance and scarcity there is the golden mean of sufficiency.

We fully realize that this vision is so different from our usual horizons as to require a sea change in us and in our environment. It takes a real effort of the imagination. After all, are we not supposed, obsessively, always to want *more*? This is the conclusion effectively reached by Paul Margulies, founder of *Anthroposophy Working*, while observing the dynamics of Rocco's desires. Rocco is the gangster in the movie "Key Largo" who, in response to Bogart's challenge, *"I know what you want. You want more,"* blurts out: *"Yeah, that's it, I want more."*

In the scramble to divide either the fruits of scarcity or those of abundance, some acquire more than they need and others do not have enough.

Enough. Is not that what we are really after? Do we not hope to have always enough of whatever we want, whatever we need? When there is enough, wants and needs become one. Of course, we are and we must remain the ones to define how much is enough for us; yet, this is not absurd individualism. By ourselves, we will never be able to achieve much. We need to join forces with others. We even need to institutionalize our beliefs. We need to create appropriate institutions to help us practice all our virtues. We need to create institutions that become intermediaries between us and the state: Institutions that enter into combat with our own worst individual instincts as well as the worst instincts of society as a whole.

Instead, are not too many existing institutions helping the modern world to go fast forward into social disorganization? The peculiar forms of this disintegration might be totally different from one country to another, but the general trend is evident. In the North as well as in the South, in the East as well as in the West, we bemoan some aspects of contemporary life. The very roots of each one of our ancient civilizations are being threatened by forces that no longer operate from the outside in. They operate from inside our very soul.

How to stem this tide? We submit that the key tool is Organization.

❋ ❋ ❋

We need to create new institutions in conformity with a new principle, a principle that we like to call Functional Integration. This is a form of organization that attempts to obtain the complementary benefits of vertical or horizontal integration as well as those of total independence. The Functional Integration (FI) Model attempts to gather activities together that are already related in accordance to their function. This is a new form of organization that is designed to lead to *social harmony and civic responsibility*. After all, do we not all share a common goal? Simply put, is not this goal the achievement of a civilized society?

Figure 3 suggests the forms this type of integration might assume within the seafood industry. Let us conceive of all participants in the seafood industry as owning in common all the hardware: From fishing boats to seafood processing plants; from institutes for the industry to educate the consumer, and be educated by the consumer, to laboratories for the research and development of all possible means of utilization of renewable marine resources; from trucks to stores. The hardware would be under the steward-ship of a group of people organized into a SuperESOP, whose Board of Directors is elected by all the owners. The owners exercise all the rights and enjoy all the privileges of owners, as the stockholders of democratic organizations do and ought to do. The SuperESOP would attend to the financing and maintenance requirements of the hardware, and independent teams of entrepreneurs would be making that hardware operational, by leasing it — from whom? from themselves. If each team organizes itself with the assistance of individual ESOPs, so much the better. The essential point is that the independence of each team is fully preserved *by concentrating the operation of functions, rather than concentrating control over people.*

FUNCTIONAL INTEGRATION
(SuperESOP)

COMMON OWNERSHIP OF ALL HARDWARE

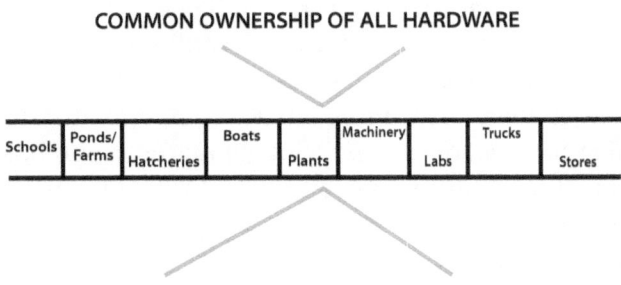

Schools	Ponds/ Farms	Hatcheries	Boats	Plants	Machinery	Labs	Trucks	Stores

LEASED BY INDEPENDENT TEAMS OF OWNERS

Functional Integration Within the Seafood Industry
Figure 3

The nearest equivalent to this type of social integration is a shopping mall that would be owned by all owners and employees of stores operating within the mall. This is in contrast to the conventional structure in which the malls are owned and operated by independent concerns, in which instance stores simply rent space within the mall, pay rent, and are provided with all the services that are needed in common. In this case, quite rightly, all capital gains (or losses) that accrue from the operation of the mall belong to the owners of the mall. In the FI Model, capital gains or losses accrue to owners of the hardware; and whatever profits accrue from the rental of the hardware belong only to the teams that rent the hardware. Beyond the legitimate concerns of health, safety, and public welfare, the state, or the public in general, has no say on any of the operations of the FI Model.

This structure might not be born full blown. It might be necessary to assemble it piece by piece. And there might be two or more SuperESOPs for each port. But, clearly, the more trust, the more cohesion, the more benefits. If, through a SuperESOP, the participants in the industry own as much of the hardware as possible, many things can be done more efficiently. At a bare minimum:

The SuperESOP can enforce the requirements of quality assurance to the consumer: This assurance can be provided only if the various elements of the industry collaborate with each other. Today this collaboration occurs quite rarely, and when it does it is mostly due to chance: One processor here, two fishermen there;

The SuperESOP can enforce efficiency standards for the utilization of each and every piece of hardware undreamed of by individual entrepreneurs. Unnecessary duplication of equipment and even operations would cease. For instance, boats might be treated like airplanes, they would not be waiting for the crew to rest before they would be turned around to go fishing again. And the boats might not need to be the same as those of today. They might be smaller, faster, more efficiently operated and equipped;

The SuperESOP can reach efficiency standards in purchasing supplies and equipment, borrowing money, and attending to all other financing requirements of a modern business — including purchasing insurance — that individual entrepreneurs cannot obtain;

The SuperESOP can set up maintenance schedules of all machinery and equipment in a way that individual entrepreneurs cannot achieve;

The SuperESOP can create and administer a first rate information system regarding marketing and biological data with the aim of rationalizing the capture and raising of each species as well as the timing of landings of fish, thus ensuring that temporary gluts — with their depressing effects on pricing — would no longer occur;

The SuperESOP can nurture first rate research and development laboratories. Special attention could be given especially to development, thus easing the process of technology transfer from the laboratory to the industry;

The SuperESOP can foster specialization of activities that small, independent, individual entrepreneurs cannot achieve. A boat owner, a fish farmer, or a seafood processor today has to be at least an expert in finances, engineering, and real estate. What do these operations have to do with catching fish, raising it, or processing it? With a SuperESOP, the boat owner, fish farmer, and the seafood processor would simply organize a team of people and devote all their time and expertise to catching the fish, raising it, and processing it. And all teams would preserve their independence at the same time. Whatever money the team that leases boats or fish farms or stores makes is its own money, its own reward.

This model of social and economic integration can be applied to any set of industrial or commercial enterprises. To name one specific example, one day it might be possible to organize along these lines commercial establishments on Main Street of any city or town in the United States. The first such SuperESOP might even be called "Main Street USA".

∗ ∗ ∗

So far, we have dealt with largely mundane issues. Can we now elevate the discussion a notch or two? Let us think about the issues in the broadest possible terms for a moment. At the core, the issues dealt with here are not technical issues at all. They are issues of economic justice. And issues of liberty. Issues of liberty and justice for all.

We have been repeating these words for a few centuries now. And some might say that they have led to the excesses of the French Revolution and the Red Revolution. In the United States, those excesses are parodied in the excesses of the "Age of Entitlements." The way to avoid all such excesses is not to leave the content of the expression "liberty and justice for all" to the imagination, but to define it precisely. The economic content of that expression can be defined by these four rights: 1. *The right of access to land and natural resources*; 2. *The right of access to national credit*; 3. *The right to own the fruits of one's labor*; and, 4. *The right to protect the blessings of one's wealth.*

And then these rights have to be anchored to the reality outside us as well as to the reality inside us. As believers, we reserve the right to speak of God, but we fully accept the wish of others who might want to speak of Nature or Chance. For us, the most fundamental proposition to consider is this: *To think that God would not provide for all his children is blasphemy.* For others who might prefer to speak in secular terms, we would like to submit the following equivalent reasoning: To think that Nature or Chance would not provide for all their children is contrary to the factual propositions that Nature is bountiful and Chance is infinite.

Leaving the reality outside us well alone, we can now attempt to relate our discussion to the reality inside us, by asking: In practical terms, what is the sin that all of us who share the biases of environmental extremists and financial apologists commit? We submit that, to the extent we share those biases, to that extent we sin against all virtues. We sin against the four cardinal virtues, because we lack *prudence, justice, temperance*, and *fortitude*. We sin against the three intellectual virtues, because we lack *wisdom, science*, and *understanding*. We sin against the three theological virtues, because we lack *hope, faith*, and, last but most, *charity*.

Yes, if we want the renewal of our fisheries and the renewal of our entire practice of economic growth, we must be quite serious about the practice of our virtues. Our virtues, as St. Thomas Aquinas said, are "the peak of power."

✳ ✳ ✳

Let us turn our sights once again to more worldly issues, and consider the experiential condition. Were those who adhere to extreme forms of environmentalism and financial apologetics reaching their most cherished goals, we would have reason to pause. But the proof of the pudding is empirical indeed. To the extent that we are infected with the strain of environmental extremism and financial apologetics, to that extent we consistently end up defeating our own purposes. If legitimate demands for goods and employment are not fulfilled, greater needs are created and their satisfaction is eventually shifted down the slippery slope of welfare and third-party payors, industrial grants and subsidies, tax reductions and tax evasion. There, waste reigns. As in all self-fulfilling prophecies, scarcity is thus attained. The detailed chain of events that leads to this conclusion can be much refined; but the gross effects are all too evident. Look at the physical landscape. Are we saving the rain forest? Have we saved the downtown of our cities? Are we preserving the integrity of the suburbs? Look at the financial landscape. Do we ever achieve the goal of a stable value of money? We seem to be going from one financial upheaval to another. And we never seem able to taste the sweetness of economic serenity.

That is the ultimate reason why, while appreciating their good reasons, we cannot join the ranks of environmental extremists and financial apologists. Despite their good intentions, they are unwittingly helping to destroy what they love most: Precisely the *natural* world — a world in which there is room for everything and everyone — a world in which there is *enough* of everything for everyone.

If the results achieved by following the biases of environmental extremism and financial apologetics are unsatisfactory, ought we not to strive to reach a better balance between their concerns and those of society? In each specific case, let us define the work to be done, and let us do it. We began this century with the passage of important environmental *and* financial legislation. Was that not an attempt to embrace both realities? Was that not an attempt to realize America's promise to achieve a society in which the ancient ideals of truth, beauty, and goodness could blossom? Let us return to this challenge as the century concludes, and a new millennium arises on the horizon.

NOTES

1. Data published after these pages were written confirm the validity of our analysis. The reader might be especially interested in these three statements from a recent Science report concerning the dynamics of 128 fish stocks. One: "Spring-spawning Icelandic herring constitute the only population we examined in which the fishery collapsed and remained *commercially* extinct" (italics added). Two: "In (the case of Pacific sardines and Georges Bank herring), no recovery was observed for decades, but now both stocks are appearing to increase." Three: "We conclude that the effects of overfishing are, at this point, still generally reversible."

2. Is not self-reliance one of the most characteristic traits of the early American character? Is not self-reliance Emerson's "central doctrine"? Ought we feel free to jettison such a trait so cavalierly today, just because we think we live in a post-industrial world?

3. How to express the unity of the issues in the most succinct way? Environmentalists like to take a leaf from Henry David Thoreau. But do they forget that Thoreau was not simply against environmental degradation but also against social injustice?

Bibliography

For more detailed statements on some of the issues treated in this article, see the following publications by C. Gorga: "The Productivity Standard: A True Golden Standard" (with Norman G. Kurland), *in* Dawn M. Kurland (ed.), *Every Worker an Owner: A Revolutionary Free Enterprise Challenge to Marxism*, Washington, D.C.: Center for Economic and Social Justice, 1987, pp. 83-86; , "Bold New Directions in Politics and Economics," *The Human Economy Newsletter*, March 1991, 12 (1) 3-6, 12; "Four Economic Rights: Social Renewal Through Economic Justice for All," *Social Justice Review*, January-February 1994, 85 (1-2) 3-6; "Quality Assurance: Internal and External Organizational Requirements," and "Quality Assurance: Internal and External Financing Opportunities," in Gilbert Sylvia, Ann L. Shriver, and Michael T. Morrissey (eds.), *Quality Control and Quality Assurance for Seafood*, (Corvallis, OR: Oregon State University, 1994), 109-114; 158-163; "Aquaculture, Marketing of Underutilized Species and Depletion of Species," in David S. Liao (ed.), *International Cooperation for Fisheries and Aquaculture Development: Proceedings of the 7th Biennial Conference of the International Institute of Fisheries Economics and Trade*, Vol. 2, (Keelung, Taiwan, R.O.C.: Institute of Fisheries Economics, National Taiwan Ocean University, 1995), 235-241. And, with Louis J. Ronsivalli, Quality Assurance of Seafood (New York: Van Nostrand Reinhold, 1988).

On ESOPs and private insurance for capital credit, see Louis O. Kelso (with Mortimer J. Adler), *The Capitalist Manifesto* (New York: Random House, 1958); on CSOPs, see Louis O. Kelso (with Patricia Hetter Kelso), *Democracy and Economic Power* (Cambridge, MA: Ballinger Publishing Company, 1986).

Paul Margulies on the "Civilization of More," in "For the Love of Freedom Not For Fear of Communism," *Shoreline* November 1988, 3-5.

R. A. Myers, N. J. Barrowman, J. A. Hutchings, A. A. Rosenberg, "Population Dynamics of Exploited Fish Stocks at Low Population Levels," *Science*, Vol. 269, No. 5227, 25 August 1995, 1106-1108.

Lena Novello on her father's dictum, in a public speech at the Gloucester Fisheries Forum on September 16, 1994.

Charles G. Washburn, *The Life of John W. Weeks* (Boston and New York: Houghton Mifflin Company, 1928).

The Creators of Poverty

by Carmine Gorga
Gloucester Daily Times, **Symposium**, December 18, 1998, p. A10

I can hardly contain myself. After years of studying the issue at a not-inconsiderable depth, I have found in an unsuspected source an insight that clears up the issue of the cause of poverty in a definitive and powerful way. The source of this insight is neither a treatise in economics, nor a work in sociology, nor a tome in the theory of justice. The source is a paper published in "Spiritual Life," — a periodical of Carmelite spirituality — in the Fall of 1997. The author is Suzanne Mayer. The title is: "Songs of the City of God: Merton, Social Justice, And the Psalms."

The author prefaces her essay with this quote from Thomas Merton's "Bread in the Wilderness": "The Psalms are the songs of (the) City of God.... Singing them, we become more fully incorporated into the mystery of God's action in human history." Recalling that the Psalms are the "ancient prayers of Israel" ascending "like incense before the altar of God," she proposes to "explore 'the mystery of God's action in human history' through the vision the Psalms give of divine justice and through the covenant call to all humanity to enter into this process."

These are some of the Psalms she quotes. Ps. 10:2: "In arrogance the wicked hotly pursue the poor..." Ps. 37:14: "The wicked draw the sword and bend their bows, to bring down the poor and the needy..."

How do you read these Psalms? I read them in this way: Poverty is created, not by the rich, but by the wicked. What a liberating thesis.

So often repeated, most of us have assumed it to be true. We have assumed that poverty is caused by the rich. Even I who, as those who have worked with me, ever listened to my words, or read any of my writings can attest, has never used one word against the rich, even I had never penetrated the issue as through this reading. In fact, most of my efforts were unfocused and must have seemed quixotic to many just because I have always refused to point the finger at "the rich."

Let us be honest. We have all assumed that poverty exists because of the rich. Indeed, have not many rich people themselves assumed that to be true? Certainly, society as a whole in its organized political effort has trained all its guns in that direction — and the reaction from the rich has, of course, been to resist that effort.

That most political discourse and action has for centuries been dominated by that assumption is not worth discussing at length. Much more interesting is another question. What is a fair assessment of the result of all
that effort?

Do we not find that every now and then one faction wins a few painful
battles, but that the war is constantly lost by all?

Are we not, generation after generation, faced with the same age-old
problem of poverty? There are times when we become so exhausted by this
burden that we refuse even to discuss it any more. But the problem remains
stubbornly there. And it gnarls our soul. Not much joy, not much enjoyment of what we possess can be had, if we somehow keep in the back of our
minds the suspicion that we have not done nearly enough to alleviate the
pain and suffering of men and women who unwillingly live in poverty.

How can we tackle such an endemic condition? Is the situation hope-
less? I believe that the first ray of light, and hope, can be grasped if we really try to learn about poverty, starting with splitting the problem into
absolute and relative poverty. This is an important distinction. Relative
poverty is the existential condition for which there will always be someone richer than others. The feast is a movable feast, indeed. That does not
matter at all. Not one iota. What matters is that those who have less be not
deprived of the conditions for a dignified and free life. When poverty of
material conditions impinges on our freedom and our dignity, then we are
suffering from absolute poverty. Then the quality of life of society as a
whole is impoverished. Freedom and dignity are absolute qualities. No one
can be deprived of them or we are all deprived of them — to say the least, we
are all deprived of the joys of a guiltless life.

What changes when we distinguish between relative and absolute
poverty? What changes when we make the wicked culpable for the existence of absolute poverty? Everything changes — and the problem becomes
abruptly soluble. Let us look only at a few effects on us, through the lenses
of some of the effects on the political stump and the religious pulpit.

Our political discourse changes. Our eyes are no longer focused on the
behavior of the rich and the behavior of the poor. That polarization in our
political life, with people taking sides between the two poles and making
the other the enemy, vanishes. We all know the hatred generated by the
"undeserving poor." How many pieces of legislation are passed on the
strength of that hatred! How many punitive agencies exist in the vain attempt at enforcing those laws!

Though less spoken about, how much hatred is directed against "the undeserving rich"? Is not most of our tax code written on the assumption that the rich have taken something away from others? The wicked rich are most certainly engaged in those practices. But are all the rich wicked? And are there not poor people who are wicked? Our political discourse is purged of many impurities, and our political action becomes much more pointed, if we keep those two basic distinctions in the back of our minds. Our finger is pointed in only one direction, the proper direction.

The religious pulpit and the political stump can finally become allies — on an equal footing. The split that has plagued society, it seems forever, is healed. Ultimate goals remain different. One is concerned more with the metaphysical life and the other more with the physical life, but the struggle, in this life, on this earth, becomes one and the same: resistance against wicked actions.

Is it easy to identify the wicked? No. Absolutely not. As distinguished from the rich and the poor who can be easily identified, the wicked cannot be easily identified by others. But the wicked themselves know who they are. (At moments of deepest insight, we know that we are all wicked, at least sporadically, at least in part. In those moments we also know that some people do not know they are wicked: hence the need for moral and technical instruction, because without knowledge of good and evil, there is no "sin.")

The root to the solution of the problem of poverty is no longer found in punishment of the rich or punishment of the poor, or both. The solution can be found only in that eternal prescription for happiness: love your neighbor; love your God; and if you love them both, you will eventually cease to be wicked and you will even love yourself.

Thus the schism within the very soul of the religious people as well as the soul of the political people and, ultimately, the soul of each citizen is healed. The religious people can be concerned only with affairs of the moral life and the eternal life: they can eventually get out of "the social action." The political people can be concerned only with providing a framework for the "good government," namely the just government, within which we can take care of all our earthly needs. And we will all succeed. The political people will no longer be dealing with wicked people in sheep's skin coming out of the synagogues, the churches, and the mosques. The few — always few — vastly wicked people will no longer intermingle with the good people. They will isolate themselves; they will ostracize themselves. Only when self purged, will they come back. Without insurmountable obstacles posed by the wicked, the majority of the people will satisfy all the needs that can and must be taken care of.

Poverty is a moral issue. As such it can be solved. But, then, just because poverty is a moral issue, do we not run against the hard fact that wickedness is an intrinsic part of human nature? I was myself under this impression until recently when, in a discussion with Father John Hughes of Fitchburg, MA, the issue was clarified for me. I pushed him to admit the inevitability of wickedness. But the goodness that is in him, resisted my push. He still declared himself optimistic that the human race will eventually shunt wickedness aside. It was then that it occurred to me. Yes, the potential for being wicked will always be with us. That is inherent in our human nature; otherwise we would not be free — free to choose between good and evil. But do we have to choose evil? Do we have to destroy ourselves in the process? Not at all. Our struggle will be to resist wickedness. Our millennium has committed more wicked acts than all other millenniums combined, perhaps. We have had our fill. We can now gain control of ourselves and mold ancient aspirations into a Movement Toward Goodness (MTG). This is a challenging task indeed. We need all our wits to succeed.

Between 1968 and 1973, Mr. Gorga was director of planning and economic development at Action Inc., the local agency conducting the "War on Poverty." Currently, he is president of Polis-tics, Inc., a community development firm whose work can be sighted at www.polis-tics.com.

Toward the Definition of Economic Rights

by Carmine Gorga

Reprinted with permission from
Journal of Markets and Morality
Volume 2, Number 1 • Spring 1999 (88-101)

Introduction

With the assistance of a rigorous analysis of a long sweep of history by Daniel Rush Finn,[1] the central legal dilemma of our age can be identified as follows: We either redefine property rights or we define economic rights. This essay attempts to define economic rights.

Currently, the terms economic rights, property rights, and entitlements are treated as nearly interchangeable synonyms. We will see that these entities are, in fact, connected to one another by many subtle links of timing sequence and by many overlapping intellectual conditions determining their respective identities. In the process, distinctions will emerge that separate these three entities from each other and firmly implant economic rights within the structure of the theory of justice.

From a practical point of view, the judgment that economic rights are neither entitlements nor the same entity as property rights leads to a fundamental realization. Since no accepted definition of economic rights can be found in theory, there is no rationale for the exercise of economic rights in practice. There is observable evidence of access to economic resources, but, clearly, the fact of access is not the same as the right of access.

The task of defining economic rights assumes particular importance because these rights occupy a pivotal position in an integrated system of social thought. They can be conceived not only as the focal point of economic policy and economic theory, but they can be construed as the keystone in the arch of economic justice. To anticipate the conclusion of this essay, only those who exercise economic rights can be said to participate in the economic process in full dignity and self-reliance.

Toward the Definition of Economic Rights

To clarify issues concerning the definition of economic rights, it might be useful to begin with an overview of three factual distinctions between economic rights, property rights, and entitlements. These distinctions can be taken as facts at this stage of the discussion but they will be justified in the course of the argument. First, the content of these three entities is different. The object of property rights are marketable things, tangible or intangible things such as material goods and services. The object of entitlements are human needs, from food to shelter to health. The object of economic rights are economic needs. Second, the legal form of these three entities is different. Property rights are concrete legal titles over existing wealth; economic rights are abstract legal claims over future wealth; and entitlements are moral claims on wealth that legally belong to others. Finally, the quantity that they measure is variable. While both property rights and entitlements relate to existing wealth, and therefore a necessarily finite quantity, economic rights relate to future wealth, an unknown and elastic–if not a potentially infinite–quantity.

Economic rights can be defined as follows: Economic rights are rights of access to resources–such as land, labor, physical, and financial capital–that are essential for the creation, legal appropriation, and market exchange of goods and services. Economic rights are self-evident. However, for their full recognition, economic rights require at least three conditions: (1) they require a knowledge of basic economic needs for a person to operate in the economic world; (2) they require a knowledge of their legal characteristics; and (3) they have to be fully integrated into the theory of justice. This essay attempts to articulate a framework that satisfies these three conditions.

Basic Economic Needs

The basic economic needs of any human being extend over one or more functions that are related to the creation, legal appropriation, and market exchange of goods and services. These needs have traditionally been satisfied through access to labor and land, which also includes natural resources. In the modern world, one must include access to physical as well as financial capital among the prerequisites of an independent and productive economic life.

There is no economic activity that does not require labor, land, and natural resources to be carried out. No poet or painter, let alone an industrialist, can perform any function without access to these resources. Furthermore, once money is seen as a means of exchange, it will be conceived to include all forms of wealth, whether physical or financial wealth. Then it can be seen how, even in a condition of barter, money is essential to carrying out any market function. And equally essential to carrying out any economic function today is access to physical capital, whether it is a pen, a computer, or a shovel. In previous times, poets may have subsisted on berries and may have been able to produce their own papyrus on which to scratch their poems. Today, we have restricted our own capabilities through the acquisition of specialized knowledge and so, in order to function properly in the economic sphere, we need access to physical capital that is generally owned by others. To put it restrictively, access to labor, land, natural resources, financial, and physical capital is essential to the performance of any economic function–whether it is production, legal appropriation, or market exchange of wealth. Indeed, access to these resources is essential to the very existence of human life.

This is generally well-known. What is not known–and, if known, not readily granted–is the legal fact that only productive people acquire by right the title to marketable products and services, a title that is independent of other people's will. And what is openly disputed is the claim that only productive people have the legal as well as the practical means to exchange goods and services in the market. The great tension that exists in the field of entitlements is the attempt to overthrow these basic legal and economic realities.

In accordance with these complex practical and theoretical conditions, four economic rights can be isolated from other potential rights, which must be placed at the foundation of a modern economic policy that is concerned with the production, legal acquisition, and exchange of marketable goods and services. These four rights are formulated in correspondence with the factors of production of classical economic analysis; namely, land, labor, and capital–with capital being specified in both its financial and physical aspects. These rights belong to each human being, and can be expressed in these terms:

- The right of access to land and natural resources
- The right of access to national credit
- The right to own the fruits of one's labor
- The right to protect one's wealth

This system of rights can be subdivided in a variety of ways. To be established singly and jointly, these rights have to be justified on many grounds. In some of my earlier work,[2] readers can find the contours of the economic, political, and moral rationale for these rights. Our primary focus here has to do with the legal grounds of these rights.

Some Legal Characteristics of Economic Rights

Economic rights are rights of access to resources that are essential for the creation, legal appropriation, and market exchange of goods and services. In order to obtain a more precise understanding of this definition, the legal characteristics of economic rights can be pinpointed as follows.

Economic Rights Distinct From Property Rights and Entitlements

Economic rights can be clearly distinguished from property rights, once it has been acknowledged that economic rights are the necessary precondition for the creation and the legal establishment of property rights and entitlements. Property rights cannot be identified with economic rights. Property rights are the bundle of dominion rights over existing goods and services that are demanded for the fulfillment of human needs. Economic rights, on the other hand, are rights of access to resources that are needed to create future goods and services. This differentiation is transparent when economic resources are not owned by anyone at the time they are energized to serve in the production process. For instance, in the process of creating consumer goods, one can fish or hunt for animals that are still held in the commons, and the only legal tool that one needs is the right of access to those resources. Moreover, one can make use of a financial resource such as credit–an entity that manifests itself as the power to create money not exclusively by a government agency but by private parties as well. Indeed, by looking deeper into the subject it becomes evident that the power to create money belongs to the people exclusively, and the role of government agencies is confined to administering that function properly. The differentiation between economic rights and property rights holds even when resources are owned by someone else at the time they are acquired and energized to serve in the production process. The bundle of legal prerequisites involved in accessing those resources constitutes the set of economic rights. Thus, the process of creating new wealth, of legally acquiring ownership or transferring ownership of wealth, involves the exercise of economic rights. Ownership of specific items of wealth involves the exercise of property rights. Property rights are static; economic rights are dynamic. Property rights involve stocks of wealth; economic rights involve flows of wealth.

Entitlements must be distinguished from economic rights. Entitlements transfer the possession of specific property (e.g., money or things) and property rights from one person to another–forcibly, if necessary, under penalty of retribution from an agency of the state. An example of this power is exercised by the Internal Revenue Service. Entitlements relate to existing wealth.

Both property rights and entitlements have a clear market value and are social to the extent that if society did not exist, property rights not only would not exist but would not be necessary to human existence. Property rights and entitlements are social and alienable, while economic rights are innate and inalienable. Since economic rights are inextricably linked to the basic requirements of life, they accompany the very existence of life; and unless one wants to live the life of enslavement–a condition that is not legally permissible in a civilized society–they are also not alienable. Succinctly put, provided economic rights are in vigorous existence, the denial of an entitlement or a property right would not necessarily imply a denial of the right to life. With due qualifications, singly and jointly, the denial of the right of access to land and natural resources, the denial of the right of access to national credit, the denial of the right to enjoy the fruits of one's labor, and the denial of the right to protect one's property, essentially amounts to a denial of the rights to life and liberty, and certainly to the denial of civilized life and liberty.

The major differences between economic rights, property rights, and entitlements can be summarized this way: Economic rights represent a legal claim on potential property rights; property rights represent a legal claim on wealth that is already in existence; and entitlements represent a moral claim on wealth that is legally owned by others.

The Differentiation Between Private Rights and Public (or Constitutional) Rights

The proposed set of economic rights offers the interesting theoretical possibility of establishing the category of public rights within the theory of justice. For some reason, the category of public rights does not exist in any of the texts or the standard reference books of Anglo-Saxon legal literature. Therefore, it seems that in order to realize this possibility, we need to go back to Immanuel Kant's Philosophy of Law,[3] where the foundation for the distinction between public and private rights is clearly defined. However, it is important to realize that Kant left the category of public rights as an empty set. He concluded his analysis by stating that "... the Matter of Private Right is, in short, the very same in both"–namely, in the "sphere of private right" as in the "sphere of public right."[4]

The acceptance of economic rights would give content to the category of public rights, and would help to differentiate between public and private rights within the field of economic justice. This differentiation would be useful not only in establishing continuity of thought with the range of political freedom where most public rights are fully recognized. The immediate usefulness of the category of public rights would consist in clearly distinguishing property rights from economic rights. Property rights would be categorized as private rights and economic rights as public rights. If the category of public rights were unacceptable for some reason, then economic rights could be classified as constitutional rights.

Another Difference Between Property Rights and Economic Rights

If the distinction between private and public (or constitutional) rights is accepted, one can further clarify the essential differences that exist between property rights and economic rights. By confining property rights to the category of private rights and assigning economic rights to the category of public (or constitutional) rights, one could clearly see that property rights regarding a specific item of wealth belong to us exclusively on either a personal or an individual basis. Economic rights, instead, are those that belong to everyone on a universal basis.

To eliminate a potential source of confusion, it is necessary to classify the right to ownership in general as an ancillary economic right and therefore as a public right–a right belonging to everyone. While the right of ownership over a specific piece of property would always be classified as a property right and therefore as a private right, economic rights, instead, would belong exclusively to the category of public (or constitutional) rights.

These are not simply intellectual distinctions. They have a solid foundation in fact. While property rights restrict other peoples' freedom, because they necessarily exclude people from using specific pieces of property, economic rights enlarge the range of freedom for everyone. Economic rights are similar to voting rights. Voting rights do not restrict the freedom of anyone; rather, they enlarge the range of freedom of everyone.

The Differentiation Between Rights in Posse and Rights in Esse

Public (or constitutional) rights are potentialities; they are rights in posse. For example, the right to vote is a potential right and not the actual act of voting. Public (or constitutional) rights are recognized by the community on behalf of all its citizens. Private rights, on the other hand, are granted by the community to individual persons exclusively. Thus, economic rights are rights in posse and property rights are rights in esse.

In these theoretical questions, the issue of the practical usefulness of economic rights is embedded. Succinctly stated, their usefulness rests on the fact that they represent a legal claim on future property rights. In other words, economic rights, as many other rights, represent legal potentialities. To distinguish them from other rights, these potentialities perform a specific function. They represent opportunities to create wealth. Thus, their exercise allows people to exist in the economic sphere with full dignity and a degree of interdependence. Since, by nature, economic rights are universal they represent a fair distribution of opportunities to create future wealth.

Rights and Responsibilities

From Giuseppe Mazzini[5] to Oliver Wendell Holmes,[6] it has been recognized that the very essence of rights is that they imply responsibilities. There are various reasons for the existence of an indissoluble link between these two entities. The first reason can be found in the very nature of rights observed in the full glory of social and communal relations. If rights are innate, they belong to all human beings universally. Therefore, since the community does not possess them, when it assigns them to each individual person–i.e., when their title is conferred by society–the community must request a quid pro quo as compensation for all other people. The quid is the responsibility. It is the assignment of responsibilities that, given community relationships, provides legal legitimacy to the assignment of rights.

Then there is the issue of moral legitimacy. Society cannot give rights away without simultaneously assigning responsibilities. Responsibilities, so understood, confer moral justification for rights. One justification for this linkage can be found in the domain of political science. David E. Stephens, a moral theologian, once suggested the following to me in a letter: "If one has responsibilities but no corresponding rights, then one is bound by and a victim of necessity—in the form of some kind of tyranny. If one has rights and no corresponding responsibilities, then one is unaccountably free, a state of anarchy." He went on to make an important philosophical argument: "Yet, in both cases the linkage between right and responsibility is inescapable: If one is bound by necessity, either one has a responsibility to conform to necessity or to suffer the alternative sanctions. If one is unaccountably free, then either one is self-accountable or self-destructive. Barring destruction of the party or parties in either state, some responsibility or some rights must coordinate with the state of necessity or freedom. Between these polar states, a full spectrum of proportionality of coordinated rights and responsibilities are to be found."

A society that wants to be civilized must link people together through a set of mutual rights and responsibilities. Human relationships then become legal because they are moral, and they are moral because they are legal. From one perspective, responsibilities are the quid pro quo that diminishes the reasons for society to ever take rights away from individual human beings, and thus binds society to the individual person. From the other side, responsibilities represent what is given back to society, and thus bind the individual person to society. In either case, responsibilities provide the moral justification for rights. If the right balance is found, the statesman builds not only upon a moral foundation but he also ensures stability for the future. Members of society will not desire to alter those relationships.

Corresponding Economic Responsibilities

Responsibilities cannot be superimposed upon rights arbitrarily. Rather, they are an inherent part of them, and are time- and place-specific. If the rights are conceptual, then the responsibilities must be conceptual. Yet, as soon as the exercise of rights becomes concrete, their inherent obligations become legal obligations—obligations, that is, enforceable in a court of law.

All too briefly, since the arguments belong mostly to the field of economic analysis and economic policy, the responsibilities that one might want to associate with the four economic rights enunciated above can be pinpointed as follows. In correspondence with the right of access to natural resources, there ought to be the duty to pay taxes for the use of those resources. The basic rationale for this duty is not only that natural resources are a common good and the good of all requires that they be equitably shared, but that the payment of taxes is a token compensation for the exclusion of others from the use of those resources. Furthermore, the rationale is that much–but by no means all–of the value of one's property derives from communal efforts (e.g., the provision of water, sewer, and electric lines; schools, theaters, and museums). The rationale is also that by paying taxes on land and natural resources one eliminates the incentive to hoard those resources and thus, with full compensation, one makes the resources that are hoarded potentially part of the commonwealth through voluntary market exchanges. The alternative is clear: One can hold on to the land but one must pay taxes on those holdings. Taxes on land and natural resources cannot be construed as "takings." Quite simply, they represent payment for the provision of public services received directly by the owner of the land. The extent to which taxes on land and natural resources should exceed the value of the public goods received can be ascribed to payment for the social and economic benefits of the absence of hoarding.

In correspondence with the right of access to national credit there ought to be the duty to repay the loan. The exercise of this right should be subjected to the following restrictions: (1) Access should be limited to capital credit to create new wealth (consumer credit, credit for paper transactions, as well as credit for transfer of ownership titles would not qualify); (2) It should be issued to benefit all participants in the enterprise; and (3) It should be issued at cost. The rationale for the basic duty to repay the loan is that national credit is a common good. Failure to repay the loan causes the pool of common resources to be drained. Worse yet, due to inflationary effects, by not repaying the loan one debases the currency to the detriment of everyone–the abuser of the right included.

Corresponding to the third right mentioned above, the right to own the fruits of one's labor, there ought to be the duty to meet the obligations outlined in the performance of the work. Likewise, corresponding to the right to protect one's wealth, there ought to be the duty to respect other people's wealth.

A brief note regarding the implementation of these duties should be appended here. As it can be seen from this list, the obligations are not obligations of the state. If the state does not have economic rights to apportion, it cannot assume economic obligations to fulfill. The obligations flow from individual human beings to other human beings. The state can only administer the policies that make for an easy fulfillment of those obligations.

Theory and Practice

The natural mutuality of interests and concerns among human beings makes for an integration of rights and responsibilities. We have seen that this integration is such an essential part of the theory of economic rights one might conclude that the link forms an implicit contract. However, does this imply that the theory is always respected in practice? Since the law does not have a soul, since it does not have an essence of its own, there is no ultimate justification in the law for this linkage. The justifications we have found occur in the domain of morality, sociology, politics, and philosophy, but not in the law. The law is a tool, in fact, a neutral tool of society. In the end, the law can accomplish anything society wants it to accomplish. Hence, there is no legal justification for rights to be tied to responsibilities. Indeed, since rights are social entities, they are a two-edged sword. Society giveth; society can take away. Society can only grant privileges. Society cannot grant rights; it can only recognize them. But society can prevent their exercise.

The link between theory and practice can be dissolved; yet if the link is a natural one, many problems will arise from its dissolution. Rather than the administration of universal rights, one shall find the granting of factional privileges. Rather than the protection of the laws, one shall find a favoritism imposed by force. Rather than freedom for all, one shall find libertinism for the few. Rather than social integration, one shall eventually find social disintegration. Liberty and stability exist only in a regimen of just laws. For moral, sociological, and political reasons it is advisable that rights be indissolubly tied to responsibilities. With such a burden lying on the propriety of the link between rights and responsibilities, one must make sure that the theory is indeed sound.

Economic Rights Within the Theory of Justice

We will examine five tests of legal validity that the proposed economic rights must pass before they can be accepted as true public (or constitutional) rights. Thereafter, we will see whether they conform with established principles of economic justice. Finally, we will see what sort of place they might eventually occupy within the structure of the theory of justice.

Some Theoretical Perspectives

For these rights and responsibilities to be accepted, they must pass a number of theoretical tests that belong to the legal understanding of justice. First, do the proposed rights and responsibilities yield the essential elements of "the original position" envisioned by Rawls?[7] Second, do they meet the requirements of the "reverse theory" enunciated by Nozick?[8] Recognizing that "particular rights over things fill the space of rights, leaving no room for general rights to be in a certain material condition," Nozick postulates: "The reverse theory would place only such universally held general 'rights to' achieve goals or to be in a certain material condition into its substructure so as to determine all else; to my knowledge no serious attempt has been made to state this 'reverse' theory."[9]

A third theoretical test of validity can be construed in relation to the Principle of Generic Consistency, which has been carefully designed and cogently argued for by Alan Gewirth.[10] Will the above set of four rights and responsibilities pass this test? Gewirth's principle to "Act in accord with the generic rights of your recipients as well as of yourself"[11] is an attempt to synthesize the logical requirements advanced by Rawls with those of Nozick.

There are many other tests of validity. The next that might be considered is based on the conditions for the existence of a "system of rights" as specified by Rex Martin.[12] Can those rights function as a system of rights? One final test comes to mind. Are the proposed rights and responsibilities properly "integrated within a robust vision of a very traditional Catholic concern, namely, the common good," as Finn recommends?[13]

The Principles of Justice
For the proposed economic rights and responsibilities eventually to become an integral part of the theory of justice they have to be expressions of sound legal and philosophical principles. The most important test that those four rights and responsibilities, singly and jointly, have to sustain is this: Are those rights built on the basis of solid principles? The essential principles submitted for scrutiny are:

- Each specific right shall make us free (the intellectual, rationalist argument);
- Each specific right shall be universal (the idealist as well as the utilitarian argument);
- Each specific right shall be fair (the emotional, naturalistic, transcendentalist argument);

- Each specific right shall be enforceable in a court of law (the positivist argument);
- Each specific right shall create social order (the political and aesthetic argument).

Only a few questions can be raised here to point toward the necessary analysis that must be done to determine the correspondence of those rights with the above principles: (1) Is each one of those rights intimately related to the question of truth–and hence to freedom in general–as well as to issues of economic freedom in particular? (2) Is each one of those rights an expression of universality and even of universal utilitarianism? (3) Is each one of those rights related to natural rights theory? (4) Can each right also be justified in terms of positivism? (5) Does each right have the potentiality to contribute to social as well as intellectual harmony?

A Place Within the Theory of Justice

If the proposed rights and responsibilities pass the specific tests of legal validity mentioned above and if they pass the theoretical test of concordance with basic principles of philosophy, in order to become fully accepted, they have to occupy a specific place within the theory of justice. Is there such a place for them?

A place for economic rights and responsibilities within the structure of the theory of justice will be found only if two requirements are met. First, one must adhere to the ancient division of this body of knowledge into two fields: political justice and economic justice. With regard to economic justice, we must add to it a new plank: participative justice.

From Aristotle to the late Middle Ages, and within the Catholic tradition up to Monsignor Ryan's work in the twentieth century, the theory of economic justice was thought to be composed of two major parts, distributive and commutative justice–with the latter presenting rules of justice that applied to the exchange of goods and services. The right to participate in the production of wealth must have seemed so natural, so innate in human beings, that no need was felt to specify it in writing. With the progressive closure of the commons, the full development of a monetary economy, and the propensity to cluster immense concentrations of wealth in a few hands, the economic conditions of the world have, indeed, changed. The right to be an active participant, rather than being relegated to the margin of economic life is a right that needs to be asserted.

Implementation of the requirements of participative justice is imperative today. Taking the lead from the seminal economic policy analysis of Louis O. Kelso,[14] this addition to the theory of economic justice can be justified from many points of view. Its moral rationale can be most clearly found in the social teaching of the Roman Catholic Church. In Centesimus Annus, for instance, Pope John Paul II calls for a "society of free work, of enterprise and of participation."[15] In the preceding paragraph he specifies: "Inseparable from that required 'something' (which is due to man because he is man) is the possibility to survive and at the same time to make an active contribution to the common good of humanity."[16]

Some of the legal rationale for this addition is provided by Nozick with his principle of "justice in acquisition."[17] The economic rationale can be found in the revision of Keynes' model first envisaged by this writer in the summer of 1965, and gradually developed ever since. This work yields the equivalence of production to distribution to consumption.[18] In accordance with these results the test is as follows: Can the proposed system of rights be justified, through a series of iterations, by the requirements of participative, distributive, and commutative justice?

All too briefly, without the exercise of the proposed four rights, people are not free to participate in the economic process. They are not put in a position of parity in relation to the apportionment of shares in the process of the distribution of wealth. If people do not participate in the production process or are at a disadvantage in the process of the distribution of wealth, then they are automatically at a disadvantage in the process of the exchange of wealth. It would be naive to see the latter set of needs as involving only problems of consumerism; one must enlarge the scope to encompass problems of monopoly and hoarding of wealth. Note Monsignor John A. Ryan's major work, Distributive Justice: The Right and Wrong of Our Present Distribution of Wealth,[19] where he builds on the solid tradition of the past but without ignoring the problems that are still with us today. For instance, this work contains a legal and economic analysis of the minimum wage that is far superior to anything existing in the current literature on the subject.[20]

In summary, the proposed four economic rights offer the opportunity to complete the structure of the theory of economic justice. The structure can be built upon three planks: participative justice, distributive justice, and commutative justice. But the three component parts of the structure do not operate sequentially. As in a physical structure, they operate synchronously, and the theory becomes a powerful engine of decision and analysis.

Conclusion

There are many indications today that, while public struggles over the last few centuries were mostly concerned with issues of political justice, the current struggle is one of economic justice. Foundational to this struggle is the issue of defining economic rights. This article has sought to define these rights as rights of access to essential resources in the process of production, distribution, and the exchange of wealth. It is through access to those resources that one creates property and property rights. By regressing the search of the legal title of ownership to present wealth, one is led to the realization that this was the reality in the ancient past as it still is today.

The practical thrust of this essay consists in transforming the fact of access to economic resources into the right of access to economic resources. Rich and poor alike–the rich to an obviously greater degree than the poor–live in a legal regimen that is one of privilege. They acquire access to economic resources as a fact–not as a right. This is the ultimate source of instability in the modern polity. The fact of access has to be transformed into a universal right. If rich and poor alike are to live under a regimen of laws, economic rights have to be defined and exercised universally.

This article has sought to provide an understanding of basic economic needs that are met by those rights. It has also described an understanding of the legal characteristics of economic rights. Throughout we have suggested that the theory of economic justice should be seen as composed of participative justice, distributive justice, and commutative justice–three planks that have to be treated not as three sequential segments but as three synchronous parts whose requirements are either satisfied simultaneously or not at all.[21]

NOTES

1. Daniel Rush Finn, "Catholic Social Thought on Property: An Urgent Need for Extension and Renewal." Paper presented at the conference on "The Legacy of Msgr. John A. Ryan," University of Saint Thomas, 1995.

2. Carmine Gorga, "The Revised Keynes' Model," Atlantic Economic Journal 10 (September 1982): 52; "Bold New Directions in Politics and Economics," The Humane Economy Newsletter 12 (March 1991): 3 – 6, 12; "Quality Assurance: Internal and External Financing Opportunities," in Quality Control and Quality Assurance for Seafood, eds. Gilbert Sylvia, Ann L. Shriver, and Michael T. Morrisey (Corvallis, Oreg.: Oregon State University, 1994), 158 – 63; "Four Economic Rights: Social Renewal

Through Economic Justice For All," Social Justice Review 85 (January/February 1994): 3 — 6; Carmine Gorga and Norman G. Kurland, "The Productivity Standard: A True Golden Standard," in Every Worker An Owner: A Revolutionary Free Enterprise Challenge to Marxism, ed. Dawn M. Kurland (Washington, D.C.: Center for Economic and Social Justice, 1987), 83 — 6; Carmine Gorga and Stuart B. Weeks, "Fisheries Renewal: A Renewal of the Soul of Business," The Catholic Social Science Review 2 (1997): 145 — 62.

3. Immanuel Kant, "Philosophy of Law," in The Great Legal Philosophers: Selected Readings in Jurisprudence, ed. Clarence Morris (Philadelphia: University of Pennsylvania Press, 1959).

4. Ibid., 252.

5. Giuseppe Mazzini, The Duties of Man (London: Chapman and Hall, 1862).

6. Oliver Wendell Holmes, "Uncollected Letters," in The Wisdom of the Supreme Court, ed. Percival E. Jackson (Norman, Okla.: University of Oklahoma Press, 1962), 398.

7. John Rawls, A Theory of Justice (Cambridge, Mass.: Harvard University Press, 1971), 12, 72, 136, 538.

8. Robert Nozick, Anarchy, State, and Utopia (New York: Basic Books, 1974), 238.

9. Ibid.

10. Alan Gewirth, "Economic Justice: Concepts and Criteria," in Economic Justice: Private Rights and Public Responsibilities, ed. Kenneth Kipnis and Diana T. Meyers (Totowa, N.J.: Rowman & Allanheld, 1985).

11. Ibid., 19.

12. Rex Martin, Rawls and Rights (Lawrence, Kans.: University of Kansas Press, 1985), 114 — 8, 129.

13. Finn, "Catholic Social Thought on Property."

14. Louis O. Kelso and Mortimer Adler, The Capitalist Manifesto (New York: Random House, 1958), chap. 5; Louis O. Kelso and Patricia Hetter, Two — Factor Theory: The Economics of Reality (New York: Vintage Books, 1967), 10, 28, 32.

15. John Paul II, Encyclical Letter Centesimus Annus (May 15, 1991), no. 35.

16. Ibid., no. 34.

17. Nozick, Anarchy, State, and Utopia, 150ff., esp. 168.

18. Gorga, "The Revised Keynes' Model."

19. John A. Ryan, Distributive Justice: The Right and Wrong of Our Present Distribution of Wealth (New York: Macmillan and Company, 1942 [orig. 1916]).

20. Ibid., 249 — 302. The historic emphasis there is on the living wage.

21. I would like to acknowledge Professor Michael J. Naughton, who invited me to participate in the conference on "The Legacy of Msgr. John A. Ryan," University of Saint Thomas, 1995, and Professor Robert G. Kennedy, who exhibited enormous patience with my unexpected delays in completing this article. I have benefited from the constructive criticism of Janis D. Stelluto, David E. Stephens, Stuart B. Weeks, and David S. Wise.

On the Equivalence of Matter to Energy and to Spirit

Reprinted with permission from *Transactions on Advanced Research* July 2007 | Volume 3 | Number 2 | ISSN 1820 — 4511: 40-45.
The original publication is available at http://internetjournals.net/journals/tar/TAR2007july.pdf

Carmine Gorga

Carmine Gorga is with Concordians.org Inc. (e-mail: cgorga@jhu.edu)

Abstract

A basic assumption in logic is that the principle of equivalence formulates a relation among three terms. Yet, there is no recognized third term in physics that completes the established relation of equivalence between matter and energy. This paper suggests that the third term to which both matter and energy are equivalent can be posited to be spirit. Spirit is defined both as the link-as glue-that holds matter and energy together and as Spirit, a notion that is akin to the spirit of God, which is by definition everywhere. All three terms might eventually be measured by a calorimeter. If this application of the principle of equivalence is accepted, physics is transformed from a linear into a relational discipline. And then everything will change in the "two cultures", namely in both the physical and the social sciences.

Index Terms

Equivalence, equivalence of matter to energy, equivalence of matter to energy and to spirit, linear rationalism, relationalism

1. *Introduction*

Einstein established a relation of equivalence between matter and energy [1]. An equivalence relation is composed of three distinct and separate terms. To the knowledge of this writer, so far there is no identified third term to which both matter and energy are equivalent. Hence the relationship is not formally valid yet. This paper proposes that the third term of the equivalence be posited to be spirit.

After observing some of the canonical requirements of the equivalence relation and the fundamental advantages of casting our thought processes into this format for the force it brings to our reasoning, we shall first note the shortcomings of some potential solutions to the lack of formal validity of the equivalence of matter to energy and then we shall try to obtain an operational definition for the word spirit. Only then shall we observe some of the consequences of accepting the proposal of making spirit the third term of the equivalence.

If the proposal stands to all the tests of validity, this solution will eventually yield two considerable benefits. It will transform physics from a linear into a relational discipline. It will also tend toward the reunification of the physical with the social sciences.

2. *Problem Statement*

Matter and energy are two terms. $E = mc^2$ is not an equivalence relation; c^2 is not a third term: c^2 is a unit of measure (of speed). As logicians know, to be valid, an equivalence relation must be composed of three terms. The three terms have to be reflexive (namely identical to themselves throughout the discourse), symmetric (one observes the same entity from two points of view in order to obtain a deeper understanding of both entities), and transitive (a third term must exist to which both terms are equivalent in order to eschew the confines of circular reasoning and to complete the analysis). With the assistance of the equivalence relation the analysis does not start from an arbitrary point nor does it end at an arbitrary point, but is rigorously interlocked.

These observations can be made more evident by specifying the progress of our thought processes and by casting them into a set of figures. Science eschews all singularities. There is a good reason for this practice. A single point, a single observation does not lead to an objective, replicable analysis or experiment. Analysis begins with the observation of two events. Yet, the observation of two events necessarily leads to circularity of reasoning.

Once we are faced with only two observations, we are obliged to observe all possibilities. Hence the mind is led back to the exploration of all potential outcomes of the position of Point B on the circumference of the circle in relation to Point A at the center of the circle. This is a process that eventually leads to a reversal of one's position and then to a return to the original position-and no certainty is necessarily acquired in the process. Therefore, science asks for a third term. The third term points the research in the right direction. However, if the third term is placed in a linear position, the end result might be a dispersal of the thought process into the empty infinity of an enlarged circle. Linearity leads to *progressio ad infinitum*.

It is the equivalence relation that restrains the analysis from collapsing into infinity by constraining the terms into an interlocked relationship as in its standard configuration: A⟷B⟷C. The equivalence relation starts in logic and has the widest possible range of applications. All forms of syllogism are based on the equivalence relation. Hence the relation of equivalence is well known to the literati. The equivalence relation is also part and parcel of all mathematics textbooks. It stands at the very foundation of mathematics, in which three fingers of my hand (3 of base 10 number system) are equivalent to the word/number/symbol (three, 3, or III) and to the three apples in front of my eyes. A triangle is based on the equivalence relation. The whole of trigonometry is based on the equivalence relation. Indeed, as R. G. D. Allen pointed out, the rules of equivalence "hold" also for the relation of "equality (=)" [2].

In brief, there are many reasons why it is essential to cast any scientific analysis in the format proposed by the rules of logic in general, and the principle of equivalence in particular. A few of them, not necessarily in their order of importance, are as follows. Logic, as a whole, provides objective criteria for the evaluation of any proposition; most disagreement, as is well known, disappears as soon as the magic words are pronounced: "But that is not logically tenable." Logic provides guidance to our analysis; without it, we are rudderless. Guided by rules of logic, we know whether or not we have completed our analysis. Logic makes it possible to replicate the reasoning or the experiment.

From the above it inexorably follows that the fundamental relationship that Einstein established between matter and energy is yet incomplete. Two terms do not make an equivalence relation. The relationship between matter and energy is completed only when a third element is found to which both matter and energy are equivalent.

3. Inadequacy of Some Possible Solutions

There are no explicit formulations of a third term to which both matter and energy are equivalent. As pointed out above, c^2 is not a third term, but a unit of measurement of speed that has nearly nothing to do with light. It happens to be the speed of light; hence, at best, it is an attribute of light. By extension, it might be assumed that mc^2 contains in it, not just the meaning of matter, but also-implicitly-the meaning of light. Even if c^2 stood for light, it cannot be the third term because light is a form of energy (clearly in the wave conception of light; or a form of matter in the particle conception of light). Thus, whether light is an intrinsic component of E or m, it cannot at the same time be an extrinsic term to which either E or mc^2 might be equivalent. It cannot appear as an addition to either side of the equation, without creating double counting and without violating the first requirement that each term of the equivalence must be reflexive, namely identical to itself throughout the observation. The addition of the term light does not make the construction symmetric; one cannot change the term light with the term energy (or matter) and obtain positive results: one does not gain a better understanding of either matter or energy. Neither does that addition make the terms of the construction transitive: from light one necessarily goes back to either matter or energy-not to both. These considerations can also be put in common language: a part cannot be confused with the whole. If light is part of energy or part of matter, light cannot be equivalent either to energy or to matter, because this definition would run into the impossibility of equating a part with the whole. Since matter and energy, to be equivalent to each other, must be whole units, namely units or entities all complete in themselves, the third term must also be a whole unit, a whole entity. It cannot be a part of a whole.

The same considerations apply if the term third is assumed to be derived from the equation $E = hv$, where E is energy, h is Planck's constant (which is equal to 1 and thus disappears from the equations of physics), and v is the measure of the frequency of energy radiation emitted as photons, rather than the speed of light.

A more abstract set of considerations are necessary to dispel the notion that space (like the old ether and the futuristic "higher order") might be the third element of the equivalence. The third element has to have an existence of its own. Take away matter and/or energy and space disappears from our field of observation. Hence it cannot be the third element that would make the equivalence of matter to energy a valid relationship. We must search for a third term to which both matter and energy are equivalent.

3. *Findings*

This paper proposes that the search for the third term to complete the equivalence of matter to energy is exhausted with the introduction of spirit into the relationship. This is the answer that Fritjof Capra [3] inspired. One then obtains the following equivalence: matter ◄─► spirit ◄─► energy. This is a relationship that reads: matter is equivalent to spirit and spirit is equivalent to energy. This is a complete relationship of equivalence, which can be defined as the Relational Reality, and it can be diagrammed using these established protocols:

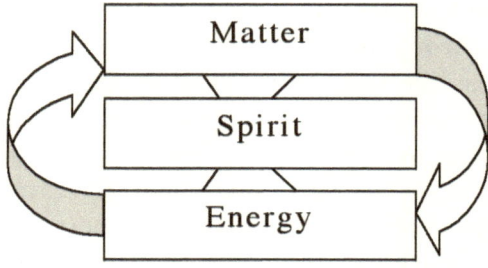

Figure 1. The Relational Reality

Figure 1 can be interpreted not only to mean that matter transforms itself into energy and energy into matter, but-at the very least-especially along these lines: The physical world in which we live has to be observed first from the point of view of matter and then from the point of view of energy. The essential prerequisite is to see these two aspects of reality not in linear fashion, but in a relational mode, namely as two separate and distinct viewpoints of the same reality. When that is done, one can also see that the total reality in which our daily existence is immersed can be grasped only if it is observed, not only from the viewpoint of matter and energy, but also from the viewpoint of spirit. One enters into the stone with a hammer; into the energy of the stone with a cyclotron; and into its spirit with prayer.

Thus we come back to the very roots of our civilization. Our ancestral ancestors-not unlike many brothers and sisters in many civilizations of today-started their analysis of the world neither from matter nor, certainly, from energy. It is fairly certain that they started their analysis of the world form the point of view of spirit.

But what is spirit? Can we obtain a precise definition of this term? Can we obtain an operational definition of this term?

4. *On the Definition of Spirit*

Spirit is incommensurable. Therefore, it is difficult to define. Once it is realized, as we shall more clearly see below, that mathematics, the most precise of all sciences proceeds on the basis of two incommensurable entities, namely zero and infinity, this inherent difficulty that is presented by the word spirit ought not to be of much concern to a physicist. That said, we shall try to identify some of the characteristics of spirit. As used in this paper, spirit is a relation, the relation that binds matter to energy. It keeps them both factually together and intellectually separate from each other. With the word spirit, we can stop thinking of the universe as a linear relationship in which matter somehow passes into energy, and we can start conceiving of the universe of matter being in organic relationship with the world of energy. We can study the objective reality first as a world of matter and then as a world of energy. These are all enclosed worlds of their own. If we conceive of both matter and energy as two entities, indeed as two worlds, in their own, without their individual link to spirit, they would both be in fatal conflict with each other. Instead, we notice near perfect and continuous harmony between the two entities. This we might say is an attempted definition of spirit in the small, as in "the spirit of this stone": spirit is the link, the glue that holds matter and energy together.

By trying to define spirit in the large, as an infinite entity into which both matter and energy are encompassed, and indeed as an infinite entity in which we-observers-are all encompassed, we might gain a greater control over the forces of this world by regaining the sense of what used to be called the "sacred". Only if the earth is seen as sacred again will we feel obliged to respect its inner existence. It is through the word spirit that we reach a better understanding of both matter and energy. Through that word, we enter deeply into their essence and we get in close contact with each of them. In an age in which we are discovering the essential importance of a sound ecological management of the planets, the word spirit will incite us to gain a greater respect for the world of matter as well as the world of energy than we have at present.

Thus the word spirit has a theoretical as well as an operational validity. And then it can inexorably be observed that the infinity of spirit manifests itself to us most clearly as both matter and energy. Hence, the preeminence of the study of physics in today's culture is no longer surprising.

5. *An Extension of the Word Spirit*

But spirit does not manifest itself only as matter and energy. It also manifests itself, indeed, as spirit. Man's mind has forever been engaged in the attempt to define "spirit". We must admit that the task has eluded us. And there is a very good reason why the task is destined to elude us forever. Spirit is not an intellectual affair, hence it can never be caught by the intellect. Since it is an intensely personal relation, indeed an intensely personal affair, the essence of the word spirit can only be caught by our feelings. This is the fundamental reason why approximation to the understanding and explanation of spirit have been in the past the prerogative of mystics, theologians, philosophers, literati, and musicians. As the practitioners of these disciplines have forever made an attempt to convey their understanding of spirit to all other people who may be interested in the topic, so physicists in the future-as they have indeed done in the past (see, e.g., Aristotle and Thomas Aquinas)-have to try to convey to the practitioners of the spirit the goodness, the truth, and the beauty that they discover in both matter and energy.

6. *Some Limitations of the Meaning of Spirit*

One could define spirit as Spirit, namely as God. However, this definition might be misleading; it might lead into the old pitfalls of pantheism. To avoid such dangers, it is necessary to distinguish God from God's spirit; it might be necessary to say that God is also spirit; and then one must be careful to limit God's presence in matter and energy by saying that the spirit of God is also in matter and energy, also in the stone and its energy. If God is by definition everywhere, then-given the above qualifications-it is possible to say that God is also in the stone and in its energy. And then one surprising result ensues: a very practical consequence indeed. It appears that all three entities, namely matter, energy, and spirit might share the same unit of measure: degrees of heat. One of God's characteristics is to be in essence love, Love par excellence. And is not warmth and heat one of the most endearing physical manifestations of love?

7. *Some Implications for Physics*

Not being a physicist, this writer can suggest some of the implications for physics of establishing a true equivalence between matter, energy, and spirit only at a very broad level of generality. When one multiplies the mass by the square of the speed of light, when one spins matter at the squared speed of light, one no longer observes matter but energy. One is no longer in the world of matter, but in the world of energy. One has made such a definite break between the two worlds that, in order to achieve clarity of mind and expression, one must accordingly design a new nomenclature. Using words from one world and applying them to the other leads to analogical thought, but not to innovative and incisive thought.

The second consequence that this writer can envisage is the need to jettison the old attachment to absolute quantification. Quantification in physics has always taken place within sharply defined limits. One has simply to resign to the nature of things that this is the only type of quantification that might forever be viable in physics. In order to reduce the level of apprehension about this condition, physicists will want to notice that mathematics too has always been subjected to this condition. If one does not see the number system as a linear but a relational organization of numbers, it becomes clear that mathematics is based on the following foundational equivalence: $0 \longleftrightarrow 1 \longleftrightarrow \infty$. The first impression is that mathematics has been able always to proceed with the quantification of only one of its terms: namely, the number 1. Mathematics does not, and cannot quantify either zero or infinity. And it does not matter. Indeed, on second thought, mathematics does not quantify the third of its foundational terms either; mathematics does not present us with an absolute quantification of one, but a relative quantification of one. Numbers proceed from (plus or minus) one to infinity, but they never touch infinity; the conception of the limit is there to recognize this deficiency and to allow us to work within the limits offered by reality. Thus, taking a leaf from the transition from Galileo and Newton to Einstein through Hume in relation to space and time [4], we shall not be concerned with absolute but with relative quantification.

Hence, we can safely maintain that

If the universe is infinite, we shall never weigh its mass;

If the universe is infinite, we shall never measure its length;

What we measure is its mass and its length in relation to man.

Then, man-indeed, every man and woman-is again positioned at the center of the universe.

8. *Some Conceptual Consequences*

In 1946 Einstein remarked: "The unleashed power of the atom has

changed everything save our modes of thinking" [5]. With the establishment of the equivalence of matter to spirit and to energy, everything
changes. Technically, Figure 1 establishes that while any element of reality
occupies its own distinctive position, everything is in full relationship with
everything else. Hence, as proved by the Internet, everything is indeed directly related to everything else. This complexity is better observed by rotating at ever increasing speed, not only the entire Figure 1, but also each
rectangle inside Figure 1 about its geometric center. One then obtains the
image of four circles: one, the circle of matter; two, the circle of spirit; three,
the circle of energy; four, the circle of the relational reality as a whole. This
is a Venn diagram delimited by a circle. And what is a circle, if not a two-di-
mensional image of a sphere? Ultimately, one is thus presented with a construction composed of four interpenetrating concentric spheres, one for
each point of view from which reality can be observed: the point of view of
matter, spirit, energy, and the system as a whole. An analysis of this type of
construction can be followed in detail in the humbler reality of the world
of economic justice [6] and the world of economics [7]. The mathematics
of this construction is well-known [8] and it might be useful to reproduce
it here in a very abstract form as follows:

$$a\bullet = fa(a,b,c)$$
$$b\bullet = fb(a,b,c)$$
$$c\bullet = fc(a,b,c),$$

where $a\bullet$ = rate of change in the first element of the relationship, $b\bullet$ = rate
of change in the second element of the relationship, and $c\bullet$ = rate of change
in the third element of the relationship.

From the linear world of rationalism, thus everything is transformed
into the organic world of relationalism. Above all, beyond changes of perspective in physics, if this construction of reality is accepted, the warlike relation between the "two cultures" is expected to change and eventually to
come to a screeching halt; with time, this war-with its multifarious manifestations of reductionism, materialism, and atheism, and, above all, mutual misunderstandings-will unavoidably come to a screeching halt.

While waiting for a response to these observations from the people of
science, we already know the response from the people of spirit. Poetry
and philosophy have spoken forcefully about the evident relationship between matters of the earth and matters of the spirit [9]. Since this writer is

more familiar with the Catholic tradition, he will limit himself to one quotation from within this belief system. But many other expressions come easily to mind. "Every culture," Christopher Dawson wrote, "is like a plant. It must have its roots in the earth, and for sunlight it needs to be open to the spiritual. At the present moment we are busy cutting its roots and shutting out all light from above" [10].

If mathematicians and physicists, following strict rules of logic that they already obey in all steps of their reasoning, can be convinced that their own fields-as moral theologians insist-are all immersed into the world of spirit, all other scientists, especially social scientists, will not take long to follow suit. After all, it was Einstein who said: "Science without religion is lame, religion without science is blind" [11].

9. CONCLUSION

There are many indications that the world of linear, rational, Cartesian logic has come to an end-see, e.g., John Lukacs, *At the End of an Age* [12]. This is a world in which reality is reduced to isolated atoms. The principle of equivalence is a ready-made tool that allows us to escape the strictures of Cartesian logic and leads us into the world of relational logic, a world in which everything is naturally related to everything else. This paper has used this principle and reached some novel conclusions in relation to physics and mathematics. In the process, it has laid the groundwork for healing the ongoing schism between the "two cultures".

A POSTSCRIPT

The reader might be interested to know that this paper was not written with the Shroud of Turin in mind. Yet, at one point it became apparent to this writer that the paper makes the Shroud a logical and "natural" necessity. Even the Transfiguration and the appearance of Jesus in the Cenacle become understandable, because-if this reasoning is right-Jesus is, was, and will forever be the perfect union of matter and energy and spirit. And, of course, accepting this reasoning one can see that the consecrated communion host is real.

If this reasoning is accepted to be theologically and logically valid, it leads to a further observation. The study of singularities is not concluded by the study of matter alone, or energy alone, or spirit alone. It is the integration of the three worlds that might yield a better understanding of singularities as well as a better understanding of the world as a whole.

The study of singularities cannot be eschewed by science. Science cannot thus limit itself. Indeed, as various technical studies of the Shroud of Turin prove, science has an essential role to play in the analysis and the distinction of true from false singularities.

ACKNOWLEDGMENTS
The author wishes to acknowledge the technical assistance received from his long-standing collaborator, Louis J. Ronsivalli, an MIT food science technologist, and a most positive feedback from Dr. F. Hadi Madjid, a Harvard physicist. The paper has greatly benefited from comments and recommendations from six referees on an earlier draft. Thanks also go to Jonathan F. Gorga for invaluable editorial assistance.

REFERENCES
Einstein, A. (1905). "Ist die Trägheit eines Körpers von seinem Energieinhalt abhängig?" (Does the Inertia of a Body Depend upon its Energy-Content?). *Annalen der Physik*. Ser. 4, Vol. 18, pp. 639-641. See also, [1935 (1971)]. "Elementary Derivation of the Equivalence of Mass and Energy". American Mathematical Society, *Bulletin*. Vol. 41, pp. 223-30. In R. W. Clark. *Einstein-The Life and Times*. New York and Cleveland: World Publishing, p. 538; see also pp. 98-103, 115-120, 126, 141, 144, 268, 537, and 587.

Allen, R.G. D. (1970). *Mathematical Economics*, 2nd edn. London and New York: Macmillan, St. Martin's, p. 748.

Capra, F. (1980). *The Tao of Physics*. New York: Bantam Books.

Cf. Feinstein, J. S. (2006). *The Nature of Creative Development*. Stanford: Stanford Business Books, esp. pp. 303-315 and 322-328.

Einstein, A. (1946). In Nathan O., and Norden, H. eds., *Einstein on Peace*. New York: Avnet Books, 1981 ed, p. 376, from a pamphlet published by Beyond War in 1985 entitled *A New Way of Thinking*.

Gorga, C. (1999). "Toward the Definition of Economic Rights", *Journal of Markets and Morality* Vol. 2, No. 1, pp. 88-101.

Gorga, C. (2002). *The Economic Process: An Instantaneous Non-Newtonian*

Picture. University Press of America, Lanham, Md., and Oxford.

Thompson, J. M. T. (1986). *Nonlinear Dynamics and Chaos, Geometric Methods for Engineers and Scientists.* New York: Wiley.

For poetry, Walt Whitman's work should suffice. For philosophy, see. e.g., Hegel, G. W. (1807). *The Phenomenology of Spirit* and Emerson, R. W. *The Natural History of the Intellect* (or *The Natural History of the Spirit)* unpublished.

Dawson, C. In Catholic Educator's Resource Center (CERC), *Bi-Weekly Update*, November 5, 2004. At www.catholiceducation.org.

Einstein, A. (1941). *"Science, Philosophy and Religion: a Symposium".* From *The Quotation Page* at *http://www.quotationspage.com/quote/24949.html.*

Lukacs, J. (2002): *At the End of an Age.* New Haven and London: Yale University Press.

Brief Biographical Sketch of the Author
Carmine Gorga is a former Fulbright scholar and the recipient of a Council of Europe Scholarship for his dissertation on "The Political Thought of Louis D. Brandeis." Using age-old principles of logic and epistemology, in a book and a series of papers Dr. Gorga has transformed the linear world of economic theory into a relational discipline in which everything is related to everything else-internally as well as externally. He was assisted in this endeavor by many people, notably for twenty-seven years by Professor Franco Modigliani, a Nobel laureate in economics at MIT. The resulting work, *The Economic Process: An Instantaneous Non-Newtonian Picture,* was published in 2002. For reviews, see http://www.carmine-gorga.us/id18.htm" http://www.carmine-gorga.us/id18.htm. During the last few years, Mr. Gorga has concentrated his attention on matters of methodology for the reunification of the sciences.

Concordian Economics:
Tools to Return Relevance to Economics

Reprinted with permission from *Forum for Social Economics* (http://dx.doi.org/10.1007/s12143-008-9017-6), May 2008. The original publication is available at springerlink.com" www.springerlink.com.

By Carmine Gorga*

Abstract With the help of planes and solids, this paper presents an enlargement of the field of observation of economic theory. Through this transformation, the distribution of ownership rights to money and wealth assumes a central position in economic analysis. Thus social relevance is returned to economics. The validity of this operation is confirmed by the return of the millenarian field of economic justice to its traditional function as guidance to economic policy. The paper then presents four sets of economic rights and responsibilities that offer the potential of translating principles of economic justice into the complexities of the modern world.

Keywords economic theory, economic policy, economic practice, economic justice, economic rights and economic responsibilities, social relevance.

As problems of human and natural ecology mount up, there is growing in mainstream economics the conception of economics for economics sake. The tendency is to see economics as an autonomous discipline isolated from other sciences, and yet dominating all other social sciences. No matter what concerned people within and without the economics profession maintain, the tendency is to neglect those concerns because mainstream economics has an unstoppable inner force of its own that makes it impossible to change course. This paper assumes that this tendency is due not to the will of any individual economist but to the sheer power of their tools of economic analysis. The action is involuntary. The process is mechanical (*cf PAER*).

The process is not without consequences. Economic theory has lost control of itself. Perhaps no one has made the case stronger than Alan Blinder

(1999), who has said: "…too much of what young scholars write these days is 'theoretical drivel, mathematically elegant but not about anything real.'" As a direct consequence, economic theory has become splintered into various schools, which vie for their own preferred policies. Because of the current disarray, monetary policy has largely been left to the bankers; fiscal policy to the politicians; and hardly anyone speaks of labor or land or industrial policy any longer. In a word, by becoming detached from reality, both economic theory and policy risk becoming socially ineffective-which does not mean that economic practices are not causing social consequences of their own.

This paper offers a set of new tools that is capable of changing this course of action. Through these tools social relevance reveals itself as an integral part of the constitution of economic theory, policy, and practice. To be specified at the outset, the new tools do not reject but incorporate the old tools of analysis. Using planes and solids in space, in addition to points and lines, economic theory automatically encompasses a larger social reality and returns to the fold of socially relevant sciences with authority to suggest desirable policies and practices.

While the proposed tools in economic theory are the result of forty years of analysis published in Gorga (1982, 2002), desirable policies and practices are distilled from a program of action presented in Gorga (1959, 1964, 1987, 1991a, 1994, 1997, 1999, 2002, and 2007). More extensive treatments can be found in the writings of Benjamin Franklin, Henry George, Louis D. Brandeis, and Louis O. Kelso-with their works, necessarily all their works, read in rapid succession and not any of them as a stand-alone effort. Standing alone, these works are open to debilitating objections. Together, they become an impregnable fortress.

TOOLS TO CONTROL ECONOMIC THEORY

Mainstream economic theory is an impressive intellectual construction with its own internal logic. Its structure is a bastion impervious to any external influence; it has become a mathematical science, and as such it is autonomous of any influence that does not enter into its logical structure. The intellectual apparatus of mainstream economic theory, once deconstructed, revolves around the following tool kit, which we propose to preserve and to build upon.

Existing Tool Kit

As everyone knows, economics is built on the theory of supply and demand. The demand of most everything increases as its price decreases; and the supply of everything increases as its price increases. This is the bare structure of most theories in economics, from the theory of growth to the theory of money. To appreciate the full force of this method of analysis one needs to realize that the lines of supply and demand represent sets of numbers-in turn derived from functions of two variables, prices and costs-and then one must see those schedules in movement. As they move up or down, right or left, they meet each other at different points on the Cartesian grid and determine a specific equilibrium of prices and quantities offered and accepted of any item of wealth in the market, from bread to gold. The basic characteristics of this framework of analysis become evident upon reflection. The focus of attention is on the market exchange; all that goes on before or after the exchange lies outside the purview of the analyst. The mainstream economist qua economist can only analyze, forecast, and report on present or likely future tendencies toward equilibrium of items of wealth that are offered in the market in exchange for other items of wealth, be they currency or pet rocks. The consequences that follow from market exchanges lie mostly outside the purview of this framework of analysis. Is the production of items being exchanged in the market causing physical damage, or moral depravation? Is the distribution of ownership rights over items being exchanged causing a concentration of wealth into too few hands? Is the consumption of items being exchanged causing ecological disaster? These are all familiar questions that are at the heart of the economist's concern. Yet, they can at best be acknowledged by the economist, but they will unavoidably be dismissed as belonging to other fields of analysis such as politics, ecology, morality, and the law, fields that lie outside the expertise and control of the economist.

The analysis becomes more complex daily by the sheer weight of accumulated data; hence equations multiply, econometric applications become more sophisticated, and theorems concerning the characteristics of economic relationships become more and more subtle; indeed, there now seems to be a model for every economic activity-and, lately, for many non-economic activities as well; and if the information is missing or it does not quite fit the case, there is the stand-by option of "as if" assumptions. Impressive as these techniques are, beyond all refinements in the state of the art of mainstream economic analysis, most economists admit to its basic limitations; not only that, they also admit that economic theory has been in a state of crisis at least since the publication of Keynes' *General Theory* in 1936. (What did Keynes say is a question that has plagued the profession ever since.) Three of the most recent recognitions of the crisis span the arc from acknowledgment of the limits of mainstream economics (Mankiw 2006) to criticism about the relevance of mainstream economic theory (Manicas 2007) to the belief that economic theory has improved and that it is expected to improve over time (Warsh 2006).

As the history of minor and major theoretical revolutions and counter-revolutions proves, economists are ready to try nearly any stop-gap measure to resolve the crisis-provided the proposed measure does not affect the structure of the theory. This position is non-negotiable; and it is not the purpose of this paper to negotiate it. What is presented for discussion is a far simpler proposition: if we want more comprehensive and more accurate results, we need different tools of analysis. In addition to points and lines, we shall be using planes and solids in space: at first, only rectangles and spheres.

The consequences of this transformation are far-reaching. Rather than attempting to create an improved mainstream theory, we shall incorporate its vital and functioning core into a new framework of analysis which, for a number of consilient reasons, this writer likes to call Concordian economics: as we will see below, the structure makes room for the perspective of each one of the various schools dominating today's economic analysis; it opens its doors to inputs from various other intellectual disciplines; and it extends itself in a seamless web to cover economic policies and economic practices.

New Tools in Economic Theory

Through laborious logico-mathematical steps (Gorga 2002: 41-158), one obtains a restructure of mainstream economic theory (Gorga 1982) and its gradual transformation into Concordian economics. While the book presents a description of that transformation with its resultant new mathematical models (Gorga 2002: 25, 38, 71, 74-6, 121-25, 129-37, 153-58, 168-70, 264, 303-20), the present paper reproduces the core of that ground with primary assistance from geometry; thereafter, it extends the analysis to cover economic policy as well as economic practices for implementation of selected economic policies.

The key results of Concordian economic analysis are these. In order to eliminate a set of innate logical contradictions at the very foundation of economic analysis, the nexus between saving and investment is broken and it is replaced by the complementary relation between Investment defined as all productive wealth and Saving defined as all nonproductive wealth-a term that is better replaced with Hoarding.[1] The analysis starts anew on the basis of the proposition that Investment is Income minus Hoarding. Furthermore, since money and financial instruments are not wealth, but only represent wealth, in macro, as distinguished from microeconomics, one cannot add money to real wealth.[2] The two entities have to be kept separate. And then the question arises: What is the relationship between the two? From Aristotle to the Doctors of the Church there was no doubt as to the answer to this question. During this long stretch of time, much economic analysis was built on the equivalence of money and goods in the exchange. It was the distinction between the two and their linkage in the relation of equivalence that provided the objective base for the determination of conditions of justice in the exchange of wealth. If we accept this answer, to satisfy well-known requirements of the principle of equivalence, we search for a third element to link monetary and real wealth together and we find it in the set of rules and regulations that in every society governs the distribution of ownership rights over real and monetary wealth-and we do not stray away from pure economic theory, because we are presented with the monetary value of those rights. The following diagram (Gorga 2002: 36, 163, 314) incorporates these results; it represents the integration of these values on one plane, in this fashion:

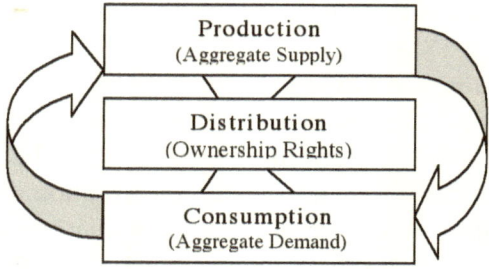

Figure 1. The Economic Process

In this figure, the values of "production", namely the values of all real wealth produced over a specified unit of time are assembled into one category of thought that is recognized as aggregate supply. (It is to be noticed that this unit is "pure" because it contains only stocks of real wealth and no monetary wealth. It is also to be noted that in a more complete treatment this value ought to be observed from the point of view of demand as well as supply: thus we ought to have an analysis of the demand and supply of the production of all real wealth.) We follow the same procedure for the values of monetary wealth, thus firmly separating real wealth from monetary wealth, and we call the result "consumption" or aggregate demand. (Ditto for the treatment of all monetary values, which here are not observed from the point of view of supply: The question of the quantity of monetary values created lies outside the scope of this presentation.) We finally repeat the procedure for the aggregate values of ownership rights over real and monetary wealth, and we call the result "distribution" of ownership rights. (At this juncture we assume that the values of ownership rights over real wealth are identical to the values over monetary wealth). In sum, we have enlarged our field of observation from points and lines to planes and interactions among planes; and, rather than leaving the question of the interaction between demand and supply open (cf. Klein 1970: 143), we have continuously specified-and distinguished one from the other-the demand and supply of (a) real goods, (b) monetary instruments, and (c) values of ownership rights over real and monetary wealth.

Figure 1 reads as follows. When real goods and services pass from producers to consumers, monetary instruments of a corresponding value pass from consumers to producers. Then one cycle of the economic process is completed-and it is accompanied by the silent exchange of values of ownership rights over monetary and real wealth. Both money and goods change hands. The unit of account can be the economy of one person, one nation, or the world. In macroeconomics, the exchange occurs neither between two insignificant commodities (*cf.* Schumpeter 1936) as in microeconomics nor between any two forms of financial instruments as in the economics of Wall Street. In macroeconomics, fully respecting the laws of supply and demand the total production of real wealth is exchanged for the total availability of financial resources-as in Keynes' principle of effective demand (see Brady 1996). Finally, in this figure the exchange visibly occurs under a regimen of social and legal relationships: ownership is apportioned at the moment of creation of wealth; and only owners can legally exchange wealth.

An effective way to analyze the instantaneous relationships captured by Figure 1 is to reduce it all to the economics of only one person. A person who snaps the apple from a tree, vs. gathering seeds, for instance, while respecting as always the rules of supply and demand commits an act of production. This person automatically apportions the ownership of the apple to the self, which means that this person is legally empowered, as it were, to sell the apple to the self. Thereafter, this person is free to eat the apple-or sell it to others. One of the merits of Figure 1 is that it describes the economic process as a whole. Everything is instantaneously related to everything else. Thus we run away from the shattered world of the schools and go back to the world of Classical economists who knew that economics is composed of the integration of Production, Distribution, and Consumption of wealth. This integration can be made more specific by a more extensive and updated reading of the terms, along these lines: The Theory of Production-namely a pure and robust production function-is concerned with the production of real goods and services (as might be studied by Supply-Side economists); the Theory of Distribution is concerned with the distribution of the value of ownership rights over real and monetary wealth (as might be studied by Institutionalists); and the Theory of Consumption is concerned with the consumption-or expenditure-of monetary, *i.e.,* financial instruments (as might be studied by Demand-Side economists). More importantly, by recognizing that Figure 1 is the flat image of a sphere we bring the mathematics and geometry of economics up to the standards that prevail among modern engineers and scientists (see, *e.g.,* Thompson 1986: 36), namely:

Synthetic Model of the Economic System as a Whole
(From Gorga 1991b)

$$p\bullet = fp(p,d,c)$$
$$d\bullet = fd(p,d,c)$$
$$c\bullet = fc(p,d,c)$$

where

p• stands for rate of change in total production
d• for rate of change in the values of distribution of ownership rights
c• for rate of change in total expenditure.

And, most important for our immediate purposes, we can see that the theory of distribution of income and wealth now occupies a very central position in economics. All that relates to the distribution of ownership of income and wealth becomes an immediate and integral concern of economic theory-no longer an afterthought or an issue placed at the margins of economic science. Related issues of social relevance of economics can no longer be shunned aside by the economist on the assumption that they are external to economic theory. These are indeed issues that lie at the very core of economic theory; and one does not stray away from mathematical and quantifiable theory either. What is to be measured and evaluated is the economic value of ownership rights over income and wealth-and the different economic effects of different patterns of distribution of income and wealth. Decisions relative to these issues are taken during the very process of production and exchange of wealth; they are not something to be concerned with only after the more impellent problems of production and exchange are resolved, as assumed in Keynesian economics and, mutatis mutandis, in mainstream economics, see, *e.g.,* Klein ([1947] 1968: 187). The concern about the social relevance of economics-as all Institutionalists have devoutly wished-is now brought within the purview of the economist.

Issues of distribution of economic values of income and wealth are not givens; they lie at the very core of the economic process and are determined by the inner workings of this process. On Mars the situation might be different; on earth, people create not only real or physical wealth-they also assign values to this wealth. Indeed, it is economists (and accountants) who, assisted by the laws of supply and demand, assign these values as best they can. Lawyers only validate these statements by transforming them in negotiable legal instruments that are called ownership rights. These rights might belong to an individual person, to a corporation, or to the state; but they legally belong to someone. And an exchange of real wealth for monetary wealth involves at the same time an exchange of the value of ownership rights over real and monetary wealth. It is thus that, no matter the disclaimer by many economists, economic values are created and are created at the very core of the economic process.

TOOLS TO CONTROL ECONOMIC POLICY

Having discovered that the distribution of ownership rights over income and wealth is an integral part of economic theory, the question becomes: What are the tools to obtain the desired pattern of distribution of income and wealth? This is the eminent question of economic policy. Economic theory tells us that, once this pattern is set, most other questions of economic policy are automatically settled. The answer to the question is well known.

Existing Tool Kit

Even though the historic roots of economics lie in moral philosophy, economists have lately assumed that they have nothing to contribute to the discussion concerning the selection of patterns of distribution of income and wealth. They have left the field to lawyers, ethicists, philosophers, sociologists, and political scientists. Mainstream economists believe that they do not have-and, what is more important, they ought not to have-any tools to control the pattern of distribution of income and wealth. Mainstream economists assume that this is a given, namely a determination that is and ought to be left to society as a whole. Economics, as pure science, as an autonomous mathematical science, is supposed to analyze the effects of various societal decisions, but not to intervene in those decisions. It is a direct consequence of this assumption that economic theory is fast becoming socially irrelevant.

Under these conditions, the discussion on economic policy falls into a trap. The discussion becomes the property of various schools of economics, each purporting the benefits of its own dictates and none being able to convince the other schools of the validity of its positions.

We do not need to put a step on this slippery slope. Once it is established that the pattern of distribution of income and wealth is an integral part of economic theory, the analysis is restricted to this question: How can we translate economic theory into economic policy? In the paragraphs below we will offer a set of new/old tools for consideration. This set calls for the construction of the theory of *economic* justice, and therefore economists will discover that they have much to contribute to it. This is the high road to re-establish social relevance to economics.

Proposed Tools to Control Economic Policy

A mere glance at the history of economic thought makes us glean this proposition: The transmission belt that for millennia carried economic theory into economic policy is the doctrine of economic justice. While remaining astonishingly constant from Aristotle to the Doctors of the Church (see, *e.g.,* Wood 2002: 83), this understanding allowed for continuous adaptations to the circumstances of the moment. The doctrine of economic justice was divided into two planks: distributive and commutative justice. Distributive justice guided rules and regulations that govern the division of wealth as it is created; commutative justice guided rules and regulations that govern the transferal of wealth between buyers and sellers at the moment of the exchange. While the Doctors of the Church left much room for discretion in the determination of distributive justice to the parties involved in the economic process, they reached a firm and revolutionary conclusion about the dictates of commutative justice. The commutation of wealth, namely the exchange, occurs in accordance with principles of justice, they discovered, only if it reflects a free market price: a price determined in a market that is not dominated by either governmental or private monopolistic forces (see, *e.g.,* Schumpeter 1954: 98-99).

While this formula appears simple, it envelops great complexities. With it, the Doctors of the Church unified the social requirements of freedom with those of morality in economics; and it was the exercise of morality that yielded freedom. The application of this formula created the essential conditions for the enterprise system to be as free as it could be at the time.

Over time, this ordered set of priorities was twisted around and its power dissolved. Through insistence on unfettered economic freedom, the unity of freedom and morality-with its inherent social relevance-was shattered and the doctrine of economic justice was lost in the fog of time.

Truth to tell, the dissolution of the doctrine of economic justice was facilitated by the fact that it was never presented with a visible head. People with direct or indirect access to land and natural resources participated in the economic process as a matter of fact through well-established privileges and as a consequence of unspoken sets of rights (indirectly, access to land and natural resources was secured through the commons: for millennia the safety valve to preserve the dignity of the poor). Hence, it never occurred to Aristotle or any of the Doctors of the Church to make explicit the requirements of a third plank that might be called participative justice (Gorga 1999, 2007). For a great variety of reasons, those conditions are no longer in existence. Today, one has to beg in order to participate in the economic process. And if one does not take part in it, one is marginalized; one is shunted to the margins of society. Hence the plank of participative justice, as it is increasingly recognized from many quarters, must be explicitly formulated. When participative justice is added to the other two planks, the doctrine is completed and transformed into the theory of economic justice. Once that is done, one is presented with a framework of analysis that can be represented in this fashion:

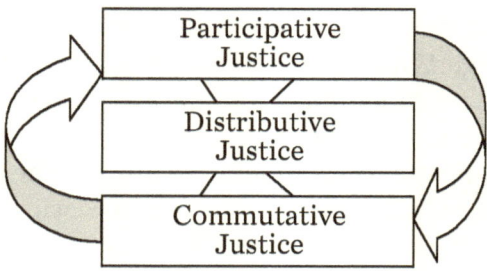

Figure 2. Economic Justice

Figure 2 reads as follows. Participation in the economic process is a matter of justice, because only men and women who participate in the production of wealth are entitled to the distribution of ownership of a share of the wealth created through their participation.[3] A just commutation of wealth, a just exchange, is implicit in the very distribution of wealth in accordance with one's participation; but, of course, the principle of commutative justice extends itself to cover the exchange of wealth just created for other wealth existing on the market. It is in accordance with these objective principles that the pattern of distribution of current income and wealth is and ought to be determined. Economists can render these calculations very precise.

But economists have much broader tasks than these. Figure 2 is a mirror image of Figure 1. If the distribution of ownership rights is an inherent part of the economic process, as we have seen in the previous section, economic justice becomes a natural extension of economic theory. Indeed, one can just as soon separate economic theory from economic justice as one can separate a person from her shadow. (The forced separation of these two entities has ineluctable consequences of its own that ought to be of great interest to the investigative powers of the economist.) Given this condition, a minimum set of questions to be asked by economists in the formulation and evaluation of any economic policy might be: Does the proposed policy favor participation in the creation of wealth? Does it allow for a fair distribution of the wealth thus created? Does it allow for a fair transfer of wealth from one person or group to another? Much could be said on these issues, but since much is already well known, we shall shun away from broad and elaborate discussions of these issues.

The wisdom of staying away from broad and elaborate discussions, however, does not necessarily require staying away from the specifics of the case. The specific question is: How can we transfer the principles of economic justice into the complexities of the modern economy?

Needless to say, this is a question that is not formally and comprehensively raised in mainstream theory. This is a question that arises naturally and forcefully within the context of the structure of Concordian economics.

TOOLS TO CONTROL ECONOMIC PRACTICES

In the section on economic theory we have seen how does the economic system create wealth, how its value is determined by economists and accountants, and how its value is then transformed in ownership rights by lawyers. In the section on economic policy we have observed how economic justice determines the apportionment of those ownership rights. In this section we shall observe how the economic system operates in practice.

Lack of an Existing Tool Kit

"High" mainstream theory is silent on the practices of economics. This neglect is not due to chance; rather, it is due to the assumption that, since economic practices are determined by society at large and are supposedly controlled by allied social disciplines, they lie outside the economist's field of expertise. Indeed, having abandoned the field to lawyers, and ethicists, and philosophers, and sociologists, and political scientists, mainstream economists have become passive takers of a proposition that lies at the very core of the issue. This is the proposition that present ownership rights provide practical rules for the distribution of future ownership rights. The proposition has long legs, because it determines the pattern of future distribution of income and wealth. Economists observe every day the manifold negative consequences of this belief, but feel powerless to even address the issues. This is another juncture at which, by taking themselves out of the discussion, economists are threatening to make economics a socially irrelevant discipline.

To regain their power, economists have only to look at it as an economic, rather than a legal, political, or moral issue. If they do that, they discover that their assumptions are faulty. The error is elementary. The reasoning is circular. In order to enter and to break this circular form of argumentation, namely that present property rights determine future property rights, economists need to remember that property rights are pieces of paper: a piece of paper does not-and cannot-create real wealth. It is not even the *exercise* of property rights that creates real wealth. Property rights are a bundle of rights that link human beings to things. Their current owners may wish as hard as they can, it is not in the nature of property rights to create wealth.

It is not the use of property rights, but the use of property-namely, the use of real goods and services-that creates new wealth. The distinction is fundamental. The discussion is shifted away from the abstract legal field on to a concrete field. The discussion is focused on the observation of the economic reality. The use of real goods and services to create new wealth is infused, not by property rights, but by the exercise of economic power. To an economic power corresponds an economic right. As specified below, temporally, logically, economically, and legally, economic rights precede property rights. Economic rights are the generators, the fathers and the mothers, of property rights. The nature of economic rights becomes clear when the two rights, economic rights and property rights, are observed as separate and distinct entities, and then both rights are placed in contraposition with entitlements. The three terms are often used as synonyms. They are not. As specified in Gorga (1999),

> First, the content of these three entities is different. The object of property rights are *marketable things,* tangible or intangible things such as material goods and services. The object of entitlements are *human needs,* from food to shelter to health. The object of economic rights are *economic needs.* Second, the legal form of these three entities is different. Property rights are *concrete legal* titles over existing wealth; economic rights are *abstract legal* claims over future wealth; and entitlements are *moral* claims on wealth that legally belong to others. Finally, the quantity that they measure is variable. While both property rights and entitlements relate to existing wealth, and therefore a necessarily finite quantity, economic rights relate to future wealth, an unknown and elastic-if not a potentially infinite-quantity.

Economically, and consequently legally, real wealth is created by the exercise of economic rights-indeed, economic rights and economic responsibilities, as we shall see. Hence economists are fully entitled to extend their competence to the field of economic rights and economic responsibilities. Economists will discover that the field is wholly within their range of expertise and responsibility. At the end of this journey, economists shall be able to offer to lawyers, ethicists, and philosophers, as well as political scientists and politicians, this proposition: Future ownership rights are determined, not by property rights, but by economic rights-indeed, they are determined by economic rights and economic responsibilities. Thus the closed circuit that at present imprisons economic theory, the proposition that property rights beget property rights, is broken. Economists are in charge of economic issues.

New Tools to Control Economic Practices

The transmission belt that carries principles of economic justice into the complexity of modern economic life, and shapes objective guidelines for the formulation and evaluation of just economic policies is the presence of economic rights and economic responsibilities (ERs&ERs), both lodged in the same person at the same time. These two conditions need to be clarified. Economic rights and responsibilities need to be lodged into the same person, otherwise one does not follow an economic discourse in which everything is strictly related to everything else; rather, one follows escapism: if my father, my uncle, or the state is responsible for my welfare, we are lost, as Keynes used to say, "in a haze where nothing is clear and everything is possible" (Keynes 1936: 292). The second condition is equally important. Economic rights are rooted, not in abstract morality, but in our own concrete economic responsibilities (*cf.* Gorga 1999).

ERs&ERs come forward in response to the well-known requirements of the factors of production identified by Classical economists as land, capital, and labor-with the addition of a modern distinction between financial and physical capital. Guided by these economic needs, our focus of attention is on the satisfaction of the plank of participative justice; successive iterations that are mostly skipped in this presentation would reveal that the same rights and responsibilities satisfy also the requirements of the planks of distributive justice and commutative justice. A minimal set of economic rights and corresponding responsibilities is as follows:

1. *We all have the right of access to land and natural resources.* This is a natural right. It belongs to us just in virtue of our humanness. Land and natural resources are our original commons. They belong to us all. This is an essential right, because without the possibility of exercising it, we are deprived of the possibility of participating in the economic process. And without this participation, we are marginalized; we are made dependent on the good will of others. The most direct way of securing this right in the complexity of the modern world is neither through squatting nor through expropriation; rather, it is through the exercise of **the responsibility to pay taxes** for the exclusive use of those resources that are under our com-

mand-with a corresponding reduction of taxes on buildings and man-made improvements on the land. The exercise of the responsibility to pay taxes on land has a double function: It secures our right to the use of the resources that are under our command and it also makes room for others to access land and natural resources that they need. Land taxation is the economic bridge between hoarding, namely the accumulation of idle land, and the right of access to that land with its natural resources. Paying taxes on the value of land and natural resources gradually encourages dis-hoarding, hence it lowers the price of the land, and correspondingly opens up the resources of that land to all those who need them and can make use of them. Worrisome hoarding is especially that which occurs both downtown and in the belt surrounding major cities and towns. It is to leapfrog over this belt that people go to the suburbs in search for affordable land, thus creating overstretched lines of communication and protection and overlong commuting lines-with consequent waste of fuel that overtaxes non-renewable resources, the ozone layer, the pocketbook, and the nervous system. Paying taxes on land value is a most fair form of taxation, because it implies returning to the community part of the value that is created, not by the individual owner, but by the community. Land that sits idle does not produce income, true; yet, it produces capital appreciation over time: Rare is the case of capital loss; and even when that occurs, the relative loss tends to be smaller than the loss on other assets. (To see how this pair of ERs&ERs meets also the requirements of distributive and commutative justice, let us simply consider that, if one avoids taxes, the total tax load is not going to be distributed fairly among the population. And if one avoids taxes, one obtains something-*i.e.,* private control over a quantity of resources-for which one does not offer proportionate compensation to the rest of the community.)

2. *We all have the right of access to national credit.* Since national credit is the power of a nation to create money, and since the value of money is given by the value of wealth left over by past generations and the creativity of every person in a nation, national credit is the last frontier, the last commons. Without access to credit today one is made economically impotent. Worse, since this advantage is granted to the privileged few, it is automatically denied to the majority of the population who are henceforth condemned to pay a higher rate of interest, if they obtain credit at all. Of course, such a loan should be extended only on the basis of **the responsibility to repay the loan**. And these loans will have a high chance of being

repaid because they ought to be issued at cost and issued exclusively to individually owned enterprises, Employee Stock Ownership Plans (ESOPs), and cooperatives, as well as states and municipalities, and issued exclusively for capital formation, namely for the creation of new wealth-not to buy financial paper, consumer goods or goods to be hoarded or to cover administrative expenses of states and municipalities. Capital credit liberates people, while consumer credit enslaves them.

3. *We all have the right to the fruits of our labor.* This right should not be limited to the right to obtain only a wage. It should be extended to cover the other major fruit of economic growth over time: capital appreciation-as well as being subject to capital loss, of course. The only justification for reserving capital appreciation for stockholders, the owners of a corporation, and excluding workers from it, can be found in the fact that loans are given only to owners of past wealth (the Catch-22 of today's economic reasoning: "save and invest and you too can become rich"-as if this proposition were either economically feasible or ecologically sustainable.) But from now on this right can be extended to people who do not have prior wealth through the right of access to national credit-especially by legally transforming workers into owners through individually owned enterprises, Employee Stock Ownership Plans (ESOPs), and cooperatives. Of course, this full right should be extended only in correspondence with **the responsibility to offer services** of value equivalent to projected compensation. And there will be an outpouring of such services because, while in a command and control economy workers are requested to check their brain at the factory gates, in a socially responsible economy-an economy in which rights are exercised on the basis of responsibilities-workers/owners are legally, socially, and psychologically empowered to exercise their brain fully at their work post.

4. *We all have the right to protect our wealth.* This right seems to be universally accepted, except in one case that matters most: in the case of the trustification process, the process used especially after the Civil War in the United States to create corporate trusts and repeated in a hundred subtle variations ever since. (People feel free, not only to acquire shares of the stock of one corporation, but free to use that stock to acquire another whole corporation by all forms of trusts, mergers, and acquisition. The very idea of the corporation, forever a public entity, has thus been privatized and monetized.) There are two ways in which corporations grow: One is through internal growth, and this approach ought to be protected in no un-

certain terms; the other is through external purchase and, with limits, this manifestation ought to be prohibited in no uncertain terms. Why? Because this prohibition is the only certain way to protect the wealth of present owners. And if it is assumed that most stockholders of the modern corporation are happy to have their shares bought and sold on the market, it must be granted that growth-by-purchase takes wealth away from workers who have contributed to create that value-and many times, in the trustification process, lose their work site as well. All in the name of efficiency-a misnomer that stands for private financial gain generated at the expense of shifting costs onto the shoulders of the community at large. Of course, this right ought to be purchased only at the cost of **the responsibility to respect the wealth of others**. These are two-way streets. We cannot even attempt to restrain the Pac-Man economy, while we use Pac-Man instruments.

These economic rights and responsibilities can be exercised by anyone who does not only want to receive economic justice, but also wants to grant economic justice to others. Indeed, these are the essential conditions for the establishment of economic justice, as well as the establishment of a free enterprise system, in the modern world. As a consequence of the dynamics of the implementation of these four marginal changes in our current practices, economic freedom will be expanded to embrace all who want to subject themselves to the rigors of the economic process-and then the few remaining hard cases can be easily taken care of by charity. No. There is no compulsion in any of the above suggestions. The landowner can pay more taxes and control more land or can escape the tax levy altogether by reducing land ownership to zero; the applicant for a national loan can escape the constraints suggested for access to national credit by tapping into private capital markets; the worker can escape the responsibilities of ownership by vying for a job rather than an equity position; and the owner of physical capital can escape the constraints implicit in the proposed anti-trust policy by remaining below the trigger of an agreed-upon threshold for growth-by-purchase prohibition. This prohibition should apply to the largest corporations first and be gradually expanded to include eventually all except, let us say, corporations engaged in intrastate or regional commerce.

Intellectually, the proposed economic rights and economic responsibilities perform functions outlined in the conception of "general abstract rules" by Hayek (1960: 153), the "original position" by Rawls (1971: 12, 72,

136, 538), the "reverse theory" by Nozick (1974: 238), and the "Principle of Generic Consistency" by Gewirth (1985: 19); practically, they will function as Gladwell's (2000) "tipping points". Ultimately, it was a poet, Vincent Ferrini (2002), who caught the essence of economic rights and economic responsibilities by identifying their ability to provide "the answers to universal poverty and the anxieties of the affluent."

Operating as tipping points in our *modus vivendi*, ERs&ERs will set in motion a process of interdependence that respects the reality of economic affairs, and the reality of human relationships. Recognizing that most people and most businesses always act morally, the increasing number of "bad apples" that at times seem to receive all the attention (and envious support) of a superficial intellectual world will be recognized as dangerous exceptions, perhaps ostracized, but certainly no longer applauded. Once the tendencies of these people are kept in check, all wealth will be distributed, not equally-that is meaningless utopianism-but fairly. The assurance for this result resides in the transformation of the current social contract into a legal contract: when landowners pay their share of land taxes, they will sell their hoards and access to land and natural resources will automatically be opened up for most people; when people will get access to national credit, many will become independent entrepreneurs; when workers are transformed into owners, they will have the legal tools to demand a fair distribution of income; when growth-by-purchase will mostly become a forbidden activity, most corporations and most employee/owners will preserve their independence. These measures, by consistently curbing the excesses of the few for a period of at least ten years, will cumulatively lead to a fair distribution of income and wealth. To reassure ourselves of this outcome, let us comprehensively look at the issues from another point of view. If land owners were to use their possessions of land and natural resources efficiently (with efficiency measured through lower private capitalization and higher effective demand), would there be such wanting in the world? If national credit were made available to all entrepreneurs at cost, would we not translate the immanent reservoir of creative powers into economically profitable ventures? If workers were transformed into worker/owners, would we not increase our extant productive capacity incommensurably? If corporate growth-by-purchase-with accompanying translation of that economic power into corruption of our political system-were curbed, would we not obtain less concentration of economic power into a few hands?

All four ERs&ERs naturally lead to a fairer distribution of income than prevails today. Eventually, with a fair distribution of income and wealth, there will no longer be any need for redistributive programs, which are an expression of double utopianism (first, people as if living in la-la land are allowed to accumulate much, no matter how; and then they are expected to peacefully discharge their ill-gotten wealth). Preserving their current wealth, the rich will grow richer at a steady but slower pace; and the poor will no longer be poor, because they will have all they need. Lacking fuel at both ends, violent oscillations in the business cycle will be abated.

We will thus recover the essential truth of economics. This is the truth that there are two conditions of growth: economic freedom and economic justice, as concrete expressions of freedom and morality. Both are essential. The relationship between the two is quite clear: While freedom does not necessarily bring justice with it, justice unavoidably brings freedom. One can abuse freedom by denying freedom to others, one can never abuse justice. Hence, the initial condition of freedom for all is proof positive of the existence of economic justice in the land. This is economics that is socially relevant. And the relevance is not an afterthought. The relevance is implicit. The social import of economic theory is realized when the distribution of ownership rights is seen as an integral part of its constitution; and the social import of economic justice and economic rights and responsibilities is simply stated: We must prevent all foreseeable injustices from occurring. Once an injustice has occurred, there is nothing that can be done to undo the dastard deed. This is the bosom of realism.

One last question: Is the proposed program of action the latest expression of utopianism? The curt answer is: No. Utopianism has consistently been based on the wishful thinking of a single person. The proposed program of action results from filling in the gaps of a millenarian train of thought that, in a seamless web, extends itself at least from morality to economic theory and from there-through economic justice-to economic policy and practice. Utopianism promises immediate results, as if by magic. This proposed program of action asks for concerted, protracted effort. Whatever life Utopianism has, it is based on the fanatical following of a small group of people who try to force it upon the will of the multitudes. The proposed program of action is expected to be readily understood and spontaneously implemented by the multitudes.

CONCLUSION

The lament that economics lacks social relevance assumes many forms, but these are mostly centered on the treatment of issues of distribution of income and wealth. We have found that these issues are not even investigated by economists today because they assume that they lie beyond the field of economics. Hence, by placing this issue at the very core of economics, we have given back social relevance first to economic theory, then to economic policy, and finally to economic practices. Without ever abandoning the field of economics, we have established a continuity of discourse between three stepping stones in economic analysis. We have followed this line of reasoning. Since money and financial instruments are not wealth, but only represent wealth, in macroeconomics one cannot add money to real wealth. The two have to be kept separate. This condition raises the question about the relation between money and real wealth. As in the economics tradition from Aristotle to the Doctors of the Church, we have recognized that money and real wealth must be equivalent in value. But equivalence is a formal relation among three terms. What is the third term? The third term that links money to real wealth is the economic value of ownership rights; hence, we have presented a restructure of economic theory that reflects the need to study not only the monetary economy but also the real and the legal economy at the same time. From this new framework of analysis, novel answers are given to the question: How is the distribution of ownership rights achieved today, and how "should" it be achieved? An investigation of the economic, rather than the legal, moral, or philosophical aspects of this question leads to the transformation of an age-old doctrine into the theory of economic justice and to the discovery that the creation of wealth is achieved, not through the exercise of property rights, which are static, but through the exercise of well-defined economic rights and economic responsibilities, which take care of the dynamic needs of the economic world.

FOOTNOTES

Every step of the way in Concordian economics, decisions are taken following relentlessly the dictates of fundamental rules of logic. For instance, analysis reveals that since current definitions of saving and investment contain items that are productive (farmed land) and items that are nonproductive (fallow land) of further wealth, both saving and investment respect neither the principle of identity nor the principle of non-contradiction and therefore they cannot be equivalent to each other, as they ought to be for their relation of equality to be formally valid (see, e.g., Allen 1970: 748).

The separation of real wealth from monetary wealth is an integral part of the transformation of Keynes' model into the series of mathematical models that provide structure to Concordian economics. This is a procedure that, outlined with the help of geometry (Gorga 2002: 32-37), starts with the enlargement of the definition of consumption from expenditure on consumer goods to spending in all its manifestations (*ibid.*, 139-50), passes through the definition of money (*ibid.*, 222) and the monetary formulation of the Flows Model (*ibid.*, 309-12), and ends with the establishment of the equivalence of the processes of production, distribution, and consumption (*ibid.*, 312-19). The description of these three processes and the economic process as a whole form the substance of Concordian economic theory (*ibid.*, 159-234).

What to do with the widow, the orphan, and the handicapped is a moral issue. Economics does not do anything for them. Indeed, as proved by the history of the world, even in the richest of the communities at the height of the business cycle, economics cannot do anything for them. Their number can become so overwhelming, their needs so vast, that even charity becomes powerless. Economics cannot do anything for the widow, the orphan, and the handicapped-unless, of course, they own stocks and bonds. But then they are not poor; they do not need any assistance through morality. They are capitalists and by the virtue of being capitalists, by the virtue of owning the machines, they participate-through remote control of the machines-by right in the economic process.

REFERENCES

Allen, R. G. D. (1970) *Mathematical Economic,* 2nd ed., London and New York: Macmillan, St. Martin's.

Blinder, A. (1999) Quoted in "Students Seek Some Reality Amid the Math Of Economics," by Michael M. Weinstein, *The New York Times*, September 18, 1999, pp. A17, A19.

Brady, M.E. (1996) "A Comparison-Contrast of J.M. Keynes' Mathematical Modeling Approach in *The General Theory* with some of his *General Theory* interpreters, especially J.E. Meade", *History of Economics Review* (25): 129-158.

Fanfani, A. (2003) *Catholicism, Protestantism, and Capitalism*, Norfolk, VA: IHS Press.

Ferrini, V. (2002) "Gorga worthy of note", *Gloucester Daily Times*. December 11, A6.

Gewirth, A. (1985) "Economic Justice: Concepts and Criteria," in K. Kipnis and D. T. Meyers, (eds.) *Economic Justice: Private Rights and Public Responsibilities*, Totowa, N.J.: Rowman & Allanheld.

Gladwell, M. (2000) *The Tipping Point: How Little Things Can Make a Big Difference,* NY: Little, Brown & Company.

Gorga, C. (1959) *A Synthesis of the Political Thought of Louis D. Brandeis.* Graduation Dissertation University of Naples.

Gorga, C. (1964) "Not Simply a National Fund, but a Stabilization and Development Fund", *Mondo Economico* 19(14): 14-16.

Gorga, C. (1982) "The Revised Keynes' Model" (an Abstract), *Atlantic Economic Journal* 10(3): 52.

Gorga, C. and Kurland, N. G. (1987) "The Productivity Standard: A True Golden Standard," in *Every Worker An Owner: A Revolutionary Free Enterprise Challenge to Marxism,* D. M. Kurland (ed.) Washington, DC: Center for Economic and Social Justice.

Gorga, C. (1991a) "The Dynamics of the Economic System," unpub. man.

Gorga, C. (1991b) "Bold New Directions in Politics and Economics," *The Human Economy Newsletter,* 12(1): 3-6, 12.

Gorga, C. 1994. "Four Economic Rights: Social Renewal Through Economic

Justice for All," *Social Justice Rev.* 85(1-2): 3-6.

Gorga, C. and Weeks, S. B. (1997) "Fisheries Renewal: A Renewal of the Soul of Business," *Catholic Social Science Rev.* 2: 145-161.

Gorga, C. (1999) "Toward the Definition of Economic Rights," *Journal of Markets and Morality,* 2(1): 88-101.

Gorga, C. (2002) *The Economic Process: An Instantaneous Non-Newtonian Picture,* Lanham, MD. and Oxford: University Press of America.

Gorga, C. (2007) "Economic Justice," in *Catholic Social Thought, Social Science, and Social Policy: An Encyclopedia,* Lanham, MD: Scarecrow Press.

Hayek, F. A. (1960) *The Constitution of Liberty*, Chicago: University of Chicago Press.

Keynes, J. M. (1936) *The General Theory of Employment, Interest, and Money*, NY: Harcourt.

Klein, L. R. (1968 [1947]) *The Keynesian Revolution*, 2nd ed. New York: Macmillan 1968.

Klein, L. R. (1970) "The Use of Econometric Models as a Guide to Economic Policy," in *Selected Readings in Econometrics*. Cambridge and London: MIT Press.

Manicas, P. T. (2007) "Endogenous Growth Theory: The Most Recent 'Revolution' in Economics," *post-autistic economics review* 41:39-53.

Mankiw, N. G. (2006) "The Macroeconomist as Scientist and Engineer," *Journal of Economic Perspectives* 20:29-46.

Nozick, R. (1974) *Anarchy, State, and Utopia*, NY: Basic Books.

Rawls, J. (1971) *A Theory of Justice*, Cambridge, MA: Harvard University Press.

Schumpeter, J. A. (1936) "The general theory of employment, interest and money," *Journal of American Statistical Association* (31): 791-95.

Schumpeter, J. A. (1954) *History of Economic Analysis,* NY: Oxford University Press.

Thompson, J. M. T. (1986) *Nonlinear Dynamics and Chaos, Geometric Methods for Engineers and Scientists,* New York: Wiley.

Warsh, D. (2006) *Knowledge and the Wealth of Nations: A Story of Economic Discovery*, New York: Norton.

Wood, D. (2002) *Medieval Economic Thought*, Cambridge, UK: Cambridge University Press.

ACKNOWLEDGMENTS

This paper is uniquely due to several maieutic interventions, truly beyond the call of duty, by Dr. Wilfred Dolfsma. I also would like to acknowledge a clarification brought to this paper by Godfrey Dunkley. If this paper has become a cogent presentation less exposed to potential debilitating criticism of single points, it is due to innumerable constructive suggestions by two referees of *Forum*. A more detailed background for this paper is contained in "The Economics of Jubilation", an unpublished monograph that has been well received by such a diverse audience as Dr. Michael E. Brady, Dr. John C. Rao, Professor William J. Baumol, and Professor Roger H. Gordon. That work, in turn, is based on a framework of analysis which was greatly assisted for 27 years by Professor Franco Modigliani and 21 years by Professor Meyer L. Burstein, among others.

* Carmine Gorga is a former Fulbright scholar and the recipient of a Council of Europe Scholarship for his dissertation on "The Political Thought of Louis D. Brandeis." Dr. Gorga has transformed the linear world of economic theory into a relational discipline in which everything is related to everything else-internally as well as externally. He was assisted in this endeavor by many people, notably for twenty-seven years by Professor Franco Modigliani, a Nobel laureate in economics from MIT. The resulting work, *The Economic Process: An Instantaneous Non-Newtonian Picture,* was pub-

lished in 2002. During the last few years, Mr. Gorga has concentrated his attention on the requirements for the unification of economic theory and policy. For details, see www.carmine-gorga.us" www.carmine-gorga.us.

Unemployment

Reprinted with permission from *Encyclopedia of Catholic Social Thought, Social Science, and Social Policy* (Lanham, MD: Scarecrow Press, *2007*).

Unemployment is the scourge of the modern age. It is unequivocally a scourge, if you are unemployed and have no other source of income. It is a scourge especially because, in most countries, you are even psychologically assaulted as being lazy.

Unemployment is a scourge for the statistician because there are no safe and secure-i.e., scientific-methods for measuring this condition.

Unemployment is a scourge for the economist because, as Professor Franco Modigliani wrote, "Indeed, the modeling of wage behavior remains to this day the Achilles heel of macroeconomic analysis."[1]

Unemployment is a scourge for the politician because votes are received when the electorate is satisfied. How can an unemployed person be satisfied?

Unemployment is a scourge for the moralist because, in the cacophony of sounds surrounding the technical aspects of the issue, the powers of the moralist are paralyzed. As *Gaudium et Spes* (at 27) did, the moralist can fulminate against the practice of treating workers "as mere tools for profit", but offers no solution.

The Catholic Church has been consistently in search of a just and lasting solution to the scourge of unemployment, and it is fervently hoped that it will eventually find it by picking up threads of its own actions and thought processes.

Back in the Middle Ages, an age intellectually dominated by the Church, if not in ages much older than those, there was no unemployment. All people who needed and wanted to work found a job. Some jobs were more satisfying than others, of course, but that is immaterial. Most land owners did not need to work, because most of the people worked for them. And to the poor was available not only the hand-outs from the monasteries and the hospices, there also was the safety valve of independent work on the commons-the mountains and the oceans. When the commons were enclosed, then unemployment exploded as a new factor in human life: the unemployed were compelled to abandon the villages and gathered in the cities where they had some safety in numbers.

The gallop to unemployment became a stampede ever since joint stock ownership and limited liability made corporations the most common form of business operation. By definition, this form of business enterprise decreases economic independence for the many. Relations become more complex and more impersonal. While the owners of the corporation benefit from economies of scale and the efficiencies of physical capital, employees of the corporation, legally, are not an integral part of the corporation: they are outside contractors who receive a wage in exchange for services performed. The legal relationship ends there.

Whatever capital accumulation occurs over time accrues only to the owners of the corporation.

Thus labor becomes a commodity and the ownership and control of financial capital is concentrated into the hands of the few. One hundred legal and financial practices make this an organic system, impenetrable from the outside, which yields most benefits and most ills in the modern age.

A return to the past is not feasible. The corporation is here to stay. And the Church, having inherited it mostly from the Roman legal system and having consistently endorsed it throughout the ages because of the numerous benefits it bestows upon society,[2] can only be expected to reinforce the institution of private property.

But the corporation can be used properly. Hence the Church has traditionally encouraged the individual ownership of business enterprises as well as cooperatives and might in the future encourage Employee Stock Ownership Plans (ESOPs). This practice is especially noteworthy because its creator, Louis O. Kelso, adopted an ingenious method of using credit to transform employees from outside contractors to owners of the corporation in which they work. From outsiders, they become insiders-without undermining property values of existing owners.[3]

A just and lasting solution to the scourge of unemployment lies in the transformation of workers into owners, because ownership respects the dictates of human dignity and those of efficiency: owners, quite simply, are more efficient than workers. Thus, in a properly ordered society, the unemployed become workers, workers become owners, and owners retire from the life of business to devote their energies to the life of the arts and the spirit.

Carmine Gorga

NOTES

1 Franco Modigliani, "Introduction." *The Collected Papers of Franco Modigliani, Vol. 1, Essays in Macroeconomics*. Edited by Andrew Abel. Cambridge, MA: The MIT Press, 1980.

2 See, e.g., St. Thomas Aquinas' *Summa Theologica*, II-II q. 66.

3 For details on ESOPs, see Binary Economics.

Technology

Reprinted with permission from
Encyclopedia of Catholic Social Thought, Social Science, and Social Policy
(Lanham, MD: Scarecrow Press, *2007*)

When God created things, He declared them "good" one after the other. When God created man, in His "image and likeness", He remained silent. The reason why God did not pronounce man good clearly is that man has the freedom to be bad. How can we apply this great lesson to that which we, imperfect human beings, create?

Three caveats seem to cover the field of innovation evaluation. First, since we create the innovation, we must expect that it contains positive as well as negative elements; therefore we must choose a "culture of life" over a "culture of death". Second, the innovation has to be for the benefit of all. Third, while God opted to leave us free once He created us, we should never relinquish our control over technology. If a technological innovation runs the risk of getting out of control, we should not bring it into existence — no matter its expected benefits.

It is unlikely that any external committee of ethicists can pass satis-factory judgments over delicate and complex matters involved in the de-tailed knowledge of science and technology. It is, and ought to be, the responsibility of the creator(s) of the innovation to pass such judgments.

Since responsibility can never be separated from control over the power to make appropriate decisions, it can be seen that the discussion re-garding issues of technology starts with science — deep and exhaustive knowledge of the effects of technology. It soon moves over onto ethics. And it ends in economics. The ultimate social problem of our age is this: How to grant full moral and legal power over technological decisions to the cre-ators of technology?

The short answer is that through individual ownership, cooperatives, and Employee Stock Ownership Plans (ESOPS), creators of technology ought to be made the owners of technology.

Carmine Gorga

For extracts of the Magisterium's position on various technologies, see *Compendium of the Social Doctrine of the Church,* Pontifical Council for Justice and Peace (Washington, D.C.: USCCB Publishing, 2005).

What Is Vital
in Binary Economics

Reprinted with permission from *Encyclopedia of Catholic Social Thought, Social Science, and Social Policy* (Lanham, MD: Scarecrow Press, 2007).

When placed in the context of economic policy and economic justice, the core of Binary economics reveals itself as one of the most genial and beneficial advancements in human thought ever. It is the product of one seminal thinker, Louis O. Kelso.

Kelso's output was considerable, was assisted by a variety of collaborators, and has been expanded upon by numerous contributors. The literature on Binary economics, in other words, is large and has given rise to a variety of controversies. The vital core of Binary economics, however, in its simplest form can be reduced to a financial mechanism called the Employee Stock Ownership Plan (ESOP). This core is of enduring value. It affects a variety of disciplines and human endeavors.

The ESOP is a trust fund. If a corporation establishes an ESOP, if the corporation distributes its profits to its stockholders (rather than reinvesting them in other ventures or using them to fund its own future activities), and if the corporation borrows money through the ESOP to fund its future operations, when the ESOP repays the loan it acquires stock that corresponds to the economic value created by all participants in the corporation-and this value is equitably distributed among all participants in accordance with their individual contribution. This is the financial mechanism through which employees, without diluting the value of existing stockholders, can gradually become part owners of their place of work.

The ESOP is not a method to re-distribute income or wealth that has been created in the past. On the contrary, ESOPs attack the need for the redistribution of wealth at one of its sources. There is an inequitable accumulation of wealth among the owners of the corporations, because workers are outside contractors; the wage contract exhausts the legal relationship with the corporation; capital accumulation accrues only to stockholders. Thus the rich get richer, many workers do not receive a living wage, and it is up to the taxpayer to sustain the living conditions of the multitudes.

The ESOP is a method to distribute the wealth that is being created at present-and a method to distribute it equitably among all those who participate in its creation in accordance with their degree of participation.

The ESOP provides a solution also to another major conundrum of the day. Under present institutional arrangements, full employment tends to lead to higher wages and to unacceptable levels of inflation, essentially because *wages are a distribution of future profits*. If and when, through ESOPs, private ownership of the corporations is as widespread as possible, one distributes profits only as they occur. Therefore, a just distribution of profits under those conditions will never lead to inflation.

A third inner strength of ESOPs lies in their inherent efficiency. It is undeniable that owners, single independent owners, work harder than most workers. It is this incentive that ESOPs carry with them, when they are properly applied.

Potentially, ESOPs are especially powerful tools of economic justice. By transforming workers (and possibly even consumers) into owners, ESOPs are an essential component of participative justice. By recognizing that only owners have the legal power to affect a fair distribution of income and wealth, ESOPs are an essential component of distributive justice. By recognizing that only fair owners have an economic incentive to establish fair prices in the market, ESOPs are an essential component of commutative justice.

Because of these major social and economic benefits of the proper application of ESOP financing-yes, improper applications are legion-the legislators in the United States have extended considerable tax advantages to those who use this mechanism. Other advantages can conceivably be extended to ESOPs if they are used as effective tools of monetary policy.

Many documents of the Church call for the transformation of workers into owners, but none more clearly than the 1919 Program for Social Reconstruction of the U. S. Catholic Bishops, which states that "the full possibilities of increased production will not be realized so long as the majority of workers remain mere wage earners. The majority must somehow become owners, at least in part, of the instruments of production."
[1] ESOPs are the technical tools to translate this aspiration of the Church

into reality. The widespread use of ESOPs will awake a new dawn for the Church and for the world.

Carmine Gorga

NOTES

1. Quoted in U. S. Catholic Bishops, *Economic Justice for All: Pastoral Letter on Catholic Social Teaching and the U. S. Economy*, 1986 [300].

Economic Justice

Reprinted with permission from *Encyclopedia of Catholic Social Thought, Social Science, and Social Policy* (Lanham, MD: Scarecrow Press, *2007*).

Underlying the doctrine of Social Justice is the Aristotelian/Thomistic division of justice into political and economic justice. The principles of distributive and commutative ("exchange") justice are part of the Church's ancestral patrimony. Since *Rerum Novarum* (# 34 and 46), the Church has been adding to them the plank of participative justice, offering thus a full-fledged theory of economic justice.

The three planks are related to the tripartite division of classical economics into production, distribution, and consumption. Simply, people who participate in production are empowered to participate in the distribution of wealth; and owners are free to exchange their share for other goods and services, invest it anew in the process of wealth creation, consume it-or give it to charitable purposes.

Anchored in morality, the theory of economic justice establishes the rules, the invisible threads-peculiar to each culture and age-that connect us by mutual rights and responsibilities (*RN* # 2, 10, 12, 13, 14, 15, 25, 37, 53, 58). These rules transform wealth from a material entity into a force that affects the quality of life of people and society, because property is indissolubly linked to life and liberty.

The Content of Economic Justice

The Doctors of the Church defined the principles of distributive and commutative justice. They left the plank of participative justice unspoken, for reasons to become apparent forthwith.

Participative Justice. Owning a farm was for ages the main way to participate in economic life; and, since in the Jewish, Greek, Roman, Christian, and Muslim tradition most studies were done by and for landowners, the issue of participative justice did not arise early on. Landowners did not necessarily till the land-just as stockholders do not necessarily sit at the assembly line. Over the centuries, landowners established relationships with tenants, who did the tilling and received an agreed-upon proportion of the product. The dispossessed had a right of access to the commons, through which they became landowners in fact, if not in title.

With the enclosure of the commons, the economic condition of Europe changed radically. And the need to address issues of participative justice eventually became explicit because, as Pope John Paul II maintained in *Centesimus Annus* (# 33-35), either people and nations participate in the economic process or they are marginalized-are made poor and placed at the margins of society.

One participates in an enterprise through sole proprietorship, partnership, membership in a cooperative, or holding stock in an incorporated business. These are forms of private enterprise traditionally fostered by the Church.

Workers do not participate in the life of the corporation for which they work because, legally, they are outside contractors: They offer their labor services and receive wages. The traditional support of the Church for unions is due to the recognition that labor unions tend to equalize the relationship between the individual worker and the powerful combines that have been formed during the last two centuries. But unions do not provide final protection. Hence the challenge to transform human beings into owners, launched by Leo XIII (*RN* # 46), represents the most living and vital portion of the Church's moral engagement with the socio-economic structures of contemporary society.

Distributive Justice. Participation in production is not enough. Issues of fairness in the distribution of income and wealth also need to be addressed. Rooted in the Jewish tradition of the jubilee, the doctrine of distributive justice spans the arch from consideration of grace from overpowering financial debt to perennial vigilance against monopolies. The keystone in the construction of distributive justice during the Middle Ages was the status of economic "superfluities" as legally belonging to the poor. The Church collected the surplus and made it available to the poor. No questions asked-urged St. John Chrysostom.

Commutative Justice. The definition of just price as any *competitive* price, first reached by the Doctors of the Church, forms the foundation of commutative justice. The doctrine covers condemnation of practices that run contrary to doctrine as well as encouragement of practices that foster competition in the market. Usury, defined as the exchange of money loaned for excessive interest payments, an issue very much alive in the Muslim tradition, used to be a primary target of the moral wrath of the Church. No space was left open to chance-hence the practice of guilds as administrators of fair prices, quantity, and quality was wholeheartedly embraced by the Church. In commutative justice one finds the moral justification for much contemporary anti-trust legislation.

This is the structure of economic justice in bare bones: Does an economic activity offer fair participation in production, distribution, and exchange of wealth? Then it is just. Technically, if prices of factors of production are set unfairly high, participation becomes prohibitive; if excessive values are distributed to some, these factors become overpriced and others underpriced; then the basis for objective evaluation of fair prices in the exchange of wealth vanishes. Adumbrated in these positions is the reality that unfair prices do not lead to efficiency.

Justice and Charity

Through comprehensive application of the theory of economic justice, the Church treats all members of society alike and, by protecting everyone, protects especially the poor who are otherwise abandoned to themselves and absent from the table where vital decisions are taken by the powerful and the efficient. This effect suggests the need for a clear distinction.

The call for justice is not a call for charity. While justice, according to St. Thomas Aquinas, exercises a practical (cardinal) virtue, charity exercises a theological virtue. The need for charity generally signals a failure of justice. More, in *Quadragesimo Anno* (# 4) Pope Pius XI issued a firm injunction against using charity "to veil the violation of justice".

Indeed, the full exercise of economic justice is essential to the success of charity. Only if its need is rather miniscule, the call for economic charity can be fulfilled. We are not saints. Charity, high as it is in the moral sphere, is a last resort in the economic sphere.

Carmine Gorga

Bibliography

de Roover, Raymond. *Business, Banking, and Economic Thought in Late Medieval and Early Modern Europe: Selected Studies of Raymond de Roover, ed. Julius Kirshner.* Chicago and London: The University of Chicago Press, 1974.

Gorga, Carmine. *The Economic Process: An Instantaneous Non-Newtonian Picture.* Lanham, Md. and Oxford: University Press of America, 2002.

_____. "Toward the Definition of Economic Rights," *The Journal of Markets and Morality*, Spring 1999, II (1) 88-101.

Schumpeter, Joseph A. *History of Economic Analysis.* New York: Oxford University Press, 1954.

Tierney, Brian. *Medieval Poor Law: A Sketch of Canonical Theory and Its Application in England.* Berkeley and Los Angeles: University of California Press, 1959.

See also Justice; Economics; Binary Economics; Politics; History of Economic Justice.

A book review by Carmine Gorga

Frugality: Rebalancing Material and Spiritual Values in Economic Life

Bouckaert, Luk, Opdebeeck, Hendrik, and Zsolnay, Laszlo (eds.)
Peter Lang, 2008.

Reprinted with permission from the *Journal of Markets and Morality*, Fall 2008 (forthcoming).

Each essay in this important collection presents a comprehensive analysis of one aspect of the long and deep roots of frugality. Thus, under the heading entitled *Frugality in Spiritual Traditions,* Luk Bouckaert leads us to distinguish the difference between rational, spiritual, and instrumental frugality. Each leads to substantially different modes of thinking and living. With the assistance of Rafael Esteban we learn how negatively the "idolatry of consumption" affects the entire arc of development from the personal to the cultural and the communal. Francis Kadaplackal guides us to see man as a co-creator and thus returns to the frugal man a full sense of responsibility for his actions toward others and our planet. Laurie Michaelis reminds us that calls for the practice of frugality lie at the very core of the Quakers' conception of life, a conception that accepts the usefulness of business, the duty to care for others, and naturally extends itself to work for a world of peace.

Under the heading entitled *Frugality in Socio-Economic Perspective,* Dirk Geldof places the issue of overconsumption into its proper context: by giving its due to the deep psychological meaning as well as the negative aspects of consumption, he becomes entitled to propose frugality as a positive alternative that reduces the risk of global ecological collapse, smoothens the ongoing trade-off between wealth and well-being, and tilts the quantity of time spent earning money and shopping in favor of time spent on improving the quality of our life. By linking frugality to luxury, Ronald Commers and Wim Vandekerckhove give the full spectrum of the long historical conversation about the morality of production by the many for the luxury of the few. After pointing out that the danger of capitalism lies in the "commodification of everything", they explore the possibilities of stakeholdership in the full context of the global economy. Knut Ims and Ove Jakobsen, placing themselves into the Organic Worldview, make us clearly see that mainstream economics, tied as it is to the Mechanical Worldview, reduces human beings to atoms unconcerned not only with other human beings, with their society, and the world, but even unconcerned with their own psychological well-being. They suggest that frugality is an "interesting gateway" to the avoidance of the pitfalls of overconsumption and the achievement of a world in which "sustainability and life quality are the overriding goals" (170). Hendrik Opdebeeck opens with the realization of the collapse of the major assumption of the modern world: faith in progress as the alternative to the traditional vision of ethics limiting freedom-especially economic freedom. Progress was supposed to eliminate want and, with it, violence. Hence he starts the work of reconstruction by recovering the distinction between science and wisdom and translating it into the Western conception of science-for-use vs. the Eastern conception of science-for-insight and thus opens the door to the acceptance of frugality as an integral part of Buddhist economics in which issues of sustainability and life quality are essential. This, of course, is one way of recovering the validity of the Aristotelian-Thomistic conception of life. What Buddhism calls balance between opposites, Aristotle called the Golden Mean. Both are practical tools to solve complex problems of the relationship between order and freedom, for instance. By the same token, frugality becomes a tool to resolve many conflicts between our needs *and* our wants as producers and consumers, our needs *and* the needs of our community or our environment, our ethics *and* our economics, our practical needs *and* our spiritual needs.

Under the heading entitled *Frugality in Business and Economic Policy*, Herman E. Daily presents a devastating critique of mainstream economics. He points out that what we leave to future generations is not utility but throughput, namely the capacity of natural resources to produce a stream of wealth; and yet, mainstream economics does not include throughput into its calculations. This lack of knowledge deprives mainstream economics of concern for issues of sustainability, and infuses fundamental misconceptions into such key working tools as value added and production function. The author points out that the justification for much growth is the alleviation of poverty; and yet, mainstream economics does not even realize that "Insofar as poverty or welfare is a function of relative income, then growth becomes powerless to affect it" (211). It is for this lack of understanding of poverty that mainstream economics does not show great concern for issues of limits to growth. The position of mainstream economics in relation to international trade and globalization appears to be even less tenable since it contravenes a basic assumption of its own theory: capital is not supposed to move freely between nations! These arguments lead to a definite condemnation of current national and international policies concerning growth and distribution of income: how else to evaluate policies that favor debt, threaten ecological disaster, discourage import substitution, and encourage export policies that rely on single crops desired by rich countries and the depletion of natural resources of less developed countries? From this catalogue of errors distributive justice and frugality naturally spring forth for the construction of a sane economic policy. Counterintuitively, Ronald Jeurissen and Bert van de Ven address some of the conditions through which, given a change in our cultural patterns, marketing will "sell" frugality just as efficiently as today it is selling luxuries. Exciting prospect! The key that opens this prospect to realization is that "people want more time, less stress and more balance in their lives" (227). After distinguishing individual from political frugality, the authors advocate that "Frugality should therefore be based on a political economy of frugality, and it should become a political movement" (229). The precondition is that we distinguish needs from wants-not a small feat but not an impossible act either; given our innate ability to know our true self-interest, it only requires some prodding from our spiritual leaders. Major spurs along this way are already being provided by such social forces as the "slow" consumption and the environmental movement. A wealth of practical suggestions are then offered to marketers under such headings as time frugality and goods frugality, marketing responses to individual frugality, commodification of frugality, and downshifting marketing. The transformation of individual frugality into political frugality, the authors predict, will come with the exhaustion of renewable sources of energy. A substantial form of political frugality is already taking shape under the heading of corporate social responsibility (CSR), but the authors are well aware that we are a long way away from the development of this movement. Robert H. Frank analyzes the details of an apparently simple question: Does consuming more goods make people happier? The answer, supported by much scientific research data on the determinants of life-satisfaction and psychological well-being conducted by in-depth surveys and neuro-imaging analysis of brainwaves, is wholly counterintuitive: "beyond some point the answer is essentially negative" (249). One example suffices. People in a community with smaller houses and more free time are more satisfied than people in a community that lives in larger houses and less free time. The reason is self-evident, once it is analyzed: "Here again, the evidence suggests that whereas the pay-off when all have larger houses is small and fleeting, the pleasures that result from deeper social relationships are both profound and enduring" (259). The advantages of buying a larger house can be temporary, the disadvantages are permanent: one has less time to spend with friends and, since affordable houses are generally in the suburbs, one necessarily has to spend more time commuting-with all the attendant aggravations of commuting to work and even to shop. There are two plausible explanations why we deceive ourselves. First, we do not know our future reactions that well; second, pay-offs depend on relative position and, unless decisions are coordinated, the effects of individual decisions can be negated by the effects of societal decisions. "Military arms races provide perhaps the clearest illustration... when *all* spend more on weapons, no one is more secure than before" (261). This last characteristic makes the author suggest the introduction of a progressive consumption tax, a tax that would encourage us "to save more, buy less expensive houses and cars, and feel less pressure to work excessively long hours" (264). Laszlo Zsolnay closes the book by giving us a comprehensive view of Buddhism as an economic strategy that naturally leads to the practice of frugality.

Each essay is enriched by a wealth of historical, theoretical, and practical particulars that resonate within each other's presentation. Taken individually, each essay successfully makes the "spiritual case for frugality" (xi). Taken together, the voice of each writer is transformed into a roar: Frugality is not an option that one might take or leave; frugality is an economic necessity. We either live in accordance with the precepts of frugality, or we perish under a sea of debt and a heap of trash.

Carmine Gorga is president of Polis-tics Inc. of Gloucester.

A book review by Carmine Gorga

Frugality: Rebalancing Material and Spiritual Values in Economic Life

Bouckaert, Luk, Opdebeeck, Hendrik, and Zsolnay, Laszlo (eds.)
Bern: Peter Lang, 2008.

Reprinted with permission from *Social Justice Review* (forthcoming).

This book is most refreshing for being countercultural. Everyday we hear so much of the inevitability and the superiority of the present that we are tempted to stop working for a better future. Listen to what the book has to say.

There is one message delivered in two stages in this important collection of essays. At the first stage one follows the primary intent of the editors and reads each essay as an intellectual effort that successfully makes the "spiritual case" for frugality (p. xi). One then goes beyond this level of understanding and discovers that the book as a whole has made the *economic* and *political* case for frugality as well. This seems to be the implicit intent of the editors and certainly the explicit intent of the majority of the authors.

Each essay deals in-depth with one aspect of frugality. From an analysis of the negative effects of overconsumption on our spirit, our bodies, our communities, and our planet, frugality emerges as the central cure for most of the ills that envelop our current social and economic condition. In the end, we are presented with exhaustive and convincing explanations concerning the need to take frugality, not so much as a rational or an instrumental, but mainly as a spiritual tool to make us distinguish between our needs and our wants, to let us be mostly satisfied with what we have, and to deeply enjoy what we have. From Aristotle to the Stoics and, via St. Thomas Aquinas, to a modern believer such as E. F. Schumacher, we learn that frugality is an expression of the Golden Mean; this understanding of frugality in the East is expressed as the search for balance, reconciliation of opposites, and for inward and outward peace. The great merit of the book is to present the case for frugality as a way of living, not for the few, but for the many. Even though it is an automatic outward manifestation of Eastern as well as Western spirituality, frugality is not presented as an elitist practice but as a gift we can all give to ourselves. Thus, in the process of addressing experts in a variety of intellectual disciplines as well as community people, in the hands of these writers frugality becomes a tool to enrich our daily lives.

The active reader will extract all the goodness out of each essay by mentally transforming them into a unified book. For this transformation to occur a major weakness of the book has to be discounted. The authors are not naive. They know fully well the obstacles to overcome in order to introduce frugality in a modern society. Thus, taken individually, each voice is rather feeble and nearly apologetic because each author struggles against such clearly identified overpowering enemies as consumerism, luxury, and mainstream economic theory. Consumerism, for instance, is properly taken as one small part of an entire system of thought and action. As such, one cannot deal effectively with consumerism unless one places the old preaching about proper consumerism within the context of the need for reforming the entire economic system of today. And this is the fight that each author does not, and cannot, wage. For the immediate future, this final aim has been assumed by each author to be wishful thinking, an impossible dream.

Hence the underlying assumption of the book appears to be this: Yes, we know we are right; therefore we utter our words in utter sincerity. Yet, let us warn you: Do not hope against hope that you can change the system. The System, The Machine, The Matrix, is too powerful. It will fight back. It will unavoidably defeat you. So, please, do not really listen to our words. We beg you, lest you find us culpable of inciting you to an Impossible Fight, do not even try.

I have read the book with a different set of assumptions in the back of my mind. I have read it as a Third Order Carmelite. And I had to remind myself that the Carmelite charisma is not elitist, it is not for the few; it is for everyone, everyone who wants it. Thus, even if spirituality is a precondition for frugality, frugality is still for everyone.

I have read the book as a Roman Catholic who is doing work on a monograph entitled "The Economics of Jubilation". Through this research I have discovered that the economics of Moses is precisely the same as the economics of Jesus, and that the economics of Jesus is all enclosed in the parable of the talents. And when I transformed this parable into a mathematical equation I obtained this result: Investment = Income — Hoarding. Hence, I have read this book with the assumption that frugality is not an impossible ideal. All that frugality requires is the absence of hoarding. Frugality is lack of hoarding.

I have also read the book as a Concordian economist, as a believer in an economic theory in which stocks have equal weight as flows of money and real wealth, in which hoarding replaces the redundant conception of saving (remember saving is investment) and in which the theory of economic justice is an essential component of economic theory (see Gorga 1982, 2002, and 2008). Hence, I have read this book with the assumption that all that frugality presupposes is the presence of economic justice.

I have read the book slowly. One chapter at a time. Indeed, since I am a slow reader of serious literature, I have read one paragraph at a time-slowly. I have listened to each voice, carefully. Attentively, with reverence for the portion of truth unearthed and for the evident desire of the writer to impart it to me. I finished the book last night.

I woke up this morning with the transformation of the feeble voice of each writer into this roar: Frugality is not an option that one might take or leave; frugality is an economic necessity. We either live in accordance with the precepts of frugality, or we shall perish under a sea of debt and a heap of trash.

References

Gorga, C. (1982) "The Revised Keynes' Model" (an Abstract), *Atlantic Economic Journal* 10(3): 52.

Gorga, C. (2002) *The Economic Process: An Instantaneous Non-Newtonian Picture,* Lanham, MD. and Oxford: University Press of America.

Gorga, C. (2008) "Concordian Economics: Tools to Return Relevance to Economics," Forum for Social Economics (http://dx.doi.org/10.1007/s12143-008-9017-6). Reprint is available at http://www.carmine-gorga.us/id34.htm" http://www.carmine-gorga.us/id34.htm.

PART FOUR

Miscellaneous Documents

Thank God for the critics.

CG

Three gifts

If the reader has reached this point, I felt that the reader deserves a reward for endurance. Since I cannot break through these pages and offer you a physical present, I thought that I can pass along three gifts that were sent to me from heaven. They are in the form of confessions.

First confession. All throughout my life, I have had people "accusing" me of being an optimist. I have mostly borne that burden with some degree of inner pleasure. Lately, however, I have discovered that such a characterization does not fit my inner make-up. This is what I am: I am mostly happy.

Second confession. Once I made that discovery, I had to ask myself, how can I ever be so happy? There are two reasons. For most of my life, I found it very hard, so hard that I simply neglected Jesus' injunction to pray for my enemies. In the last few years, I have made an important discovery. Jesus was not only morally correct (of course, it goes without saying); being God, He was also clever. Here is what I have discovered. It is a great pleasure for me to pray for the inner peace of my enemies. Here is why: If they ever reach inner peace, they will leave me alone.

Third confession. This is the simplest one. And it is such a recent discovery that it occurred to me only this morning, and in fact it triggered my desire to jot this page down. I am mostly happy because I like to surround myself with happy people.

And I find it my responsibility to make people around me as happy as possible.

And so on and so forth.

Go forth, O reader. Become a Somist. But, of course, feel free to go back on what you have read so far. Happy reading!

August 15, 2008

Gloucester Daily Times, Thursday, April 18, 1996, A 7

'He seeks economic justice for all'

Political scientist Gorga seeks a place on the state and national agenda

By GAIL McCARTHY
Times Staff

Carmine Gorga thinks everyone in the country deserves a chance to earn enough money to live a good life.

This week, Gorga is taking part in a global Town Meeting in historic Concord to put that statement in writing, in an economic Bill of Rights.

Sitting a red leather armchair in his Middle Street home, Gorga recently talked about his mission to put "economic Justice for all" on the state and national agenda.

Residents near and far should care, because in a society where there is more economic justice, they would be fewer social ills.

The 60-year-old Fulbright scholar works for the Concord-based Center for American Studies, which organized the Global Town Meeting.

In April of 1995, Gorga was appointed Center Scholar at the non-profit, educational corporation, founded 10 years ago. The Center puts on programs for a wide range of audiences, from businessmen to international leaders.

The weeklong Town Meeting will culminate Sunday at Minuteman National Park with a presentation of the economic Bill of Rights, which will be drafted by the 50 some participants on Saturday.

The participants—including experts in economics, public policy and constitutional law—come from nationwide as well as representatives from Russia, Romania and Singapore.

The Center scheduled the event to coincide with Patriot's Day. The site of Concord was also meant to coincide with the place where the first shots of the American Revolution were fired.

Now Gorga and the Center hope to start another revolution of sorts, one of a push for "economic justice" for all.

"We're trying to create economic freedom for everyone, not a few," he said. "We have a good foundation in this country, but it has to be broadened."

Gorga said his theory has recently been called "Concordian economics," which means if the economic system works properly, it will work to the benefit of nearly everyone. The "Concordian" refers to people talking and working together.

"Our (system) now works fantastically well for a few, so we have to change that," he said. "How? By changing the legal system that allows structures of selfishness to exist in society."

He referred to the case of bonds dealer Michael Milkin, who earned $500 million in one year in the mid 1980s. More recently in the news are the top executives of health care companies who are worth in excess of Milkin's windfall after making lucrative deals.

"Society should say 'I'm sorry, you're not allowed to do that.' We could ask what do you need, $10 million? $15 million? But society needs to say there needs to be limits," Gorga said.

He said economists—who are usually employees of non-profit organizations—need to analyze the effects of such excess in detail.

The Italian-born Gorga, who received his doctorate in political science from the University of Naples, describes himself as a political scientist working as an economist working in the field of economic theory, policy and consulting.

Peter Anastas of Action, Inc., the city's anti-poverty agency, said Gorga's work was exciting and described the man "as a real visionary".

Gorga worked at Action in the 1960s and early 1970s as the Director of community development, where he undertook many efforts, including organizing the Fishermen's Wives Association. Anastas said he also did the first in-depth study of the fishing industry.

In the future, Gorga and the center hope to lobby politicians.

"This country was based on a Bill of Rights and that has held the country together," he said. "People come here from all over the world because there's a Bill of Rights. It's a fantastic environment and it's still the best county in the world."

Gorga also asks environmentalists to take a broader view.

"Maybe we need to pay more for certain products instead of just squeezing business profits. Environmentalists need to say to consumers 'you have a responsibility to accept higher costs associated with striving to have a clean environment,'" he said.

Gorga has taken his ideas to top scholars, including Nobel Laureate Franco Modigliani.

"We've have had long discussions about economic theory and he always recommends there is something of value in what I am doing," he said.

A few years ago, Gorga was searching for people who had an interest in his topic when he met center director Stuart Weeks at a conference. That led to his appointment at the center.

Gorga credited Gloucester High School social studies teacher David Wise, who he described as his "intellectual and moral supporter."

Gorga said the organizers are looking for reactions from the residents about their efforts. People can call Gorga or the Center at (508) 287 5305.

Hard Data
and Hard Reasoning
Concerning Overfishing

1. Arguments For and Against ITQs

2. Letter to Judge Kessler with attachments

3. Letter to Chairperson Hill with attachment

Arguments For and Against ITQs

by
**Dr. Carmine Gorga, Mr. Edward J. Lima, and
Dr. Damon Cummings** *

for
**Presentation at National Academy of Sciences Hearing on IFQs
Boston, Massachusetts
May 7, 1998**

Dr. Gorga's practical expertise lies in fisheries development; he is also the author, with Louis J. Ronsivalli, of *Quality Assurance of Seafood* (Van Nostrand Reinhold, 1988). Mr. Lima is the former Executive Director of the Cape Ann Fishermen's Cooperative Association, Inc. Dr. Cummings is a former Professor of Hydrodynamics and Control Theory at the Massachusetts Institute of Technology.

We are thankful to this distinguished panel of scientists for the opportunity given us to present a series of arguments for and against the institution of Individual Fishing Quotas (IFQs), especially in their incarnation as Individual Transferable Quotas (ITQs). The arguments against ITQs are based on experience and theory, and are very strong. The arguments in favor of ITQs are theoretical and do not apply to the concrete case of management of natural resources that are identified in the literature as common pool resources such as maritime fisheries.

The arguments for ITQs are arguments for privatization, the arguments for private management of wealth. They are ancient and powerful. From Aristotle to St. Thomas Aquinas most thinkers have recognized the many advantages of private management of wealth. These arguments have become even more solidified during the last half of this century through the formalization of the discussion as represented especially by the work of two Nobel laureates in economics, Kenneth Arrow and Gerard Debreu.

There is an implicit distinction in this type of argument, however, that needs to be made explicit. Since wealth, as Jean Baptiste Say especially made clear, is always social wealth, the arguments for privatization apply to social wealth that can somehow be made private. It does not apply — it should not apply, and it should have never been applied — to natural resources that, by definition, are common wealth.

Thus we start our presentation of arguments against ITQs. Following the inner rationale of these arguments, we consistently reach conclusions that — startlingly — suggest a reversal of conventional wisdom. We would doubt our own logic if our conclusions were not backed up by a long series of well-known facts that confirm the validity of this logic.

First, there is the legal argument. ITQs are issued on natural resources that are "common wealth," namely, common property of present and future generations who, by dint of geography and tradition, are somehow tied to those resources. As such, no government has any right to alienate those rights in perpetuity. Those resources are common resources. They belong to all generations, present and future ones. The government cannot alienate property that it does not own and that in fact is owned by someone else. If the government cannot alienate this property, the government cannot even give it away free of charge to anyone — as generally proposed with ITQs.

This argument is mostly presented as an argument of "natural law," and thus it gets entangled in the overall issues surrounding this brand of jurisprudence. The argument can also be presented as an argument of positive law, however. Where is the party entitled to common law rights? The answer is clear. The party is represented by those future generations that are entitled to present a "welfare bill" to a certain society. The kind and the quantity of people needing welfare assistance during the last five hundred years, the Age of Enclosures, as we might dub it, has changed to a type and size unknown to any earlier age in the history of the world. It is future generations, made pauper through enclosures, which have presented their "welfare bill" to society. These demands of future generations are generally met, not so much for practical or even moral reasons, as for the economic contribution that those generations bring to the overall welfare of society. The poor contribute their "consumers' power," a power without which many economies would not survive.

Second, there is the issue of irreversibility of the decision to create ITQs. Once ITQs are created — however illegally — they cannot be taken back. With an enormous will power that has never been exhibited so far, those rights might be taken back, but only at great cost to the general taxpayer. Why incur this future liability?

Third, there is the issue of economic dynamics. The present dynamics, in the absence of ITQs, essentially is this. Presently capital is required to enter the fisheries. However, in practice, the investment is made slowly over time in the traditional fishing communities. Young crew members work on boats until they assemble funds to enter inshore fisheries, for example lobstering, on a small scale. As they progress, they are able to invest in larger boats and work their way up to the offshore fishery. Needless to say, not all purchases constitute net additions to the fleet. Some represent only changes in ownership. The introduction of ITQs changes this traditional system entirely. The major investment in purchase of a quota must be advanced on the initial entry to the fishery. For instance, the market value of a quota for 500,000 lbs of cod per year can be estimated to be $833,330. This initial cost shifts the entire industry to a capital-intensive regime, and the industry will eventually converge to large corporation domination with the small fishing communities excluded. Let us follow the process through its major stages.

With the presence of ITQs, the internal dynamics of present fisheries economics would essentially be transformed into this. The process is self evident at the second generation pass. But it is present even if the first generation owner has not paid any price for ITQs, because the rights of exclusion of other people from the utilization of natural resources included in ITQs do automatically possess a market value. In their essence, ITQs are a means to monetize natural resources. This market value must be realized whether through direct exploitation of the property right or by sale to a third party. The dynamics of this market value has historically led to overcapitalization, namely the use of inappropriate technology to make the ITQs market value as real, as high, and as immediate as possible.

The trigger force of this dynamics is the very act of "naming," the very act of creating market value where none existed before. Does the "state" have such a power? Indeed, do people have such a power? The place where this power can be most easily observed is in monetary affairs. It is people and governments that create money. While a moment before creation nothing existed, the moment after creation everyone wants that money. Acts have consequences; to every action there is a reaction. In order to obtain this value, some *extra* effort is required — hence overcapitalization, when no overcapitalization was necessary before the creation of that market value.

That is the first stage. Stage two, all too briefly, is this. Once ITQs exclude people from fishing for certain species, where do these people get their fish? From the persons who have been granted exclusive fishing rights, naturally. But then, to meet the demand, the holders of ITQs — even while remaining within the overall limits set by the quotas — will consolidate quotas and will serially harvest bigger catches than they would have individually had to catch before the institution of ITQs. The catch must be larger because there will unavoidably be a bigger amount of waste involved in catching large catches and distributing them to a large number of people over a large geographical area. Waste will also result from the opposite effect. Since the holder of ITQs can only land X pounds per year, he will throw back any fish that are not maximum price fish, exactly the right size, fat content, etc. If the market goes down during a return from a trip, the skipper may throw the whole catch over the side after hearing the radio message from his shore captain and go fishing again when the price goes up. Also what happens when a herring trawler catches some cod? That boat has no cod quota, so will of course throw it back.

In addition to waste, and hence unavoidable ecological degradation, there are all other issues concerning prices and costs. Larger waste implies larger risks that somehow need to be covered by higher prices. Higher prices upset the equilibrium of the original economy. Some people will undoubtedly be unable to meet those prices and fall into higher degrees of deprivation. Others will stop working for themselves and go to work for others. But then they will ask for higher wages than they would have naturally paid to themselves. Hence costs of production rise and selling prices rise ever more.

In stage three one finds the elimination of less efficient competitors and the buying out of smaller and/or less efficient holders of ITQs. Thus, the market that essentially starts with the granting of small and official monopoly rights, without provision to compensate in perpetuity through taxation those who have been excluded from access to natural resources, ends up in unofficial enforcement of monopoly privileges — unless either innovative forces create new markets or, less likely and frequently, the government intervenes to break up monopolies. One needs to ask, why willingly and consciously go through these destructive economic cycles?

Fourth, there is the issue of ecological dynamics. Overcapitalization — whether in the form of machinery or heads of animals on a limited amount of land — and the use of inappropriate technology lead to what is assumed to be "the tragedy of the commons."

Fifth, the expression "the tragedy of the commons" is a mistaken metaphor. The commons have existed, literally, for thousands of years. They have always worked well for the benefit of all those who have had the right of access to them.

Sixth, commons that are transformed into private property are no longer commons. Today, they might be called ITQs, but they have traditionally been called "enclosures."

Seventh, it is enclosures that have traditionally collapsed. The "Tragedy of the Commons" always occurs **after** the enclosures are put into effect.

Eight, if language is important at least to clarity of thought, one must realize that the historically correct expression, then, is "the Tragedy of Enclosures." Will Garret Hardin incorporate this expression in his next revision of his famous article and no longer find fault with his "own conclusions"?

The source of all misunderstanding is that there was indeed a tragedy experienced by humankind during the last four to five hundred years. But this is not the tragedy of the commons. This is The Tragedy of the Enclosures. It is the ecology of the enclosures that has collapsed, and as we have all too briefly seen above, it was doomed to collapse.

Ninth, limiting our observation to our North Atlantic marine resources, we have discovered that the depletion of traditional commercial species might have been due to overfishing by predators rather than (in addition to?) by fishermen and that an observable change has occurred in the internal composition of the biomass. In other words, there is as yet no tragedy of marine resources as a whole in the North Atlantic Ocean. There is only a depletion of some highly valued commercial species of fish and their replacement with less commercially valuable species such as herring and mackerel. Trustworthy literature has also established that many species worldwide that appeared to be almost extinct have, after a lapse of time, generally been plentiful again. There is no tragedy of commons yet, because there has not been an enclosure of those areas yet. Indeed, there is no need to enclose those areas. At least, there is no urgent need to do so.

In brief, we would like to stress that, while we find no compelling reason for establishing a regime of ITQs, we find extremely compelling reasons to stay away from them. We trust that this distinguished panel of scientists will act accordingly and not be swayed by faddish opinions in support of ITQs. All predictions in support of ITQs have never been validated by the facts.

If you support ITQs, you will not only support a wrong solution to a non-existing problem, namely privatization of common resources to avoid overexploitation by small traditional fishermen. You will also stifle innovation to solve real problems with real solutions: lack of coordination and integration of management functions to avoid periodic occurrences of glut and scarcity with attendant negative consequences on costs and prices. Many such creative solutions are outlined in Elinor Ostrom's *Governing the Commons (1990),* or Susan J. Buck's *The Global Commons (1998).* In fact, we would like to suggest that, given time and perhaps some degree of protection from human and natural predators, local communities will come up with solutions that are indeed workable and to the advantage of all those concerned. For instance, here in Gloucester, MA, working within the context of Vision 2020, the planning arm of the Gloucester Fishermen's Wives Association, a sizable group of people from various walks of life, is developing a Strategic Plan for the Fisheries, a plan that — as a substitute for ITQs — includes a proposal for a new type of fisheries management system, namely, a Functional Integration Model of Management (FIMM). As against the micromanagement of any form of IFQs, with all its attendant difficulties of enforcement as stressed especially in the works of Parzival Copes, the FIMM would allow for the macro management of fisheries resources. The plan is following a bottom-up strategy, it is being formulated as a nested plan, and its focus can be drawn port by port.

The Strategic Plan is included in outline form as Attachment 1.

A brief description of the Functional Integration Model of Management is contained in a paper published with Stuart B. Weeks and entitled "Fisheries Renewal: The Renewal of the Soul of Business." The paper is included as Attachment 2.

 Both the Management Model and the Strategic Plan are based on a restructure of contemporary economic theory. This work is the result of more than thirty years of work. It includes many innovations, the most relevant of which to the present context is the insertion of **stocks as well as flows of real wealth** into the very structure of economic theory. This work has been powerfully assisted especially by Professor Franco Modigliani, the Nobel laureate in economics at MIT. An unpublished paper, included here as Attachment 3, presents an outline of this work. The paper is entitled "The Dynamics of the Economic System." An anonymous referee for *The Journal of Economic Theory* has reviewed this paper and recognized that it contains a "new analytical engine" (Referee Report, Manuscript #

91297, 12/31/91).

Attachment 4 contains a paper written with Edward J. Lima and entitled "The Depletion of Commercial Species of Wild Fish Stocks: A Natural Disaster."

Attachment 5 contains Carmine Gorga's resume. More information on Mr. Gorga's work and thought can be sighted at www.polis-tics.com.

NOTE: Some attachments are omitted here; others are presented differently.

GLOUCESTER COMMUNITY DEVELOPMENT CORPORATION

128 Main Street Gloucester, MA 01930   978.282.4344 Voice/Fax 978.282.4664
www.gloucestercdc.org   gcdc@gloucestercdc.org

May 18, 2002

Honorable Gladys Kessler
U.S. District Court
333 Constitution Avenue, N.W.
Washington, D.C. 20001-2866

Dear Judge Kessler,

What would Louis D. Brandeis recommend in relation to your pending decision concerning fisheries management? I did my dissertation on his political thought about some forty years ago. It is with some confidence, therefore, that I dare believe that he would recommend two rules: use judicial restraint; follow the living law.

Surely you have to interpret the law. But which law? A law as faulty as the Magnuson Act? A law so faulty that it is in the process of being revised by the Congress? Wisdom might suggest that you urge Congress to pass the new law ASAP.

In the meantime, what is the living law? I would suggest that the living law of the sea is telling us that the stocks of cod and haddock are on the rebound. Can human action help them along? To answer this question, we have to be guided by two factors: past history and science. I am enclosing a chart and a table of official statistics showing about one hundred years of decreases and *natural* rebounds for cod.

As to science, I am enclosing two graphs which suggest the existence of natural cycles between predators and prey. These cycles seem to occur in many natural environments. The hypothesis in the fisheries is that the relationship of predators to prey exists between groundfish and pelagics, such as herring and mackerel. On our web site, www.gloucestercdc.org, you will find that a team from the MIT System Dynamics Program is helping us evaluate this hypothesis and, in the meantime, we are also trying to establish Gloucester Fish Inc, a for-profit corporation designed to transform pelagic species into surimi — i.e., reduce the stocks of natural predators of cod.

To the glory of Louis D. Brandeis, please use judicial restraint; follow the living law of the sea.

Very grateful for granting me your attention.

Carmine Gorga
Executive Director

United Stated Atlantic Coast Cod Catch, 1880 to 1945

300 Million Pounds

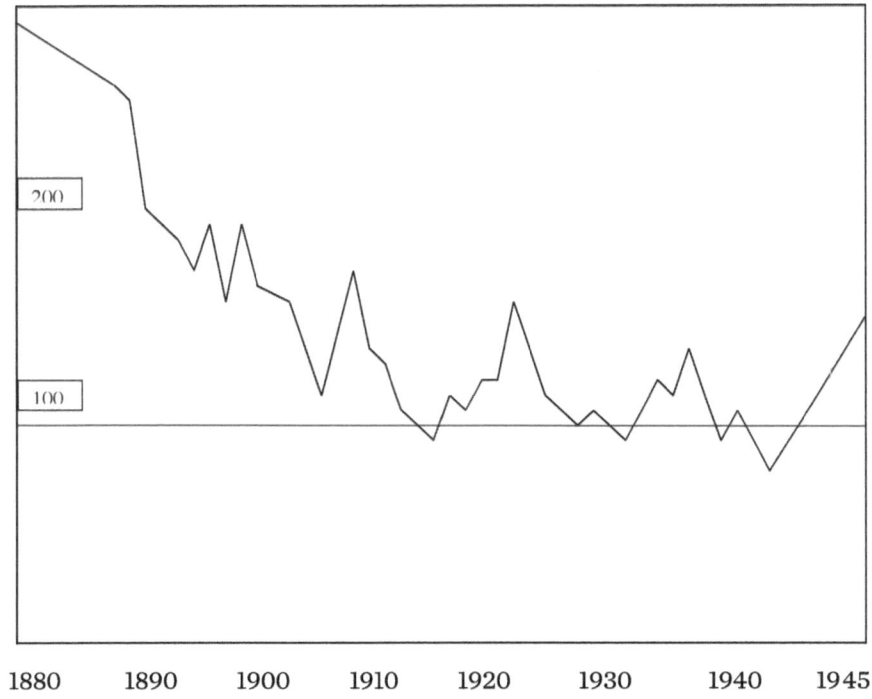

1880   1890   1900   1910   1920   1930   1940   1945

Source: New England Landings, November 1945. Department of the Interior, Fish and Wildlife Service C. F. S, 244, p. 11.

Data, in thousand of pounds, are as follows: 1887, 207,458; 1929, 86,999; 1930, 101,632; 1931, 86,276; 1937, 134,605; 1942, 65,092; 1944, 141,072; 1957, 31,911, 1962, 43,946; 1965, 35,465.

Source: Fisheries Statistics of the United States, 1965. Bureau of Commercial Fisheries, Washington, D.C. 1967; p. 131.

The Dynamics of Fish Stocks

The dynamics of fish stocks is uniquely grasped with the assistance of a Predator-Prey Model developed in 1925 by Lotka and Volterra, respectively a mathematician and a biologist. Through this model, they explained the ebbs and flows of the sardine fishery in the Adriatic sea. The model is sketched, in simplified fashion, in Figure 1.

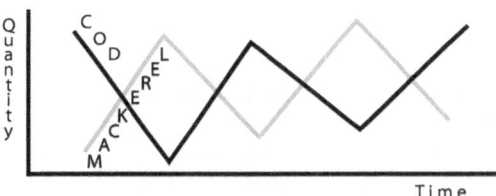

A Simplified Fish Predator-Prey Model
Figure 1

Source: C. Gorga and S. Weeks, "Fisheries Renewal: A Renewal of the Soul of Business," in *The Catholic Social Science Review*, Volume II (1997) 145-161.

The simplification consists in the elimination of the cycles in which both predators and prey either fall or rise together. The complete model can be found in ABRAHAM, R. H. AND SHAW, C. D. (1981): *Dynamics—The Geometry of Behavior. Part 1: Periodic Behavior*. Santa Cruz, CA: Aerial Press.

GLOUCESTER COMMUNITY DEVELOPMENT CORPORATION

128 Main Street   Gloucester, MA 01930   978.282.4344   Voice/ Fax 978.282.4664
www.gloucestercdc.org   email: gcdc@gloucestercdc.org

October 15, 2003

Mr. Thomas Hill
Chairperson
NEFMC
50 Water Street, Mill 2
Newburyport, MA 01950

Dear Mr. Hill,

Enclosed please find a modest proposal that I would like to add to your agenda in preparation for your forthcoming deliberations. The proposal, developed through much consultation with various constituents, is an attempt to fuse disparate interests together into a coherent unit. And, of course, it attempts to respect the letter as well as the spirit of the law.

This proposal is buttressed by the enclosed letter and attachments I sent to the Honorable Judge Kessler last year, as well as by much work that we at the Gloucester Community Development Corporation have done on the issue of the relationships between pelagics and bottom fish. This study was done by a team of volunteers from the MIT Systems Dynamics Program. The team was composed by Dr. Peter Otto, Jeroen Struben, and Sanghyun Lee under the guidance of Professor Jim Hines. Our team received in-depth hard data and wise counsel from Dr. William Overholtz at the Woods Hole Laboratory of NMFS.

My Board of Directors has instructed me to put this study at the disposal of your Council. It should be of great help to you in your forthcoming delicate decisions. You can review this study directly from our web site. I would be happy to come down to discuss especially the practical aspects of this study with you. We are well advanced in our plans to translate this study into reality. I am sure that Dr. Otto would ready to join me if you asked for his presence. He can also be reached directly at System Dynamics Group UAlbany.

Sincerely,

Carmine Gorga
Executive Director

October 2003

A Modest Proposal

The Status Quo Plus One

With my face in the mirror of Jenni Glenn's eyes during an interview the other day, I asked myself: "What would I do if I were a member of the New England Fishery Management Council?" The answer that shot back at me was: "Nothing. Absolutely nothing."

An enlightening suggestion from Stephen Demetri last Sunday allows me to clarify and mollify my position. Steve is suggesting that what we need is to add Option Five to Amendment 13: Option 5 would allow for the preservation of the status quo.

The more I look at this proposal, the more eminently reasonable it becomes.

Everyone agrees that the stocks of "bottom fish" species, such as cod and haddock, are naturally rebuilding. Those scientists who have observed the peaks and valleys in the historic catches of cod off of our coast since at least 1880—as can be seen from the chart nearby—are not surprised by this prospect. Peaks and valleys in fish stocks have occurred consistently throughout our recorded history, which confirms that we are indeed getting out of the "valley". Why not leave well enough alone? Why not allow Mother Nature to finish her work in peace?

So, let me begin all over again. If I were a member of the New England Fishery Management Council, I would look at myself in the mirror and critically analyze my choices. As a result, I would be compelled to draw the following conclusions.

The current four options of Amendment 13 provide these choices:

Option One allows me to crush the fishing industry with a stone: some of its broken bones will heal over time;

Option Two allows me to smash the fishing industry with a club: one can go on living without a limb or two for quite some time;

Option Three allows me to wound the fishing industry with a gun: the wound will be debilitating only for a few years;

Option Four allows me to dispatch the fishing industry with a machine gun: the survivors might flee for good, and the industry might never resurrect again.

It seems to me that, faced with such horrible choices (Are these CHOICES? Are these OPTIONS?), we need a fifth option. The fifth option, which the Council might have not considered yet, is a modified Demetri proposal that can be phrased somewhat like this:

WE the undersigned members of the New England Fishery Council, singly and jointly,

Recognizing that the stocks of bottom fish are naturally rebuilding themselves;

Realizing that the administrative measures already in place are achieving their goal—but a bit too slowly to suit all palates;

We propose a modest addition to the defense of the naked status quo;

We propose a compromise whose core can be stated as follows:

We Resolve:

Since the law, in the form of the Honorable Judge Gladys Kessler, is directing us to make some decision about Amendment 13, we wish to comply by adding one day to each category of days-at-sea restrictions. One day and no more.

But, what if Judge Kessler and all parties involved in this law suit will not accept our Solomonic decision?

The Council will enter into negotiations with the National Marine Fisheries Service (NMFS) and NMFS will eventually satisfy the needs of the plaintiffs (NGOs), who are properly concerned with the errors of the past. With the breathing room thus gained, neither NMFS, nor the Council, nor the various fishing communities involved will sit idly by. There is much work to be done. A better stock assessment science will be developed, better policies towards discards will be formulated, and at the same time we will all seriously work on a multispecies model of management.

The basis for this study is already available to the Council in the massive study done on behalf of the Gloucester Community Development Corporation by a team of volunteers composed of Dr. Peter Otto, Jeroen Struben, and Sanghyun Lee from the MIT Systems Dynamic Program under the direction of Professor Jim Hines.

This multispecies model suggests that we have to manage all the fisheries at once, not one at a time—sequentially. In nature, everything affects everything else at the same time. The predator-prey system that exists in nature says that if we do not manage, nay, if we do not catch, herring and mackerel, the so-called pelagics, they will overpower bottom fish species such as cod and haddock. And of course, if we overfish the pelagics, we might have a collapse of other fish species, including tuna and whales.

What we as members of the Council can say to all interested parties is this: What we need is a balance; a balanced management model; a balanced fisheries industry. If you look at the catch of pelagics in Gloucester during the last few years, a fishery that had died during the last few decades, we are on the verge of achieving this goal. Please, give us a chance to succeed; give us time.

Dear plaintiffs and defendants in this unfortunate lawsuit, any one of the options offered by Amendment 13 will kill the fishing industry. We cannot be a party to that. We know you will understand. We will vote for Option Five, the preservation of the status quo. And to respect the spirit of the law, we will impose one extra day of penalty on our fishermen. One day and no more.

My board of directors has studied this proposal and approved it unanimously. I hope that every other group in town and groups all along the coast will come to the same conclusion. I recommend to every reader to send a letter to this effect to the New England Fishery Management Council in Newburyport, MA. I hope the Council, in its wisdom, will take the same stand.

I doubt if there is any other industry in any free country of the world that is as completely regulated as the U.S. fishing industry. And yet, the fishermen who belong to the Northeast Seafood Coalition, assisted by many wise counselors, have mastered the bewildering complexity of the maze of rules and regulations, politics and science, sophisticated mathematics and discriminating geography of the ocean under which they have been operating for decades now. They are ready to offer an even more generous compromise than the one I am proposing. They are ready to accept even greater sacrifices than the ones they have experienced so far—provided they are allowed to catch fish that are underfished in other areas of the ocean. This compromise is well in tune with the latest suggestions from biologists and economists who are recommending an "area-management" approach.

Even though I praise them for their generosity, when I look at the issues from a comprehensive point of view, when I look at the issues from the point of view of the total biomass in the sea, rather than the biomass calculated species by species, I would not go that far. I would say, again, "The status quo plus one—and no more." I commend our fishermen and I urge the Council to accept their compromise, even if this compromise will indeed inflict more pain on the industry.

We have already come too dangerously close to losing our fishing industry. We need to retreat from the precipice. If we lose our fishing industry, we are going to lose our tourist industry as well. Why run this risk? Our rallying cry ought to be '"The status quo plus one—and no more."

Who ever heard of a people who have to beg to go to work!

Carmine Gorga, Ph.D.
Executive Director
Gloucester Community Development Corporation
128 Main Street,
Gloucester, MA 01930

Tiny Fish, Huge Future, Say Herring Fans

By BARBARA TAORMINA
Times staff

Reprinted with permission from *The Gloucester Daily Times*, May 21, 2001

Carmine Gorga and Ed Lima believe herring can play a leading role in Gloucester's evolving waterfront.

As the leaders of the newly formed Gloucester Community Development Corp., a local non-profit economic development organization, Gorga and Lima are making the rounds with an idea to create a new high-tech plant to process herring and other pelagic fish.

Both Gorga and Lima are members of Gloucester Initiatives, a grass-roots group of local activists committed to protecting the harbor as Gloucester's central economic resource.

Their immediate goal with the new herring plan is to get fishermen, processors and other waterfront advocates to the table to talk. The long-term goal is to transform Gloucester into a high-tech seafood processing center.

One of Gorga and Lima's first official stops was at last week's Fisheries Commission meeting where they briefly introduced their idea.

"We are looking at getting support for a herring manufacturing plant," Lima told the commission. "We are looking at creating a value-added product with a manufacturing plant that's very high- tech, very green."

The idea as it now stands is to build a plant that will process herring, mackerel and menhaden into surimi (sir-ree-me), a concentrated fish paste that is used as the basis for other seafood products.

According to Trident Seafoods, a leading U.S. producer of surimi, the process was developed in Japan almost 1,000 years ago.

Nowadays, whole fish is boned, skinned, minced, washed and strained into concentrated fish paste, which is then flash-frozen. Processors then add flavorings such as crab extract, as well as natural coloring and natural binders and stabilizers, such as starch, salt, egg white and sugar.

The surimi seafood is then shaped to look like the product it imitates, and marketed under various brand names.

Labels on surimi seafood are required by law to say "imitation" to avoid confusion with the real product.

Although Gorga and Lima have yet to start work on the details of what they estimate will be a $10 million plant, they highlighted what they believe are the proposal's key benefits.

Because the waterfront lacks the infrastructure to handle fish waste, most fish is landed and then shipped with little or no processing. A surimi plant would bring fish processing back to the waterfront, which has essentially operated as a fish transfer station for the past decade.

Processing pelagics into surimi would add approximately four times the value to the original fish product, according to Lima. Those types of potential profits make working with low-paying catches a more attractive option to fishermen and processors accustomed to earning six cents a pound or less from herring.

Surimi's value-added benefits also ease the need for huge volumes of fish needed to support a more traditional herring or mackerel manufacturing plant. Thus the risk of overfishing and depleting stocks is less of a concern.

Lima also stressed that the plant would incorporate the latest water reclamation and processing technologies that would produce little or no waste.

Gorga and Lima want to talk with anyone and everyone about the idea, but they are paying close attention to ideas and opinions from the waterfront.

"We want to put together fishermen and processors and let them argue about their needs," said Gorga. "We want them on both sides of the table surrounded by experts who can offer technical advice."

But they also intend to work closely with the city's Community Development Department, Mayor Bruce Tobey, the Cape Ann Chamber of Commerce and anyone interested in becoming involved in hammering a working proposal that will draw funding and investors.

Still, they admit that building trust and cooperation will be a difficult task.

"Saying the fishing industry is dead is almost a slogan and this is what has to be changed," said Gorga, who hopes the new idea will help boost community confidence in the waterfront. "The issue is to convince people in Gloucester that the fishing industry is alive and well and can have a brilliant future."

Sumptuous Surimi Seafood Science

by Michael Ryan
Reprinted with permission from
Common Sense for Gloucester and Cape Ann
Issue No. 10, Thursday November 29, 2001, pp. 1, 12

In Maine, Eastern Pulp & Paper Corp. — a paper manufacturer — uses waste sawdust in manufacturing its pulp, thus saving more than four million tons of virgin timber and ridding the company of unnecessarily and wastefully burning the waste saw dust. On November 25th, Maine Gov. Angus King presented the company with an environmental excellence award for its accomplishments in pollution prevention.

As forestry companies like Eastern Pulp & Paper try to abide by the regulations imposed upon them by their regulator, U.S. Environmental Protection Agency, Gloucester fishing concerns continue to struggle even to see eye to eye with their regulatory body, the National Marine Fisheries Services. Fishermen here are forced to throw overboard the majority of their catch. In the midst of stringent, suffocating regulations, a shrinking fishing fleet, continuously conflicting industry data, and blue-light special federal boat buyout programs, new fishing- and fish-related concerns are gathering momentum.

Whether due to a perceived need for a more stable business model or the result of a thousand years of success in development by Japanese fishermen and cooks, surimi and the plan Carmine Gorga, Ph.D. proposes may now be ready for implementation. But, before the wheels of the independent, for-profit company Gloucester Fish, Inc. start spinning, the non-profit, fishing industry partner Gloucester Community Development Corporation first needs to educate Gloucester fishermen, fish processing firms, and fish and seafood marketers about the benefits of joining such a collaborative.

Gorga, president of Gloucester Community Development, and an economist at Polis-tics, Inc., wishes "to bring the community together on the issues of lowering production costs and bringing equity ownership to the three players — fishermen, processors, and marketers. Each can lease the equipment, but what we're doing is forging relationships with these important people for the betterment of the community and a profitable enterprise."

Having served more than thirty-five years in community development roles, ranging from City Planner for Community Planning Services in Boston to Director of Planning and Economic Development for Action, Inc. in Gloucester, he's firm in his belief that today the community is ripe for the business model he suggested back in 1970 — a Functional Integration (FI) Model, a form of organization that attempts to obtain the complementary benefits of vertical or horizontal integration, as well as those of total independence leading to social harmony characterized by civic responsibility.

"The idea of a surimi plant becomes more acceptable if it is seen as the fulcrum to transform Gloucester into a leading seafood processing center. And we're not talking about a huge plant. The space the centrifuges require is only about the size of two small conference rooms."

In short, using his *mall* business model analogy, he wishes to foster specialization of activities that small entrepreneurs (i.e. fishermen, fish marketers, and processors) cannot achieve, or could achieve more easily collaboratively. A socialist he is not. With low costs and barriers to entry for local Gloucester fishermen, the processed pelagic product's retail price tag is estimated to fetch four times the value of the original product, and profits are to be shared by the players, according to their investment. Next month, he'll present his plan to the Founder's Forum at MIT, but, more important, he says, is the need to listen to the ideas of active local fishermen, in order to best serve the community.

Along with MIT students and related businesspeople, his initiative has the buy-in of several of Cape Ann's fishing industry experts, including Ed Lima (whose columns appear in Common Sense), Mayor Bruce Tobey and Dean Harrison, Director of Community Development, Dave Ellenton, President of World Wide Trading, Dr. Herbert Hultin, Dr. Stephen D. Kelleher, of Umass Marine Station at Hodgkins Cove, who together founded the H-K Surimi Processing Model Gloucester Fish, Inc. will rely on.

"When Angela Sanfilippo of the Gloucester Fishermen Wives told me she would support the collaborative, I felt our chances to succeed just grew by thirty-five percent; she knows and understands everything — all aspects of the businesses, outreach, and manufacturing — so I was very proud to have her with us."

Paralleling the success of surimi are the achievements of Dr. Joe Park, a faculty member in the Department of Food Science and Technology at the Oregon State University Seafood Lab. He brought international recognition to OSU as a leader in seafood science research by establishing the OSU Surimi School in 1993. Each year, the school has a long waiting list and attracts attendees from Japan, Mexico, Ireland, Chile, France, Thailand, Spain, Russia, Denmark, Sweden, Malaysia, and other countries. He established international OSU Surimi Schools in Thailand and France, which are run in alternate years, and he received a grant from the Office of International Research and Development, making the establishment of the first overseas Surimi School in Thailand possible. Dr. Park has been involved in several research projects on an international level and received funding from the Royal Thai Government to undertake a joint research project with Khon Kaen University in the use of tilapia (a species of fish) for surimi. Recently, he received a grant from the Thai Research Fund to work as a mentor for Dr. J. Yongsawatdigul at Suranaree University of Technology and also received funding and support from the Icelandic National Science Foundation for a joint research project with the University of Iceland in the utilization of seafood wastes in fish sauce production.

In the Gloucester CDC study, which encompassed March 13, 2001 to June 30, 2001, the CDC presented the outline and project summary to eighty-seven civic and political leaders, thirty-two fishing captains, and fifteen seafood processors and waterfront owners.

"The consensus has been that it is worthwhile to explore all the details required to establish the physical and financial feasibility of a surimi plant in Gloucester. The project would give Gloucester and its fishermen a great boost. A model surimi plant just went live in Iceland in September of this year, and not only is surimi being widely marketed in countries like Thailand, Japan, and Korea, it's in huge demand in countries like France, due to its versatility in taste and texture."

"There are so many opportunities beyond the marketing of surimi, too, such as oils and pharmaceuticals. Everything from the fish bones to the scales is recycled in some way, and as a value-added, there's no limit really to what you can do with it." But, again, it's not so much the inventiveness and the development of the idea of processing pelagics into surimi that brings notice to the astute potential investor, it's the labor-intensive administration of task specialization and project management.

Gorga's talking about coordinating and collaborating...among fishermen, processors, and marketers...across several industries...in Gloucester...a city lacking adequate space for waterfront manufactories, or fish processing facilities. Venturing down this road would certainly require excellent communication technologies, foundation assistance, superb management, marketing expertise, and quality assurance of fish products.

To this, he says, "We'll reach efficiency standards in purchasing supplies and equipment, borrowing monies and attending to all other financing requirements of a modern business — including purchasing insurance — that individual entrepreneurs cannot on their own obtain. We'll manage maintenance schedules of all machinery and equipment in a manner unachievable by individual entrepreneurs, and we'll administer a growing database of marketing and biological data. Such a collaborative will nurture first-rate research and development laboratories. The nearest equivalent to this type of social integration is a shopping mall that would be owned by all owners and employees of stores operating within the mall. This is in contrast to the conventional structure in which the malls are owned and operated by independent concerns, which simply rent space within the mall, pay rent, and are provided with all the services that are needed in common."

"In our case, quite rightly, all capital gains (and losses) that accrue from the operation of the mall belong to the owners of the mall. In the FI Model, capital gains or losses accrue to owners of the hardware, and whatever profits accrue from the rental of the hardware belong only to the teams that rent the hardware. The more trust, the more cohesion, the more benefits. Today, this collaboration occurs quite rarely, and when it does it is mostly due to chance — one processor here, two fishermen there."

"What will you see thirty years from now? If you go down to the Gloucester waterfront today, you can plainly see that the seafood industry is in a state of disorganization and despair. You see few fishing boats steaming out to sea to fish for cod, haddock, and flounder because of the federal regulations. You see seafood plants that, due to the decreased catch, have been forced to close. You quickly realize that wharf space left idle for a number of years begins attracting condominium and real estate developers, motels, and touristy stores. The soul of Gloucester — America's oldest fishing port — will be inalterably changed. To have true renewal of the fisheries, we need to have a thorough renewal of our economic policies and practices."

Glossary of Industry Terms:

Some terms were defined by Angela Sanfilippo of The Gloucester Fishermen Wives, while others were culled from a seafood processor's web site.

Aquaculture — Finfish or shellfish raised in fresh or saltwater pens or ponds or on growing surfaces such as ropes or posts.

Best Available Science — Unbiased information based on data that integrates current data that is less than two years old, is collected by both government and fishermen working together, utilizing the same or calibrated equipment and practices and meets generally accepted standards with no less than 80% accuracy, defined by the probability distribution function. The best available science must be used before a stock can be declared "over fished".

Biomass — the amount of living material.

Blast Freezing — Freezing by circulating cold air over batched product placed in trays or racks.

Bleeding — Severing an artery of a fish before the fish is gutted and dies to allow the heart to pump out the fish's blood. The result is a whiter fillet and higher quality meat.

Blocks — Frozen compressed slabs of fish fillets, usually without skin and bone, used as raw material for value-added products.

By-catch — Unintended catching and killing of marine life.

CSW — Chilled seawater. Seawater chilled with ice and mixed using air.

Deep Skinned — Removing the fat layer underneath the skin on oily species for milder flavor and improved shelf life; also called defatted.

FAS — Frozen at sea.

Fishing Community — US vessels, crew, people, and related businesses that earn
   income as the result of the harvesting or processing of wild fish stocks.

Fish Oil — Fatty oil from the bodies of fishes pressed from cooked fish during the manufacture of fish meal and separated by centrifuge. Used in the manufacture of many products, such as margarine, cooking oil,
   cosmetics, caulking compounds, paints, industrial coatings, lubricants, water repellents, soaps, and candles.

Fish meal — Coarsely ground powder made from the cooked flesh of fish, primarily used in animal feed especially for poultry, swine, mink, farm-raised fish, and pets.

Formed Fillets — Portions cut from blocks in such a way that they appear to be natural fillets although all are exactly the same size and shape.

Frozen-At-Sea Products — Fish and shellfish that are cleaned, processed, and frozen on board usually within hours of being caught.

Gel Strength — Mechanical strength and elasticity of the gel produced in cooked surimi.

GMPs — Good Manufacturing Practices. Federal regulations that describe proper food sanitation and handling practices. HACCP (Hazard Analysis of Critical Control Points) — The basis of a voluntary seafood inspection program overseen jointly by the National Marine Fisheries Service and the Food and Drug Administration. HACCP requires suppliers to write up and follow a program detailing all points in their manufacturing process where hazards exist.

Healthy Fishing Community — A "fishing community" that maintains sustainable participation in US fisheries and provides for the social, economic, and cultural needs of such community.

Over Fishing — That amount of fishing mortality, not including mortality or stock population declines from other causes (e.g. pollution or habitat loss, changes in physical or natural environmental conditions, predators, and unknown causes) which decrease spawning biomass to a stock level that results in decreasing stock population over time.

Pelagic — Species living in the open sea, as distinguished from benthic species living near the bottom.

Previously Frozen — Frozen seafood that has been slacked out, or thawed, for sale in that state. Must be clearly identified as "previously frozen" product to distinguish it from fresh.

Primary Processor — Refers to the first freezing/processing facility that handles freshly caught fish or shellfish.

RSW — Refrigerated Seawater. A chilling and holding system for fish that uses mechanical refrigeration to cool seawater. Boats involved in Surimi production off of Gloucester might transport pelagics in RSW containers.

Secondary Processor — Refers to a processing facility that utilizes previously frozen seafood and further processes it (into specialty cut, batter/bread, etc.) before selling.

Shelf Life — The expected amount of time a seafood product remains in high quality condition for human consumption. Variation in shelf life among species is due to composition of the seafood. In general, the higher the fat content, the more prone the product is to spoilage and flavor changes. Cold temperatures retard most of these changes.

Surimi — An odorless, white fish paste developed by the Japanese centuries ago; made from minced fish meat (usually pollock) which has been washed to remove fat, blood, pigments, and odorous substances and mixed with cryoprotectants, such as sugar and/or sorbital.

Surimi Seafood — Analog shellfish products made from surimi that has been thawed, blended with flavorings, stabilizers and colorings and then heat processed to make fibrous, flake, chunk, and composite molded products, most commonly imitating crabmeat, lobster tails, and shrimp.

Value-Added — Product that has been reprocessed and repackaged into a consumer ready form.

Vertical Integration — Refers to a company's ability to control its goods from the beginning raw state to the finished end product, including harvesting, processing, and marketing.

Yield — The amount of meat that can be recovered from a particular fish or shellfish; usually expressed as a percent.

1. Tempura -Thailand
2. Imitation Shrimp — Thailand, Korea and China.
3. Imitation Lobster Tails — Thailand and Korea
4. Imitation Crab Claw Meat — Thailand and Korea
5. Imitation Smoked Salmon Flakes & Sticks -Thailand and Korea
6. Surimi Claws — Korea and Malaysia

A fish full of dollars?

Reprinted with permission from *North Shore Sunday*
By Chad Konecky
Friday, May 2, 2003

Economist and author Carmine Gorga surveys Gloucester Harbor's dwindling small boat fleet. As executive director of the Gloucester Community Development Corporation, Gorga believes he's championing a plan that would return Gloucester fishing to Gloucester fishermen.

A Gloucester economist says a different catch — and a new way of doing business — can save the city's fishing industry. But some fishermen think he's full of carp.

There's no mistaking Dulie's Dory on Gloucester's Commercial Street for anything other than a fishermen's greasy spoon. Especially within 30 minutes of sunrise.

Weathered, stout men trickle in from predawn until around 7. These guys sport the other 5 o'clock shadow. Many have berthed boats just a couple hours earlier, snaking home between Field Rocks and Ten Pound Island in darkness. And now they're dining. In a wood-paneled, drop-ceiling shack backed up against Pavilion Beach underneath a pink-streaked sky.

Conversation is sparse. Plates overflow. The clear laminate countertop entombs a seafaring photo essay. Images of mammoth catches and monster storms, faded by time and tall tales.

A clock with lighthouses for numbers marks the morning minutes and a curiously crisp sheet of office paper offers a phone number for tax-free cigarettes. Adorning a paneled support beam overhead is a gallery of variously vivid pinup postcards — gals and thongs from faraway slices of sand and sun. Just next door is the Cape Ann Chamber of Commerce.

A cruel coincidence.

The fishing industry as Gloucester knew it and meaningful commerce appear to be in the final stages of a bitter divorce. Former fisherman Mark Godfried spins smartly on his Dory stool in confirming that.

The current federal catch limit and fishing grounds regulations on groundfish like cod, haddock, flounder, hake, pollock and whiting "are designed to create a limited number of offshore fishing companies and spell the elimination of the small-boat fleet," says Godfried, 67, who fished commercially from 1975 until 1992 and now serves as a buyer at the Gloucester Seafood Display Auction. "The National Marine Fisheries Service is not truly interested in preserving this fleet."

Carmine Gorga is.

The executive director of the non-profit Gloucester Community Development Corporation, Gorga is a jovial, robust native of Salerno, Italy, part Kris Kringle and a dash of George Peppard. Two months before his 8th birthday, he watched America's liberating Fifth Army roll through his hometown and khaki remains his favorite color because of it.

At 68, the spriteish Gorga is about as unlikely a Galahad for Gloucester fishing as any Merlin could conjure. But the Fulbright scholar and Ph.D., an academic advisee of Nobel laureate economist Robert A. Mundell at Johns Hopkins University's Bologna Center, is point man for a plan.

"Trying to stop regulation of falling fish stock is like trying to stop an avalanche ," says Gorga, who advocates a retrofitted Gloucester fleet designed to target different fish stocks than cod and its bottom-dwelling neighbors, Gloucester's staple catch since 1623. "People think Gloucester fishing is a thing of the past. But it is the present. This is about attacking a fear. There are enormous economic pressures here. And they are negative pressures. So restrictive. So much scarcity. Species that are depleted. Instead, let's look at the biomass and concentrate on what's in abundance."

To Gorga, the plan is Gloucester's deliverance.

The gist: Use new federal funding to build a vertically integrated cooperative industry uniting fishermen, processing and marketing under the same roof. The product — a processed fish meat that can be powdered or spun into protein paste, either later reconstituted in water, called surimi — is part of a high-growth, worldwide niche market. And a Gloucester-born technology allows for the use of abundant, cheap bait fish once unfit for such processing, principally herring and mackerel, as the source meat. Associated oils can be marketed separately. Scales and skin can be converted to fertilizer.

A multi-layered industry of which each participant owns a share.

To at least some Gloucestermen, it's a pipe dream.

"Anybody that comes along with a cure-all plan at this point, it's a bunch of BS," says Gloucester's Dean DeCoste, a former fisherman and lobsterman, now running the ice hockey rink at South Hamilton's Pingree School. "A pair of trawlers could fish this entire ocean out here out of herring and mackerel on their own. There are no saviors. The government made a big business out of a little business and now the little business is gone."

Gorga doesn't dispute the industry's previous failings. He does insist that this new business would be exclusively a Gloucester business. Making all the difference.

A surimi tsunami

DeCoste's suggestion that independent "inshore" fishermen, guys for whom a typical trip endures 24 hours or less, haven't raised anchor on a level ocean for some time has merit. An ever-tightening federal noose around legally fishable cod grounds has choked boat captains since a dramatic, late-1980s falloff in stock necessitated radical conservation regulations by the mid-'90s.

But that doesn't mean Gorga is selling snake oil.

What's newsworthy — what hits at the essence of Gloucester's future — is that Gorga's script casts a blue-backed, silver-bellied bait fish about 12 inches long in a starring role of the port city's recovery. Which makes the most vital morsel on Gloucester waterfront these days, besides the Dory's ham, egg and onion sandwich on wheat, easily digestible. Herring is the hot topic.

Red hot.

The most user-friendly definition of surimi: The fake crabmeat in refrigerated packages at your local supermarket.

More broadly and absent flavor additives, it's processed fish. Traditionally obtained from white flesh fish, surimi is a remarkable source of protein, infuriatingly healthful and enjoys an exploding market in Asia and France as well as domestically. According to Seattle-based Trident Seafoods, a leading U.S. producer of surimi, the traditional process was developed in Japan 1,000 years ago.

How those details become relevant to Gloucester is pretty complicated. The story boils down to three parts.

First, a pair of University of Massachusetts Marine Station scientists in Gloucester, Dr. Herbert Hultin and Dr. Stephen Kelleher, have patented a method to process dark-flesh fish like herring, mackerel and menhaden, the latter commonly called pogies, into surimi.

Gorga says these fish, known as pelagic because they're catchable in a mid-water column between the surface and bottom, exist in abundance.

National Marine Fisheries Service (NMFS) data backs him up. A whopping 1.8 million metric tons of total spawning stock biomass, according to U.S. estimates, allowing for a total allowable catch (TAC) of up to 250,000 metric tons per year.

Currently, about 100,000 metric tons are being landed annually, according to the New England Fishery Management Council in Newburyport, which oversees fishery resources in federal waters off the coast of Maine, New Hampshire, Massachusetts, Rhode Island and Connecticut.

Part two: A group of Gorga-recruited smart guys from the System Dynamics Program at MIT's Sloan School of Management have concluded, given existing species data for those same fish, a sustainable volume of product could support a Gloucester fish-processing center based upon the UMass technology.

Third, Gorga introduces a means by which federal loans to local banks could finance a cooperatively owned surimi industry. This would be new government money. Money Gorga calls "national credit," a concept not yet approved, but on the horizon (see accompanying box) and right in line with the Bush administration's stimulus package.

Gorga's model, Gloucester Fishing, Inc. (GFI), would be the genuine cooperative article. Employee stock ownership. Umbrella insurance coverage, maintenance contracts and tax structure for the boats, the plant and the product's local marketers. Captains might not even own their boats at GFI, functioning more like a professional airline crew, disembarking at the end of a trip as another crew boards.

Revolutionary. But feasible?

"When you talk about fishing herring more aggressively, you're talking about eliminating the base food source of an entire food chain," says Gloucester gill net fisherman Rich Burgess, who owns five inshore groundfishing vessels, four of which are idle until June 1 due to current federal regulations. "Every other species interacts with the Atlantic herring. The stock is already in trouble. It's crazy.

"These NMFS scientists specialize in creating a crisis to justify their existence," adds Burgess. "They protected the striped bass, which feed on juvenile lobster, and now the bass exists in such abundance, the lobster stock is down. Now they say there's herring, but nobody can find any. Bottom line, we used to be able to fish 300 days a year, now it's 70. This harbor used to be packed. Today, there are maybe 25 boats. The Mafia would run a better operation than this. I'd rather deal with them."

But there's a catch

At first blush, it might seem Burgess's groundfish gripes and Gorga's mid-column Godsend are largely disparate. Not so. Like the richly complex multi-species ecosystem of the North Atlantic, the men's respective passions are interrelated.

You can't fish pelagic stock with enough yield to support a surimi plant without hauling herring. Heavy. Burgess is one of many bright folks who believe herring is nowhere near as bountiful as NMFS says. Canadian scientists estimate the North Atlantic herring total spawning stock biomass at 550,000 metric tons, less than a third of the NMFS number.

More to the point, corporate giant super-boats from out of town, some passing through the Panama Canal from the herring-depleted Pacific Northwest, are currently docked in Gloucester, trawling herring. And trawling in fishing grounds (almost certainly dragging the bottom and thereby a portion of the ground stock) that Burgess and captains like him are banned from. Foreign capital is also flowing into New England to support developing processing operations for Atlantic herring.

Carmine Gorga might be sitting on a gold mine. Or, atop a biomass bust.

"Although I'm personally unfamiliar with the details of (Gorga's community development plan), I expect those involved ... are similarly concerned with making sure the herring resource is both available and sustainable," says Glenn Roger Delaney, a Washington, D.C. lobbyist and U.S. commissioner of the International Commission for the Conservation of Atlantic Tuna, a species that feeds principally upon herring. "Poor and unrealistic planning has led to many a bust in 'gold-rush' fisheries around the world."

Gorga reckons GFI needs about $10 million to coax the surimi genie from the bottle. GFI surimi sales are projected at about $12 million annually, allowing for at least $700,000 initial reinvestment into the coop after everyone gets paid.

"These are general federal resources, a pool of commonwealth," says Gorga, who thrice tried and failed by differing means to bring a cooperative element to Gloucester fishing from 1968-'75 as director of economic development for Action, Inc., a Cape Ann non-profit anti-poverty organization. "The Federal Reserve is suggesting exactly what I'm saying. The possibility would exist for GFI to go to [Federal Reserve Bank of Boston CEO] Dr. Cathy Minehan and say, 'Can GFI have $10 million?' and she could write a check. It's a loan to the bank, then to the fishery for a specific national credit program.

"Right now, Gloucester is a pass-through port for catch," he adds. "This plant would transform Gloucester into a seafood processing center."

But GFI's surimi plant calls for 30,000 [subsequently corrected from erroneously reported 300,000] metric tons of fish, annually, meaning even taking herring to its current TAC, which might be lowered, would fulfill only half the plant's need. Fishery Management Council regs further stipulate that herring's current TAC includes 80,000 metric tons of reserve, only accessible if a southern New England fishing ground hits a 50,000 metric ton take, which has never happened.

"It's hard to get your hands around what's an appropriate scale," says state Sen. Bruce Tarr, R-Gloucester. "How much of the plant's functionality will rely on herring? Will there be enough product to keep the process flowing smoothly?"

Surimi boasts considerable appeal, nonetheless.

"Carmine's system involves a vertical integration of the industry in which the fishermen would own the processing," explains Gloucester's Damon Cummings, 65, a former MIT professor of naval architecture and now a fishermen's activist advocating technological solutions to population dynamics in association with Sailors' Snug Harbor of Boston. "The idea is, they'd make more money than if they sold pelagic catch separately on shore to processors. The (UMass) technology is crucial to the whole thing. Two plants are already operating, one in Chile and one Iceland."

Yet fishermen are a prickly lot when they perceive their livelihood, perhaps the ultimate capitalist venture, drifting toward any shore associated with socialist sensibilities.

"That's true, but there are some progressive guys in the industry who have an eye toward innovation, so I'm not so sure it can't sell here," counters Cummings. "But there is a problem with how people see fishing in the community. The obstacles aren't just crazy science at the fisheries and stocks being down. It's also a matter of perception. Many people think fishing is gone, but it's still bigger in Massachusetts than software. Carmine's is a great idea and I hope it works. We'll see."

Gorga, then, may be fighting a three-front battle: economics and ecosystem, along with heavy hearts and closed minds.

A barbed hook

Whether a sustainable and profitable pelagic population swims beneath the surface is the keystone for GFI.

"There's certainly no question that mackerel and herring stocks are the highest we've seen and that there's no problem with that stock size regarding increased exploitation of the stock without trepidation, according to our research," says Teri Frady, chief of research communication at the National Oceanic and Atmospheric Administration in Wood's Hole, Mass.

But even folks under same governmental umbrella don't endorse that notion as heartily.

"We have a Canadian assessment and a U.S. assessment that conflict, but the stock is healthy," says Lori Steele, a herring fishery analyst at Newburyport's New England Fishery Management Council (FMC). "We are committed, however, to review both assessments so our Scientific and Statistical Committee can manage the stock more effectively and make a recommendation to our Herring Plan Development Team, which would adjust TAC accordingly."

Even Gorga acknowledges Gloucester might only currently support a modest retrofitted fleet of about 10 boats.

That level of uncertainty, particularly within the same regulatory walls, could act as Kryptonite for Gorga's plan. Herring and mackerel sometimes co-mingle, making it difficult to take one without the other. According to Gloucester's CDC, the TAC for mackerel and pogies is about 500,000 metric tons, but that data may be even fuzzier than the herring estimates.

"Balance is the key," says Godfried. "If you take too much of any one species, you start a chain reaction."

Gloucester's CDC estimates it would cost $250,000 per boat to retrofit the addressable portions of the Gloucester fleet — expanding, say, a 60-foot vessel to 90 feet.

Gorga knows the federal money will likely be there to do that.

"Hard cash is very convincing," says Gorga. "It's a question of education. But a lot of people will be motivated when $10 million comes along. Once they start seeing their ownership share grow, they'll be hooked."

But how many additional nets in the water can the pelagic fishery support? Not to mention, GFI won't help guys like Burgess, whose fleet of 30- to 50-foot groundfishing boats presents no candidates for retrofitting.

In fact, herring fishing appears to be an antagonist. Both as far as the ecosystem supporting the groundfish stock rebound and via the groundfish taken unintentionally in a herring catch, called bycatch.

The Newburyport FMC confirms there is no existing data to delineate the issue of bycatch as negligible, a crisis or anywhere in between.

"We have very few observers on mid-water trawlers and the limited number of trips we have are several years old," says Tom Nies, an FMC groundfish fishery analyst.

"So we really don't know about bycatch."

That raises plenty of people's blood pressure.

"NMFS is going full speed ahead on increasing whale and mammal populations, which require herring to thrive, just as tuna, dogfish (sharks) and groundfish populations do," says Rich Ruais, executive director of the East Coast Tuna Association, who represents harpoon and rod-and-reel tuna fisherman from Maine to Florida. "NMFS hasn't researched how much herring we need to leave behind to support those populations. This is all being done blind.

"The stock assessment being touted by NMFS is that you ought to be able to walk on herring from Cape Ann to the tip of Georges Bank," adds Ruais. "What you're hearing from industry greatly disputes that. What the bottom line is, I don't think anyone knows.

"It's crazy to talk about more boats fishing herring," he says. "You've got to shut the gate for this fishery. You've got the capacity in New England right now to harvest whatever your dream TAC is. The federal estimates are what's driving the capital investment in herring and the leadership of the NMFS are the only ones who can shut that faucet off."

Ruais's gate isn't fictional. And it could well slam on Gorga.

NMFS proclaimed Sept. 16, 1999 as a conditional control date. Any permits issued for herring fishing after that date could be subjected to limited or revoked access to that fishery if stock levels drop.

If the fish aren't there, pelagic surimi becomes Odysseus's Sirens, luring GFI toward the rocks.

Tarr and measured

It's easy to see why it's hard for anyone around Gloucester to invest a ton of faith in fish stock. Particularly, say fishermen, when estimates and data streams are produced by bureaucrats who rarely, if ever, set foot on a boat.

Government regulators say spiny dogfish shark populations and cod populations are critically low. Word on Gloucester docks is, you can't drop a line in the water without hooking a dogfish and groundfish have rebounded significantly.

Quite the contrary, two 90-foot trawlers recently converted into 140-foot herring hunters — via a $5 million dollar facelift — returned to the Everett Jodrey State Fish Pier moorings in Gloucester this past Tuesday after a six-day trip without enough herring to fill a pickle jar.

"I don't think you can have a land-rush mentality and have everyone pursuing herring to the maximum extent and ignore the ecosystemic realities of the fishery in that everything is interrelated," says Tarr, noting that lobstermen are vexed by the new run on herring, which has cut into their fresh bait supply. "We need to be concerned about herring not only because of it's own resource qualities, but because it impacts other stocks very important to New England. Herring is being aggressively exploited right now."

So, putting GFI on a Providential pedestal is folly?

"There really isn't any panacea," says Tarr. "Even if Carmine's (pelagic) plant works, as we all hope it will, it won't solve all of Gloucester's problems. I'm confident at some level that it would work. The idea of having the plant support a substantial fishing fleet is wishful thinking, I believe. But the idea it might help a discrete number of vessels is a sound one. Particularly vessels fishing in a collaborative method, like a coop."

Sound. But still a tough sell.

"I'm sure the people saying herring and mackerel are the answer are well-intentioned," says Gloucester's Don Smith, who captains Burgess's 38-footer, Hollywood, routinely steaming seven hours to reach challenging seas and fishable grounds off Provincetown in a 31-year-old boat to comply with regulatory restrictions. "But it's just another bureaucratic measure. A clash of two different worlds. People telling the people who go get things how they can do it better."

E-mail reporter Chad Konecky at ckonecky@cnc.com.

New Markets Tax Credits (NMTC)

Excerpts from NMTC Debriefings, 2004

SECOND ROUND (2003-2004) NMTC ALLOCATION APPLICATION DEBRIEFING DOCUMENT

Concordians.org Inc.
Control Number: 03NMA001428

D. Community Impact Comments:

• The Applicant's strategy for serving communities of high economic distress is excellent... The Applicant clearly makes a case for the fishing villages that are in need of new economic revitalization and has a novel plan for modernizing the fishing processing industry.

• The reviewer has only some confidence in the ability of the Applicant to achieve projected impacts...

• The reviewer has only limited confidence that the applicant's strategy will catalyze additional investments in the targeted low-income communities. The vision is present with no plan of action connecting the vision to today's reality.

Quality Assurance of Seafood. — book reviews

Marine Fisheries Review, Wntr, 1989

Publication of Quality Assurance of Seafood" by Carmine Gorga and Louis J. Ronsivalli under the AVI Books imprint has been announced by Van Nostrand Reinhold, 115 Fifth Avenue, New York, NY 10003. Gorga is a fisheries consultant and Ronsivalli, retired, was a director of the NMFS Gloucester Technological Laboratory in Massachusetts. The book is published in three parts: I, assurance of seafood supply; II, assurance of seafood quality; and 3, administration and economics of quality assurance.

The authors stress that seafood quality assurance is not the same as seafood quality control; the former is a guarantee, and they use this book to provide a step-by-step review and discussion of the attitudes and steps that need to be adopted to guarantee the ultimate arbiter — the consumer — high quality fresh fish and fillets (shellfish or such products as canned, pickled, cured, or dried fish are not addressed). The book is suited for a broad audience, and it explains the various procedures in terms easily understood by processors, fishermen, as well as market owners and the consumers.

Part I presents general information on the values of seafoods, strategies for assuring the seafood supply, and the role of the U. S. government in the process. Part 2 then goes into seafood quality — how it is defined and measured, and how, why, and how fast seafood quality deteriorates. Then the authors discuss how to assure high seafood quality, discussing the roles of the fishermen, processors, retailers, and the consumers. Chapters in part 3 then outline the planning, administration, and coordination needed to assure high quality seafoods as well as the economics and economic benefits therein. Appendices discuss fish lipids, effects of decreasing temperature on the physical state of water in fish tissue, importance of accurately measuring seafood quality, spoilage rates of seafood, and provide formulae for the determination of gross profit margins and some specific costs. Indexed, the 245-page hardbound volume is available from the publisher for $42.95.

November 18, 2002

Published in the Gloucester Daily Times

A hat trick on one page

by Vincent Ferrini

Three goods glowed on the editorial page of Oct. 23:

• Cynthia Fisk's essay on how to handle terrorism, linking it to Halloween, seen at its profound obvious.

• Carmine Gorga's view that the creative class is slowly operating with the commercial class, at the very bottom and surface of the seas, in a process when seized by the fishing fathers will reap the reward lying fallow in our faces; an easy process sent or risen by the lowliest, the Pelagics. Commerce has fresh air, which comes out of the creative genius, when shared, becomes contagious, in directions rarely dreamt of.

• And Helen Lauenstein's letter, precise and exacting. Maybe this will reach the hoodwinked Democrats. The creative instinctively functions uninterrupted.

Under the Clouds of Perdition, the light is laughing.

December 11, 2002

Published in the Gloucester Daily Times

Gorga worthy of note

A book review by Vincent Ferrini, Gloucester (Poet Laureate)
reprinted by permission of Sheila Ferrini

Carmine Gorga, of the Gloucester Community Development, who studied with Nobel laureates in his discipline, is a practitioner of creative economics.

In his book, "The Economic Process," (University Press of America, 2002) he has the answers to universal poverty and the anxieties of the affluent.

The blueprint for the elimination of poverty among the masses of the planet. A manual for a healthy mind, in a healthy body, in a healthy society. Gorga is a Ph.D. authority in psychology, physics/metaphysics and his chosen center economics.

My ideal real man for the rectification of the stuck human condition. What Gloucester was, it can become again.

Today flies off before we know it and the future too. Can we make the leap and land into the promise. Without a doubt.

I read his book, the first I-IV sections were too abstract for me, incisive for the scholars, but it by passed me without establishing a landing, Part V held me to his anchor and the vessel's engine sang with the practical means for operating a spaceship into cosmic plenty.

Gloucester has a destiny for fulfilling i[t]s capabilities and resources in its jurisdictions: the island, the sea, the brains and the energies, marked to deliver the communion.

Gorga doesn't miss a shadow. He talks with the angels in the angles, a holistic seeder.

A review by Dr. Michael E. Brady*

of

The Economic Process
An Instantaneous
Non-Newtonian Picture

(University Press of America, 2002)
by Carmine Gorga

4.5 Stars-A dynamic systems (the economic system as a complex, evolving process) reinterpretation of Keynes's Y= C+ I model, July 8, 2007, at Amazon.com. Reprinted with permission.

By
Michael Emmett Brady "mandmbrady"
(Bellflower, California, United States) — See all my reviews

This book will be extremely difficult to follow for a " modern" mainstream economist brought up on general equilibrium theory (g.e.t) and the stochastic version of g.e.t based on the assumption that all the relevant variables in any macro model of the economy can be analyzed either as (or as if) they were random variables that are independently and identically distributed so that some type of normal distribution (log normal, bivariate normal, multivariate normal, etc.) can be assumed, based on the central limit theorem, to apply to the time series data generated by capitalist economies.

The writing style of the book is similar to the writing styles of Veblen, Schumpeter, Keynes, and von Hayek. This means that the reader is going to have to think carefully about the fundamental nature of capitalism as a complex system evolving through time. Gorga's (G) concern is to identify what the fundamental problem is that prevents such a system from obtaining AND MAINTAINING a full employment level of output. Why is such an economy subject to a destabilizing boom-bust business cycle over time? G is one of the very few economists to identify the fundamental problem as hoarding behavior. Hoarding means that the individual is not spending his income on consumption goods, investment goods, public goods, exported goods or imported goods. Hoarding problems will manifest themselves at the macroscopic level. Thus, involuntary unemployment can be identified as a macro problem that results from the microscopic hoarding behaviors of many individuals but will not be susceptible to a purely micro analysis based on utility maximization subject to an income constraint problem. It is an effective demand problem that shows up at the aggregate level. This, naturally, may present a major stumbling block for a modern day economist who believes that all macro behavior is merely the sum of all microbehavior.

G's framework of analysis is a reinterpretation of Keynes's syllogistic (double entry accounting) model of chapters 6(app.-65) and 10 that deals with the actual results. This is Keynes's simplist model and it can be used be demonstrate or establish the multiple equilibrium nature of the capitalist economy. Keynes' model specifies a positive relationship between consumption and investment spending(the aggregate demand side)that conflicts with the necessity for consumption goods and investment goods to be negatively related from the production side(aggregate supply side)of the analysis since full employment of all resources can only take place on the boundary of a production possibilities frontier. This boundary must have a negative slope. Keynes has introduced the possibility of a positive feedback effect. This effect is destabilizing. Speculative behavior can have catastrophic results if the commercial banking system is allowed to provide loans to speculators (hoarders) that allows them to try to leverage their private hoards so as to accumulate even more. For instance, Milton Friedman rejected Keynes's analysis because he felt that it was based on "excessive" liquidity preference. Naturally, Friedman views speculative behavior as stabilizing since he argues that it takes place under conditions of risk and not uncertainty. This distinction is fundamental Eliminating uncertainty and ignorance from decision making effectively eliminates hoarding behavior as a negative.

Keynes' model specification, however, does not allow him to specifically answer the question of why the economy is unstable. Keynes's answer is that the economy is unstable and suboptimal because of the propensity to hoard. Keynes calls this also by the name liquidity preference. Keynes can't show this in the Y=C+I model since there is no explicit role for money to play. Instead, Keynes demonstrates this in the expectations-uncertainty D-Z model of chapters 20 and 21. Keynes's result is that if L2 (the speculative demand for money) is greater than 0, you will have involuntary unemployment, which will increase as L2 increases. Gorga's reinterpretation of the Y model allows him to reach Keynes's conclusion as well as integrating it into a complex systems analysis (non Newtonian) as the economy evolves as a dynamic process over time.

G also shows that this is the major problem that has impacted all types of economies over the last 4,000 years and not just capitalist economies. This is also the major economic problem that has been identified by the Roman Catholic church during the many centuries that humans were subject to great uncertainty. Technically, it is impossible to eliminate all uncertainty which means that hoarding will be a problem. However, once identified, its negative impact can be reduced to a minimum. Keynes states this on pp. 241-42 and 351-52 but does not emphasize it for his economist audience. G emphasizes it and convincingly identifies it as the main problem.

There is one technical problem that appears throughout the book which may lead to confusion on the part of the reader. This is G's use of the symbol "=".This symbol must be interpreted to mean equivalence or equivalent to. I have deducted 1/2 of a star for this drawback. It can be remedied in a future edition. I would then give the book a 5 star rating.

---

* Michael E. Brady, Ph.D., is a lecturer in the Operations Management Dept. at California State University, Dominguez Hills. Overcoming its piecemeal presentation through chaps. 10, 19, 20, and 21-as well as two minor typographical mistakes on p. 283 and p. 305-of *The General Theory*, Dr. Brady has reconstructed the mathematical model that fully specifies Keynes' analysis of the economic system. In a series of papers and three books, he has found the answers to the question that has plagued the economics profession ever since 1936: "What did Keynes really mean?"

For additional reviews of this book, please see
www.carmine-gorga.us/id18.htm

PART FIVE

The Petition

The sacred roots of democracy:
"Where two or three are gathered in my name, there am I in their midst"
(Mt 18:20).
Even God seems to shunt aside the lonely wolf.

A Brief History

Two days to the opening of the 2007 Gloucester Sidewalk Bazaar, David Wise came to see me with a few ideas concerning a petition that we might offer to the passing crowds. I immediately agreed that it was a brilliant idea, and together we asked for the permission to have a booth on the sidewalk and prepared the following petition and its attachment.

We explained the purpose of the petition to as many people we could, as concisely as we possibly could. Many returned after signing with friends or family they encouraged to sign as well. Over the three days of the Bazaar we collected 425 signatures.

Shortly after the Sidewalk Bazaar we presented the petition to the City Clerk, Mr. Robert D. Whynott, with an enclosed letter to the Mayor and City Council. Of the 425 there were Cape Ann residents; visitors from many states; and even a few from abroad. Our City Clerk certified that there were enough legal signatures to qualify to legally present this petition to the Mayor and City Council. He transferred the documents to the City Council and a date, August 19, 2008, was set for a public hearing.

A Petition

To The Mayor
And
The Gloucester City Council

August 2007

Please Keep and sustain Downtown Gloucester economically vibrant

Name	Street	City

1._____

2._____

3._____

4._____

5._____

6._____

7._____

8._____

The Downtown Gloucester Restoration Committee
David S. Wise and Carmine Gorga
87 Middle Street, Gloucester, MA 01930 Tel. 978.283.5926
www.polis-tics.com
cgorga@polis-tics.com

How can we keep downtown Gloucester vibrant?

Shop at locally owned businesses

Continue beautification of store fronts

Continue city support of façade improvement

Search for a department store with low cost items, such as sheets, towels, pillow cases, stationary items, kitchen items, etc.

In the future, perhaps elevate Rogers Street to provide parking under it

Beautify its top and connect it with a promenade and park to the waterfront (http://polis-tics.com/id22.htm" http://polis-tics.com/id22.htm)

Let us scream with the famous Gloucester poet Charles Olson to prevent the loss of architectural and historically important buildings in Gloucester

Let us invest into the Gloucester Interdependence Fund (http://www.polis-tics.com/id23.htm" http://www.polis-tics.com/id23.htm)

Let us create Gloucester Fish Inc. (http://www.gloucestercdc.org/id32.htm" http://www.gloucester-cdc.org/id32.htm)

Let us revitalize our community spirit

The Downtown Gloucester Restoration Committee
David S. Wise and Carmine Gorga
87 Middle Street, Gloucester, MA 01930 Tel. 978.283.5926
www.polis-tics.com
cgorga@polis-tics.com
For recent articles by Carmine Gorga in the Gloucester Daily Times see Archives

The Downtown Gloucester Restoration Committee
David S. Wise and Carmine Gorga
87 Middle Street, Gloucester, MA 01930 Tel. 978.283.5926
www.polis-tics.com
cgorga@polis-tics.com

August 15, 2007

Gloucester Place City Hall
9 Dale Avenue
Gloucester, MA 01930

Dear Mayor John Bell, President James Destino, and Members of the City Council,

We would like to present to you the results of the survey we ran during the three days of the August Sidewalk Bazaar in Gloucester. After providing the public with the purpose of the survey as outlined in the enclosed attachment, we invited those interested to sign the petition.

We collected 425 signatures in the enclosed 39 pages, mostly from people living in Gloucester and Rockport, but did not discourage those from other cities to sign. Two tourists said that Forte dei Marmi in Italy is experiencing similar problems of sustaining the economic vibrancy of their downtown as in Gloucester.

We trust you will value this petition.

It will allow an integrated look at the issues facing our downtown. As suggested to the signers of the petition, there are solutions for sustaining the vibrancy of shopping in the Downtown if the experience is considered part of an integrated vision of the waterfront:

(a) exploring funding sources to raise Rogers Street and connect Main Street with the waterfront, by creating free parking below and a landscaped promenade attached to it;

(b) creating a private for-profit corporation dedicated to the development of new and innovative fish products such as Surimi and Omega-3 oils, Gloucester Fish Inc.;

(c) establishing a Gloucester Interdependence Fund, by bringing together financial resources and investing them exclusively in Gloucester. Such funds are not uncommon in Italy; see attached 1999 positive reaction from Cape Ann bank officers.

Please also have the flyer that was attached to the petition. It has more detailed suggestions and provides signers with two websites for additional, helpful information.

Sincerely,

David S. Wise   Carmine Gorga

GIC
GRLF
GRP

February 1, 1999

Carmine Gorga, Ph. D.
President, Polis-tics, Inc.
87 Middle Street
Gloucester, MA 01930

Re: Gloucester Mutual Fund

Dear Carmine,

We are writing in response to the discussion held on January 20th relative to your concept of a Gloucester Mutual Fund. After you excused yourself the other evening, the group had an opportunity to further discuss your ideas and then asked Dave Sidon to draft this response.

First and foremost, we would like to commend your selfless efforts toward establishing a common vision for Gloucester's urban restoration and recognizing that such a vision needs an economic stimulus in order to be successful. Your plan provided us with an interesting framework within which to discuss Gloucester's economic issues and potential.

As to the issue of considering the establishment of an entity such as your envisioned fund, we reached consensus that such an entity is not currently needed or viable. It seems to be premature to establish another funding source prior to establishing the restoration vision that will create the demand for such funding. Over the past few years, we, as a fraternity of local bankers, have established three new funding sources for low-interest loans. The Gloucester Investment Fund, Gloucester Revolving Loan Fund and Gloucester Revitalization Program have all been created to fill particular needs. Our experience has shown a lack of demand for all three sources. Our experience has also shown a lack of cohesive community vision surrounding these loans. To that end, the local banks will continue the community work of helping to facilitate such a vision. Without a "solid" need, we feel it would be difficult at this time to entice "solid" investment in a new entity. The concept is intriguing, but we would recommend waiting as a course of action.

Thank you again for including us in this important discussion, and please keep us informed of any input you receive from others concerning this matter.

Sincerely,

David Sidon, Executive Director, GIC/GRLF
Peter Anderson, Rockport National Bank
David Marsh, Gloucester Bank & Trust
John Pettazzoni, Gloucester Cooperative Bank
Harold Rogers, Cape Ann Savings Bank

GIC
GRLF
GRP

Meeting minutes – January 20, 1999

A special meeting of a sub-group of directors of GIC representing the local banking community was called to meet with Carmine Gorga, Ph. D., President, Polis-tics, Inc., to discuss Mr. Gorga's vision of a "*Gloucester Mutual Fund*".

The meeting was held at Cape Ann Savings Bank. In attendance were Mssrs. Gorga, Anderson, Marsh, Pettazzoni, Rogers & Sidon.

The meeting was called to order @ 4:10 pm.

Mr. Gorga prepared an agenda for the meeting which is attached hereto.

In his introductory remarks, Mr. Gorga described the need for a physical plan of urban restoration for the City of Gloucester. He described a plan incorporating tourist, fishing and commercial industry initiatives, citing community pride and Gloucester's place in history.

Mr. Gorga requested this meeting with Gloucester's bankers to describe his vision of a funding mechanism to facilitate needed urban restoration. He described an entity which he calls "Gloucester Mutual Fund" as follows:

- An independent for-profit entity
- Yearly assembly of shareholders based on a concept of one person – one vote
- The entity would be a grant facilitator and administrator
- Shareholders would be sought worldwide
- Benefits would be local – leveraging funds for loans aimed at creating new, real wealth
- Income sources – investments, loans & grants

Mr. Gorga then provided a working document describing in some detail the various provisions of the entity as he envisioned it.

Questions and comments followed at Mr. Gorga's suggestion that the purpose of meeting with the bankers was to provide a forum in which to critique his "draft" ideas.

Mr. Pettazzoni questioned the viability of attracting significant investment with a one vote-one person management mechanism.

Mr. Marsh and Mr. Sidon questioned the need for funding prior to establishing a common vision for urban renewal, citing the lack of demand for the three existing loan programs administered within GIC & GRLF.

Mr. Marsh requested clarification as to how shareholders would be rewarded for their investment. Mr. Gorga replied that stock appreciation created by an economically stronger Gloucester was the hoped for result.

Mr. Anderson echoed the comments about the need for funding, stating that he feels that the spirit of community and cooperation amongst competing banks has the economic good of Cape Ann strongly in mind, and that the local banks stand ready to work together to meet current community financing demands. He went on further to complement Mr. Gorga on his personal efforts toward creating a stronger local economy.

At 5:15 pm, Mr. Gorga excused himself.

Continued discussion resulted in consensus that the concept of creating a new separate fund at this time may not be necessary or timely in terms of attracting investment. Given the current lack of a common vision for the City or consensus among the many economic and social factions within the City, funding was considered to be premature. The group asked GIC Executive Director Sidon to draft a letter to Mr. Gorga thanking him for spawning this type of discussion and expressing the opinions of the group.

Meeting was adjourned @ 5:35 pm.

Respectfully submitted,

David Sidon, Executive Director

PART SIX

Seven Proposed Resolutions Plus One

Wouldn't it be great if the tail (Cape Ann)
were to wag the dog (the United States)?

Bruce Tobey
former Mayor of Gloucester

A Brief History

The following seven resolutions
were presented to Mayor Carolyn A. Kirk
and the City Council at a public hearing
on September 2, 2008

✳ ✳ ✳

Jonathan, our son, is a most severe editor. I wish the reader could have benefited from much more of his wisdom. Unfortunately he is busy doing other things. But let me give you one example. I had plunged right into the discussion of the seven proposed resolutions, when he shot back at me, and — being a son — you realize how much personal involvement is in an expression like this: "What do you think, you are God?" In my most fake-humble voice I said: "No, no, no." More importantly, I immediately wrote this introductory paragraph:

These resolutions are not set in concrete.
Indeed, they have to be adapted to the needs
of the Gloucester City Council
and Mayor Kirk's Administration.
They are simply recommendations.

Seven Proposed Resolutions

1. A Call to Local Bankers to Develop the Gloucester Interdependence Fund

The City Council of Gloucester, MA,

Noting that the City is endowed with a wealth of financial resources,

Noting that the City is comprehensively and competently served by a rich financial infrastructure,

Relying on the natural desire of Gloucester residents to be financially independent,

Realizing that competition between local financial institutions is conducted within the constraints of respect for the specialized niches developed by each one of them over time,

Calls upon all financial institutions within the City of Gloucester to explore possibilities of collaboration that might yield significant social and economic benefits,

Directs the Mayor of the City of Gloucester to assist local financial institutions to facilitate the creation of the Gloucester Interdependence Fund (GIF).

For a detailed analysis of the proposed operations of this fund, please see: http://www.polis-tics.com/id23.htm" http://www.polis-tics.com/id23.htm.

For an initial reaction from Gloucester bankers, please see attachment at pages 324-325.

2. A Call to City Departments, to Civic and Religious Groups to Voluntarily Create as Many Mutual Assurance Funds as Possible

The City Council of Gloucester, MA,

Recognizing that one of the ironies of life is contained in the statement that "People who do not need money have it in abundance, while people who need it very badly have it not at all,"

Recognizing that this contradictory situation leads to unspeakable hardships and even tragedy,

Recognizing that this Body and any public body does not have the tools to remedy such a complex condition, except by recognizing that there is a limit as to how much money can be raised in taxes or fees and how much can be cut back on community expenses, while keeping the various functions of the city in working order,

Recognizing that, individually, residents are limited in their ability to improve their financial condition, while jointly they might be better able to help themselves,

Recommends **that the residents of Gloucester build their own safety net by calling upon city departments, civic and religious groups to voluntarily create as many Mutual Assurance Funds as possible.**

For a brief description of mutual assurance funds, please see:
www.polis-tics.com/id17.htm" www.polis-tics.com/id17.htm.

3. A Directive to the Mayor to Study the Feasibility of Developing Dogtown Village as a Natural National Tourist Attraction and the Creation of a Tourist Center/Convention Hall/Regional Theater Complex on Blackburn Circle

The City Council of Gloucester, MA,

Realizing that attracting tourists to the waterfront might result in conflicts between the operations of the fishing industry and the interests of tourists,

Noting that Gloucester is endowed with a precious historical treasure, namely that at the center of Dogtown Common there are cellar holes and other recognizable evidence of original Colonial habitation,

Noting that other communities have either to invent or to import specimens of comparable importance,

Relying on the thirst of the American public for knowledge about authentic historical experience,

Directs the Mayor of the City of Gloucester to Study the Feasibility of Developing Dogtown Village as a Natural National Tourist Attraction and the Creation of a Tourist Center/Convention Hall/Regional Theater Complex on Blackburn Circle.

A Few Important Notes

Noting that, if historians and archaeologists are satisfied that we are already doing our best in relation to the preservation of our Dogtown Common heritage, every additional step ought to be shunted aside and thrown into the category of waste

Emphasizing that paved roads and paved parking lots should, at the very least, be characterized as inauthentic and therefore never even be conceived

Noting that, if and when a Tourist Center/Convention Hall/Regional Theater Complex on Blackburn Circle becomes a reality, the "Dogtown experience" can be made *virtual* with the assistance of interactive computer displays

Noting that the existence of our unique Dogtown Village is absent from our official tourist website as well as its inset about Gloucester History

Noting that the existence of our unique Dogtown Village is absent from official regional as well as state tourist websites

Noting that tourist brochures about our unique Dogtown Village are not in display either at the Chamber of Commerce or at two Gloucester Visitor Welcoming Centers and that one brochure is offered for $5.0

Noting that maps about Dogtown Common are produced by the Gloucester Conservation Commission and are made available upon request by removing them from manila folders inside filing cabinets and that only on the retro of one such map is there any information about the site

The City Council might want, at the very least, to call for a feasibility study to integrate the historic existence of Dogtown village into our public consciousness

And subsequently fully integrate it into the roster of unique attractions worthy to be called to the attention of our visitors in a systematic way in order to make their visit more rewarding.

The aim: The aim of this proposed tourist policy, by adding one more leg to it, is to spread among the arts and historic venues the burden that is today put by the tourist industry onto the shoulders of the fishing industry. Artists and art galleries would benefit directly for such a policy; the consciousness of our proud historic past might be enriched and might add appreciation for the blessings of living on Cape Ann.

4. A Directive to the Mayor to Study the Feasibility of a Plan of Urban Restoration

The City Council of Gloucester, MA,

Noting that the combined action of two national programs of the 1950s has left deep scars on our landscape, namely that with the construction of the superhighway through town, Route 128 Extension cut deeply into the granite of Portuguese Hill, and with the alteration of Rogers Street, Urban Renewal separated the downtown from the waterfront,

Noting that the construction design of Route 128 Extension can be healed by creating a multi-layer facility as parking to serve the needs of the proposed Blackburn Complex as well as the traffic needs of the Town of Rockport,

Noting that the construction design of Rogers Street can be healed by elevating Rogers Street — or enclosing it in a Ziggurat type of construction, thus forming a tunnel — so that free parking can be created underneath it in order to serve the needs of Main Street as well as the needs of the harbor,

Noting that the healing of these two scars would serve to restore our landscape to the organic status that existed in the past,

Advising that a fleet of jitney buses link the two proposed parking lots with destinations to downtown Gloucester, downtown Rockport, and Rocky Neck,

Conceiving also of the possibility of eliminating the scattered adjacent parking lots that exist today between Rogers Street and the harbor and consolidating them into one contiguous public park area,

Conceiving further the possibility of attaching to the elevated (or enclosed) Rogers Street, at a dropped-down level, a Gloucester Promenade with stairways leading to the park, to the waterfront, or to Main Street,

Envisaging the possibility of restoring the amenities of a pedestrian community by keeping cars and trucks under full control,

Directs to the Mayor of the City of Gloucester to Study the Feasibility of this Plan of Urban Restoration.

5. A Directive to the Mayor to Study the Feasibility of the Creation of a Main Street Corporation

The City Council of Gloucester, MA,

Recognizing, as the *Wall Street Journal* is emphatically editorializing these days, that "The hottest trend this decade in shopping-center development has gone cold." This trend concerns the building of "open-air" shopping centers as distinguished from the covered mall,

Recognizing further that a new trend is appearing, the trend toward "instantaneous-old" shopping centers, such as the one next to Farmers Market in Los Angeles or the one in Hingham, Mass.,

Recognizing further that our true-blue old downtown has all the makings of an authentic modern shopping center by linking the upper floors in order to create space for an assisted living/hotel/restaurant(s) complex on the harbor side and a supermarket/department store(s) complex on the North side of Main Street,

Recognizing finally that a Unified Downtown Corporation can be created either through voluntary action or through eminent domain,

Urges all downtown interests that a Unified Downtown Corporation be created through voluntary action, and

Instructs the Mayor of the City of Gloucester to assist all downtown interests in all possible ways in the performance of a feasibility study concerning the creation of a Unified Downtown Corporation (UDC).

Some additional notes:

To a downtown that managerially functions as a unified entity as it is in the economic reality, many opportunities will open up

> There could be common purchases of electric power
> There could be shared expenses for maintenance
> There could be a common merchandising plan

6. An Invitation to Private Entrepreneurs to Develop a Surimi Plant in Gloucester

The City Council of Gloucester, MA,

Remembering that since the closure of the Lippman Marine plant there has hardky been any sizeable harvesting of herring and mackerel in our New England waters,

Noting that for the recovery of depleted species of bottom fish it is essential that herring and mackerel, the current predators of bottom fish, be more fully harvested (see letters to Kessler and Hill, together with attachments),

Realizing that pelagics are still in abundant supply,

Realizing that a new technology for the processing of herring and mackerel into Surimi (a thousand-year old Japanese process) was developed in Gloucester at the University of Massachusetts Marine Station in Bay View by Drs. Herbert Hultin and Stephen D. Kelleher,

Realizing that a system management analysis of the feasibility of the Surimi plant has been developed by a team of doctoral candidates led by (now Drs.) Peter Otto, Sanghyun Lee, and Jeroen Struben under the guidance of Professor Jim Hines of MIT's System Dynamics Program,

Realizing that a business plan can easily be extracted from this system management study,

Relying on the hunger of the American public for healthy seafood,

Noting that if the Gloucester Interdependence Fund becomes a reality, with or without assistance from New Markets Tax Credits (NMTC), Gloucester residents will have the opportunity to own and control the use of local renewable resources,

Directs the Mayor of the City of Gloucester to Invite Private Entrepreneurs to Develop a Surimi Plant in Gloucester.

7. A Directive to Our Congressional Delegation to Amend the Magnuson-Stevens Fishery Conservation and Management Act

The City Council of Gloucester, MA,

Noting that the administration of the Magnuson-Stevens Fishery Conservation and Management Act is creating unconscionable hardship on our fishermen,

Noting that the administration of this legislation is unduly depressing the value of our harbor front,

Noting that the administration of this legislation is failing to take into account results of deep science that reveal the existence of a predator/prey model in every living habitat,

Noting that the administration of this legislation is failing to take into account the balance of payment effects that result from prohibiting the harvesting of local fish and compelling the importation of staggering quantities of seafood per year,

Regretting that the administration of this legislation is threatening the destruction of our three-hundred year old way of community life,

Directs the Mayor of the City of Gloucester to Advise Our Congressional Delegation to Amend the Magnuson-Stevens Fishery Conservation and Management Act at least to Incorporate the Predator/Prey Model of Biomass Behavior.

Some additional notes:

There are undoubtedly necessary preservation measures that need to be shared by all participants in the industry, and they should be enforced;

Yet, there are rules whose enforcement is doing damage to the pelagics as well as to the depleted bottom fish (remember, overfishing is not done be the fishermen, but by the natural predators of bottom fish) and these should be eliminated from the legislation;

Rules and regulatins ought to be a help not an impediment to the wise managemtn of the resources.

✳ ✳ ✳

+1. The Gloucester Concord Resolution

(A resolution to be presented at a more opportune moment.)

The City Council of Gloucester, MA,

Fully aware of the enormous financial needs of our community,

Painfully aware that the financial resources of taxpayers are overstretched,

Recognizing that the municipal bond market serves only temporary and illusory benefits for bondholders,

Recognizing that substantive and permanent benefits for bondholders are served by reduced municipal expenses and solvent taxpayers,

Resolves **that the City of Gloucester will borrow** *public money* **to fund duly authorized** *public works* **projects. The Treasurer is authorized to borrow public money by accessing national credit, rather than the private bond market. Thus loans are obtained at cost, rather than exorbitant interest charges. The Federal Reserve System will use national credit to create money as an asset. The loan will preferably be repaid from proceeds of increased taxes on land and natural resources (while correspondingly reducing taxes on buildings, improvements, and other assets).**

For theoretical background, please see:

Gorga, C. "Concordian Economics: Tools to Return Relevance to Economics", Forum for Social Economics, May 2008.

Gorga, C. *The Economic Process: An Instantaneous Non-Newtonian Picture* (Lanham, Md. and Oxford: University Press of America, 2002).

Gorga, C. "The Productivity Standard: A True Golden Standard" (with Norman G. Kurland), *in* Dawn M. Kurland (ed.), *Every Worker an Owner: A Revolutionary Free Enterprise Challenge to Marxism,* Washington, D.C.: Center for Economic and Social Justice, 1987, pp. 83-86.

For much pertinent — and some impertinent — additional information, please see:

www.concordresolution.org
www.monetary.org
www.webofdebt.com/articles/minnesota-bank-proposal.php
www.prosperityuk.com/prosperity/prosperity.html

See also:
money site:youtube.com
Money As Debt (1 of 5)
www.youtube.com/watch?v=DU7E3jMVtjI

PART SEVEN

Follow Up

Vox populi, vox Dei

Action/Results

O n September 2, 2008, David Wise and Carmine Gorga presented the seven proposed resolutions to the Gloucester City Council. Councillors At-Large: Joseph Ciolino, Sharon George, Sefatia A. Romeo Vice President, Bruce Tobey President. Ward Councillors: Ward I: Jason Grow, Ward II: John "Gus"Foote, Ward III: Steve Curcuru, Ward IV: Jackie Hardy, Ward V: Philip Devlin.

On September 2, 2008, the Gloucester City Council voted unanimously to send the seven proposed resolutions for study to the Planning and Development Standing Committee of the Council, Jackie Hardy: Chair. Sharon George: Vice Chair, Philip Devlin: Member.

A Summary

Depending on the interest of the audience, in their presentation David Wise and Carmine Gorga use most of the following slides because they offer a quick summary of most of the arguments put forward in this collection of essays.

A Citizen's Petition

Seven (plus one) proposed resolutions

an integrated approach
to resolve the issues
facing downtown

History

in 2007
The Downtown Gloucester Restoration Committee

was formed to offer visitors
at the Gloucester Sidewalk
Bazaar the opportunity
to sign the petition

We wish to thank the 425 residents mostly from Cape Ann who signed the petition

General Considerations

- Proposed resolutions are not set in concrete
- They have to be adapted to the needs of the Gloucester City Council and Mayor Kirk's administration
- They are simply recommendations

Under two torch lights

Wouldn't it be great
if the tail (Cape Ann)
were to wag the dog
(the United States)

**President Bruce Tobey
in his former incarnation as Mayor of Gloucester**

Allow me to ask

Wouldn't it be nice
to be the focus of
favorable national
attention?

The second torch light

It takes
a child
to raise a village
Sen. Hillary Clinton, in reverse

A child's **hard** look at finances

Reveals three things

People who do NOT need it, have money whose value is fast disappearing

People who NEED it, do not have money

To Become a Somist

- Individually, there is not one thing we an do about situations such as these
- As social human beings, many things become possible

because the world of economics is

A World of Interdependence
The Economic Process

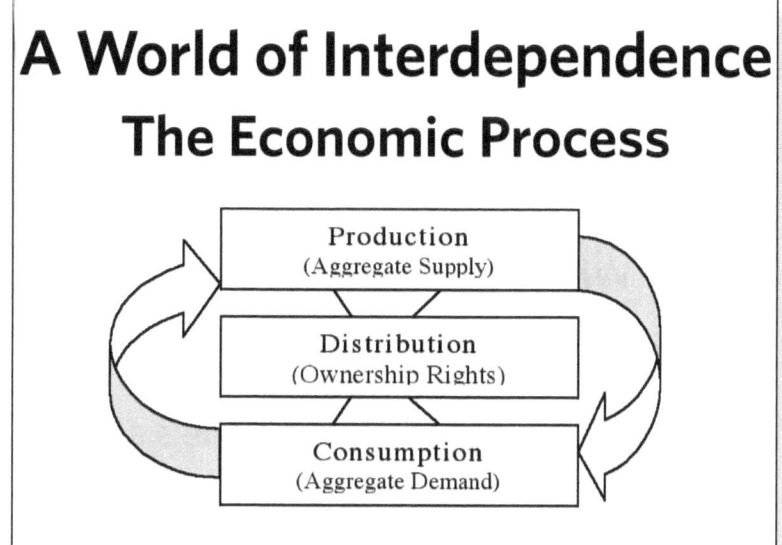

An Old Looking Glass

From

Saving = Income – Consumption

to

Investment = Income – Hoarding

Toward a new financial world

- **Gloucester Interdependence Fund**
  (Capital tithing)
  While keeping ownership

- **Gloucester Mutual Funds**
  (Income tithing)
  While preserving the right to one's share

Gloucester Interdependence Fund

- Receives money from anywhere
- Lends soley to Gloucester entrepreneurs
- Who do business in Gloucester
- Is administered by bankers and business people
- Its shares are subject to capital gains/losses
- Most benefits are indirect

Gloucester Mutual Funds

- No more than 30 members
- Members who know each other
- Funds administered by members
- The fewer the rules the better
- Contributions: mostly "mad" shopping $$
- Withdrawals: as needed
- Withdrawals returned if/when possible

Toward a new financial world

- **For Europeans, money is created by bankers**
- **For Americans, money is created by US:**

It is our money that the Fed administers

The Gloucester Concord Resolution
(Public Money for Public Works)

Resolved that the City of Gloucester will borrow **public money** to fund duly authorized **public works** projects. The Treasurer is authorized to borrow public money by accessing national credit, rather than the private bond market. Thus loans are obtained at cost, rather than exorbitant interest charges. The Federal Reserve System will use national credit to create money as an asset. The loan will preferably be repaid from proceeds of increased taxes on land and natural resources (while correspondingly reducing taxes on buildings, improvements, and othe assets).

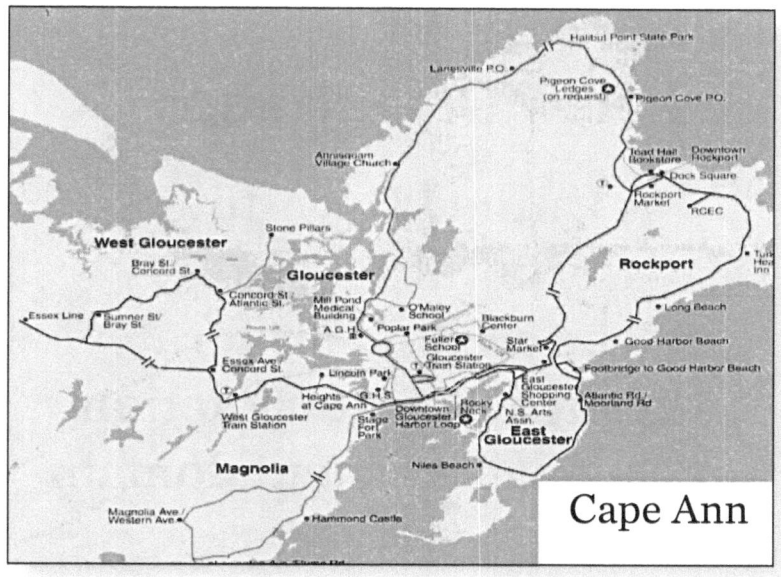

Cape Ann

Urban Restoration

- Start from Blackburn Circle
- Build a welcoming/convention hall there
- Send people walking through Dogtown
- Build multi-layered parking facility in ravine
- Elevate Rogers Street or build on its aerial rights
- Construct promenade alongside it
- Build free parking facility underneath it
- Consolidate existing parking lots into a park

New Organization

A Unified Downtown Corporation (UDC) can be created preferably through voluntary action or through eminent domain

Gloucester Fish Inc.

- Resources, the pelagics, are there
At present, they are the predators
Pelagics do the overfishing
of bottom fish
- The business plan has to be extracted from management plan prepared by System Dynamics Program at MIT

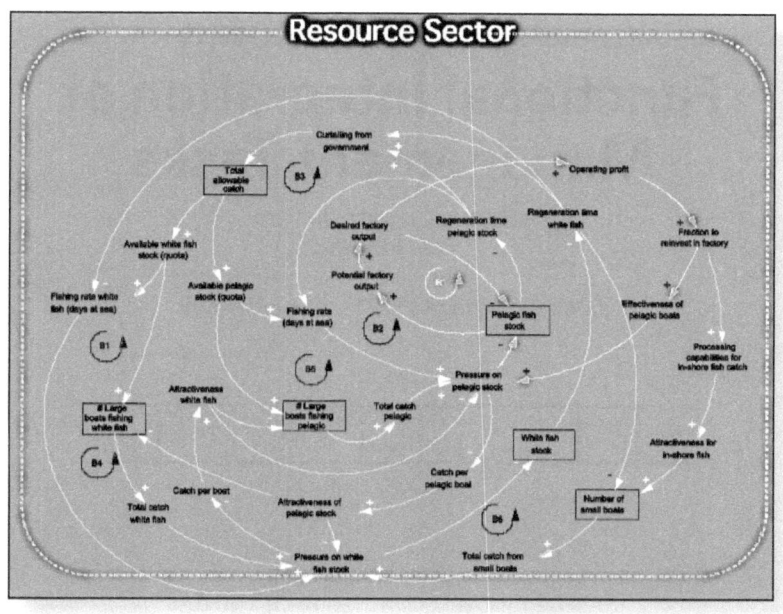

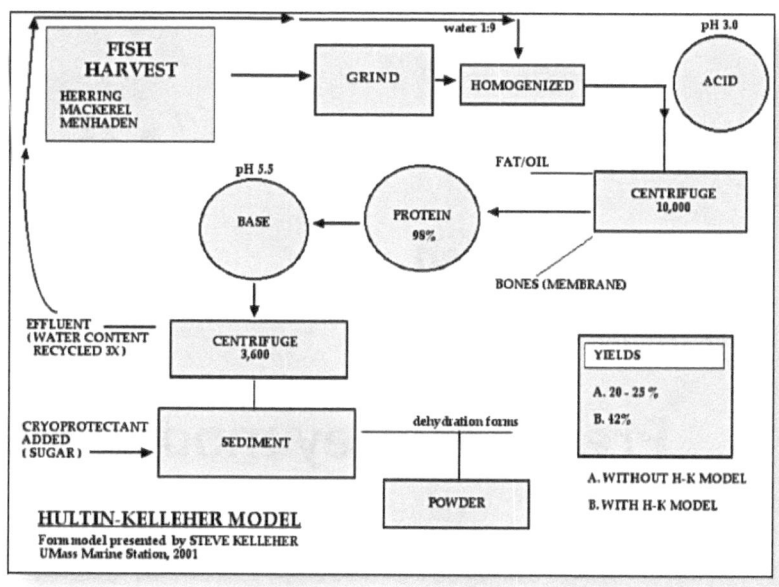

Functional Integration of Management Tasks

FUNCTIONAL INTEGRATION
(SuperESOP)

COMMON OWNERSHIP OF ALL HARDWARE

Schools	Ponds/ Farms	Hatcheries	Boats	Plants	Machinery	Labs	Trucks	Stores

LEASED BY INDEPENDENT TEAMS OF OWNERS

Magnuson-Stevens Act

- To be amended

To include at least

Predator/prey model

Reasons to Preserve Fishing Industry

- **It forms a community**
  it is not a pack of lone wolves
- **It shares joys and pains**
- **It respects other communities**
  such as old arts community
  and emerging community of engineers
- **It practices economic interdependence**
- **It is frugal, hence financially independent**
- **It practices economic justice**
- **It produces a quasi-vital food**

Additional Reasons to Preserve Fishing Industry

- **It practices sound economic values**
  Boats build houses; houses do not build boats.
  Lena Novello
- **It offers year-round work**
- **It offers good financial rewards**
- **It preserves the harbor as a regional hub**
- **It preserves 300 years of investment**
- **It helps our balance of payments**
- **It uses renewable resources**

The City Council

1. *Directs* the Mayor of the City of Gloucester to assist local financial institutions to facilitate the creation of the Gloucester Interdependence Fund (GIF)

2. *Recommends* that the residents of Gloucester build their own safety net by calling upon city departments, civic and religious groups to voluntarily create as many Mutual Assurance Funds as possible.

The City Council

3. *Directs* the Mayor of the City of Gloucester to Study the Feasibility of Developing Dogtown Village as a Natural National Tourist Attraction and the Creation of a Tourist Center/Convention Hall/Regional Theater Complex on Blackburn Circle.

4. *Directs* to the Mayor of the City of Gloucester to Study the Feasibility of this Plan of Urban Restoration.

The City Council

5. *Instructs* the Mayor of the City of Gloucester to assist all downtown interests in all possible ways in the performance of a feasibility study concerning the creation of a Unified Downtown Corporation (UDC).

6. *Directs* the Mayor of the City of Gloucester to invite Private Entrepreneurs to Develop a Surimi Plant in Gloucester.

The City Council

7. *Directs* the Mayor of the City of Gloucester to Advise Our Congressional Delegation to Amend the Magnuson-Stevens Fishery Conservation and Management Act at least to Incorporate the Predator/Prey Model of Biomass Behavior.

Resolution 7 + 1

Resolved that the City of Gloucester will borrow **public money** to fund duly authorized **public works** projects. The Treasurer is authorized to borrow public money by accessing national credit, rather than the private bond market. Thus loans are obtained at cost, rather than exorbitant interest charges. The Federal Reserve System will use national credit to create money as an asset. The loan will preferably be repaid from proceeds of increased taxes on land and natural resources (while correspondingly reducing taxes on buildings, improvements, and othe assets).

A bit of history
Life, liberty, and property

changed by Jefferson to

Life, liberty and the pursuit of happiness

Comments

If you like what you have read, tell your friends.

If you do not like what you have read, tell me. But tell me why.

You can contact me at cgorga@jhu.edu.

Thanks in advance, CG

Ready for a long goodbye?

Epilogue

Gloucester, Massachusetts, my adopted community, my polis, is divided into four parts. There is the tightly knit community of fishermen and people who live off the fishing industry; a loosely knit community of artists; a modern emerging community which, for lack of a better term, might be called a community of engineers; and then there are all the others. To fully understand Gloucester, one must understand all four parts.

The Others run the gamut from the voyeurs to the indifferent to the exploiters.

The exploiters know who they are: they take more than they give; the indifferent live entrapped in the fog of their own personality; hence, this epilogue is addressed to the voyeurs. May they come, see, but may they also understand. While they stay here, love-struck for the town, they are at the same time trying to change the ways of the town to their own liking. May they understand that, rather than living in a fantasy world of their own, they ought to go back where they came from, and when back to their place of origin, may they try to integrate the various aspects of their lives by forming a community of their own there. Trust me. There is too much pain in emigration. Much better is to change your social and economic condition right where you are. If you read this book actively, you will gather a few tools to achieve this goal.

The emerging community of engineers is the most complex to understand, because it shares characteristics with all the other communities. It has its fair share of voyeurs, indifferent, and exploiters. Above all, granted all differences, it shares characteristics with the community of fishermen and the community of artists. Just like fishermen, engineers live directly or indirectly from the powers of nature: even computer chip makers (hence Varian, for instance, at one level removed) qualify because silicon is made out of sand; and computer programmers qualify, because they belong to the creative arts. And yet, until they find their own songs and their own narrative, the community of engineers will not exist in the consciousness of the local population, because, as the Basques believe, things that are not named do not exist (as noted by Mark Kurlansky); indeed, at a deeper level still, until this emerging community finds its own identity, through finding affinity with and full participation in the local life, it will not exist even in its very own consciousness. That is work ahead of us.

The most important and immediate work is to restore the existing community of fishermen and artists to its former glory — indeed, getting it ready for future glory.

To see what a community is, we have to give a look at what a community is not. If you do not know your neighbor next door, you do not live in a community. If you do not know the name of the person in your pew, you might be worshipping your God in a holy building but you do not live in a community. If you do not live where you work, you do not live in a community. (Memo to School Committee: More engineers would live in town if the academic curriculum were more substantive; get ready for transformative actions; get ready for transferal of ownership of premises *together with* taxing powers to teachers and students; get ready to become either a Board of Directors of the School Corporation or to dissolve.)

Let me put the converse as strongly and as briefly as I can. The "individual" who lives alone is indeed a lone wolf. The emphasis is on being a wolf. As Hobbes well knew, the wolf is going to eat other wolves; and in the end it will be eaten by wolves.

Proof of community life? Well, when members die, and the conditions warrant it, whether it is the tragedy of a group of seasoned fishermen lost at sea or a lad who leaves the community unexpectedly and prematurely, all feel the void left behind in nearly equal parts. They all fill the church for the last rites. It is thus that the family directly affected bears the burden of such a loss with a proportion of ease. And then, when one person rejoices, all the members rejoice. The brave man who catches the flag at the end of the Greasy Pole, a feat of physical prowess and resilient courage that occurs on three successive days a year, that brave man is king for the year! Come to Gloucester on the Feast Day of Saint Peter; come to Gloucester on the Feast Day of Saint Joseph, and you will see joy overflowing from the home of many a fisherman and a fisherman's wife. Is this an appropriate moment for me to bare my soul by telling you that Saint Joseph is absolutely my most favorite saint? The Bible has not a single recorded word by Saint Joseph; but the Gospels are full of his recorded deeds.

The strongest proof of community life? People know most candidates for office. Politics is not vicious; politics is still mostly fair.

Allow me to frame the issue as starkly as I can. If you do not share the joys and the pains of other people, you are likely to develop into a Columbine plotter at one end of the social ladder or a Bhopal CEO at the other. You are not a Somist; you are not a man or a woman in a social context; you are not a civilized person.

Gloucester is both the oldest fishing port and the oldest art colony in the country. Both of these communities create wealth; all other economic activities, at best, add value to what is being produced in these two communities. It cannot be otherwise: Primary industries are agriculture, fishing, mining, and — as yet unacknowledged in the economics textbooks — the creative arts. Fishermen and artists (and farmers and miners and engineers) create as if out of nothing, because nothing is not Nothing, but Fullness: the fullness of matter, and matter is also spirit. And therefore theirs are some of the hardest and most imaginative activities on earth. They require skills that are acquired over long years of practice; they require patience for the exercise of those skills; they require humility in the process. This is how artists and engineers and miners and farmers and fishermen create everything almost from nothing. All the other sectors of the economy depend on what is visibly produced by the primary industries.

Serving the community of fishermen and the community of artists, some of the best craftsmen and craftswomen live in town; some of the best purveyors of services live in town. Wealthy and poor people rub shoulders at the post office and the supermarket. Life is not idyllic here; the town shows the full complement of pain, sufferance, and social ills that can be found in any community these days — or any days, for that matter. What is missing are the extremes.

The community of fishermen and the community of artists live in near total harmony with each other. One of the merits of Mark Kurlansky's new book on Gloucester, *The Last Fish Tale*, apart from the demerit of its passive acceptance of the dreadful situation facing the fisheries today, is to have highlighted this symbiotic relationship through the ages. Thus, the author not only speaks effectively about Fitz Henry (Hugh) Lane and Hopper and Hassam and Gruppé(s) and Hancock (and misses Al Duca) and Demetrios and Virginia Lee Burton and Charles Olson and Vincent Ferrini; he also depicts this incisive vignette: Charles Movalli, a Gloucester-born art critic and painter, apologizes for being in the way of fishermen working and a fisherman says, "You have your job, we have ours."

No. The artists are not all dead. The living and alive ones can be found in droves! I wish I knew them better. But here are the few I know better than others: Joe Garland keeps the heroic traditions of Gloucester alive, he is renowned especially for his celebration of the incredible life of Howard Blackburn. Peter Anastas does not only keep the legacy of Olson and Ferrini alive, he preserves the sweet scent of Gloucester of fifty years ago. You can sing along sea chanties into the sunset with Michael O'Leary; and Willy Alexander will infuse some of the wild energy of hard rock into your spine. Gordon Goetemann paints as if he were already in heaven looking down on us. Paul Goldberg's sharp eyes and innovative techniques produce photographs as vibrant as Csontváry paintings. Michele Miller can transform "common" people into heroes with photographs. And with Ernest Morin, our economist photographer, we understand not only people and places but also the economics of people and places. We even have at least two filmmakers on Cape Ann: Henry Ferrini and Andrew Stanton of Pixar Animation fame. With the inexhaustible energy of Gordon Baird, Ian McCall, Ina Hahn, Israel Horovitz, and assorted groups such as the Annisquam Village Players, we support more than two theaters here on Cape Ann. Thanks to the indefatigable David Benjamin, we enjoy yearly performances of the Cape Symphony; and thanks to the Shalin Liu Performance Center, we are enraptured by world-class music during the Rockport Chamber Music Festival. And then we have Thomas Misuraca, Sarah Wetzel, and the precious Corus Stella Maris. We also have more gem-like museums than we deserve on Cape Ann and a plethora of art galleries. The poetry scene is so rich as to have become political. And then there is the inimitable Jo-Ann Castano: she is a holographic sculptor and a tireless advocate for the arts.

And, no. We do not neglect the sports. Nor are we unappreciative of our landscape on which stand boulders at whose presence one is reminded of the birth of the earth. Neither does it escape us to notice that Gloucester is the land of the seagulls. At the end of *The Economic Process*, I wrote: "Gloucester is the place where the land meets the sea and the sky; it is the place where fishermen live; it is the place where religious liberty, the inner core of intellectual freedom, was born — at the other end of Middle Street, the street where I live." If you have followed my thoughts all the way here, welcome, dear Reader. Welcome to Gloucester. Welcome to my resplendent abode.

Where is the fountainhead of great tolerance, a tolerance that is not limited to the fishing community but exudes from all of Gloucester? Just a bit of thought and a bit of knowledge yields the answer. Both artists and fishermen are frugal; hence, avoiding debts both artists and fishermen are economically independent. At 40, Mark Carroll is reported as saying: "The reason I got into fishing in the first place was to be my own boss and to be outside." Each artist, it is well known, is an independent economic entity. What is less well known is the method of economic organization of the fishing industry: the method is called the "lay." Fishermen do not work for a wage; they work for a share of the profits. It is this economic independence that generates independence from other people's opinions, and thus forms the source of Gloucester's great tolerance.

There is no haggling as in a bazaar. There is no jockeying for position. George got a $1.0 million wage; I'm better than George; I need and deserve at least $1.2 million! The shares of the lay have been set since time immemorial. They represent commonly agreed upon societal rules of just compensation. The shares have been set forever (which does not mean that one cannot work two shifts and get double pay and eventually buy a boat of one's own. This is not the static world of the Middle Ages). The men and the women can go to work concentrating on how best to perform their self-assigned tasks. The competition is not with the other; the competition is with oneself. That is the challenge that never ends.

Thus, technically speaking, the fishermen enjoy the blessings of economic justice: they enjoy the blessings of participative justice (the work is done in common and they all share in the profit or the loss of each trip); they enjoy the blessings of distributive justice (the relative shares have been fixed from time immemorial; they are known in advance of the trip; they are not wages paid in advance of the trip, rather they are shares of profit that are executed at the end of each trip, if the trip does indeed yield a profit); they fully enjoy the blessings of commutative justice (there are no slack hands on deck; they take as much as they give). Artists, being independent entrepreneurs, bask in the same sun.

Since we live in a la-la land of Economic Unreality, the issue of just compensation bears some additional note. It is not our Mayor who sets the distributive shares of the fishermen; it is not the Chamber of Commerce, or the Manufacturers Association, or the Union that sets those shares. They have been set and respected since time immemorial because they have been found to be just. To fully appreciate the import of just compensation, let us remember that unjust compensation unavoidably leads to the many having too little and the few having too much. And since this too much is acquired unjustly, it is easily squandered. Squandered resources are resources that are not wisely reinvested to take care of the long term needs of the industry. Recently in the press there was news that the USA is losing its preeminence even over the Internet for lack of wise reinvestment practices.

This way of economic life of the fisherman needs to be nurtured, admired, possibly emulated, and spread throughout the world. The determination on the part of the fishermen is indisputable. As Vito Giacalone put it recently, "We want Gloucester to stay in the fishing business, period." And those who say that today fishermen and their allies are holding Gloucester back ought to remember that the port is a "hub" serving the region. It took 300 years to develop. Who or what is going to build such a comparable investment?

More to the point. Following the example of the fishermen, by being frugal we can all, or nearly all of us, be put on a path to financial independence. And, by recognizing the reality of economic interdependence and following the dictates of economic justice, we can all, or nearly all of us in our little village, build structures of economic independence from Wall Street and even from Washington. The search for economic independence is, after all, the path that has lead innumerable generations of people from the whole wide world to America. Economic independence is the path on which our forefathers might have set us if Jefferson, to save the union, had not been compelled to erase the word "property" from John Locke's formula: Life, Liberty, and Property. By one of those tortuous roads that human nature takes, property at that time was no longer reserved to things. The legal institution of property was extended to cover control over men and women and children. But now that the stain of color has been nearly eradicated from our consciousness, we might become so bold as to erase the words that Jefferson wrote, "the pursuit of happiness." These are words that have led us to the la-la land of entitlements. If we go back to the world of rights and responsibilities with a fresh mind, we will discover that above the rights of property stand economic rights. These are the fathers and the mothers of property rights. Economic rights and responsibilities can be extended to all, because they are natural unalienable rights.

Since it is so obvious, it goes without saying that the crowning achievement of the fishing community is to be at peace — and not war — with all other communities that live on the same stretch of land. This is proof, if proof were necessary, of the validity of Pope Paul V's maxim, "If you want peace, work for justice." When will this policy be practiced, not just talked about, all over the world?

And yet, unthinkable thought, as Vincent Ferrini put it, there are people who — locally, regionally, and nationally — are talking and working for the demise of the fishing industry. There are people who, waiting eagerly for the last fisherman to fish out of Gloucester, are making plans to build, if not condos, at least hotels and slips for yachts in the inner sanctum of Gloucester Harbor.

There are many reasons why the community ought not to give in to the cry for hotels and yachts in the inner harbor. First, there is an enormous quantity of free space for condos and yachts in the outer harbor: I am not the only one able to see a thousand masts piercing the sky there in the future. This would be a much more exciting view than even the splendidly cramped landscape of Portofino, Italy.

The second reason is a negative one and a bit technical; but not too technical. It depends on the fallacy of composition. If one owner of property in the inner harbor is granted the privilege of hosting yachts and motels and restaurants on his premises, he will certainly be richer than the neighbors. However, if all property owners are granted this privilege — and all will eventually be granted this privilege to avoid discrimination — once they all sell their land to motels and yacht visitors, they will all be in the same relative position as they are today. None will be richer than all others. Just think of watching a game in a stadium. If one person stands up in the bleachers, (s)he will have a clear and unobstructed view of the game. Yet, once all spectators stand up — and they will all eventually stand up — then no one is better off. Indeed, they will all be suffering from a worse view and tired feet.

A third reason is positive and natural. It is all enclosed in Lena Novello's famous dictum: "Boats build houses; houses do not build boats." A house is a consumer good; a motel is closer to the house than to the boat. A motel is part of the service industry. The service industry relies on the primary industries such as agriculture, fishing, and mining. If we destroy the fishing industry in Gloucester — and if we make costs of living and buying a house so expensive that fishermen and artists can no longer afford to live here — then, in the long run, we will have destroyed the source of the survival for the motel and the tourist industry as well: the very reason why tourists come here.

It takes only one scene to realize that certain uses of the land are mutually incompatible. The gorgeous blonde from the big city wakes up the morning after and says, "Pew! Where is that smell coming from? I was kept awake in the middle of the night by the noise of men going out to work. By the way, do you realize that little Tommy was almost run over by a trailer truck this morning?" There George's investment of $200 for the hotel room or the $750,000 for his two-room condo on the waterfront plummets down to zero. The people of the desert know better. They do not allow the nose of the camel under the tent, lest they want the tent destroyed. If you allow one hotel or condo on the working waterfront, the push will start for imposing restrictions on the fishermen. This is not theatricality; it is history repeated over and over again all over the world. Do read Kurlansky.

The great debate, the only debate worth having in Gloucester today is: not whether the fishing industry is declining (it is), but how to arrest the decline. The great debate, the only debate worth having is: not whether to allow hotels and yachts on the inner harbor, but how to use the fisheries resources that are there in the ocean — not to destroy them, but to manage them in a long-term sustainable fashion. The great debate worth having is how to avoid waste.

If this is the debate we want to be engaged in, then much work to be done comes easily to mind. First, we cannot afford to throw fish overboard because administrative regulations put a limit on daily catch. Once brought to the surface, a bottom fish is dead. It ought not to be thrown overboard; it must be utilized-perhaps via "pro bono" bins that go directly to a Surimi plant. Then, at this stage in the cycle, the predators of bottom fish have to be taken out of the water and a market must be found for them: the proposed Surimi plant is the natural receptacle for herring and mackerel, the natural predators of bottom fish. This is not a call to overfish herring and mackerel; this is simply a recommendation not to waste bottom fish at the table of the pelagics, the midwater fish like herring and mackerel that gobble up the larvae of bottom fish when they go up to sun and plankton and then gobble up the few codlings that survive when they go back to their friends and relatives at the bottom of the ocean; this is a recommendation not to waste the pelagics either. They naturally die; they might as well be used for the benefit of mankind. Even their biomass will collapse one day and go to waste if it is not properly harvested. When a predator's population grows to such a size that it no longer finds sufficient prey, its biomass collapses. This is the natural cycle of things. Even the lemmings, even the trees behave in such a way. Just recently, our inimitable Peter Prybot recorded for all those who have ears to hear and eyes to see that "The school sizes (of pogies, another midwater fish) were sometimes so large they even suffocated themselves, washed ashore by the millions, and temporarily putrefied the air and water of sections of shoreline, even beaches." Since a picture is worth a thousand words, I will leave at the end of this Epilogue two diagrams for the reader to observe and to study that depict the enormity of the size to which pelagics have been allowed to grow.

And the unholy alliance of bureaucrats, stunted ecologists, and ideologues is attempting to impose stricter and stricter rules and regulations even on catching pelagics? Where is the wisdom, where is the science on which such pigheaded positions are based? Why is the larger community of scientists, religious, civic, and political leaders condemning itself to be a passive onlooker? Certainly my soul is not at rest while unconscionable hardships are imposed upon and flagrant injustices are perpetrated against fishermen who do not even all speak perfect English.

Nor is my intellect at rest. How can we have fallen so low as to allow the government to usurp our unalienable rights? The ocean is one of our last commons. And yet, government officials, perhaps uneducated to the history of the commons and certainly misled by a Garrett Hardin who too late admitted that he mistook the tragedy of the commons for the tragedy of the enclosures, government officials are selling our unalienable rights to the commons to powerless fishermen who can do no more but oblige.

Truth to tell, fishermen cannot be held totally blameless for their condition either. They ought to unite. They ought to distinguish truth from the many shades of falsehood.

We saw many things clearly when Louis Ronsivalli and I wrote the paper on "The Importance of the U.S. Fishing Industry" in 1981. What we did not see is that the decline of the fishing industry was part of the deindustrialization of America and the resulting need for importation of foreign goods. But we did express our concern about the outsized contribution that fisheries imports make to the U.S. balance of payments deficit. The ultimate effect of this trend has finally become exceedingly clear: dollars that go aboard eventually come back to own and control "pieces of America."

To fully appreciate the struggle Gloucester is undergoing today, we have to enlarge our view even more. The current crisis of the fishing industry is a crisis of modernity. It is not local to Gloucester and a few other localities scattered throughout the world. It is a typical crisis. Let us quickly see how the crisis is indeed general and it is closely linked to the decadence of societies. The crisis has been repeated innumerable times in farming and mining communities all over the world. Through a combination of inner and outer forces, the family farm is replaced by the oversized corporate farm that survives economically because of its political power: because it is heavily subsidized by the government. And so the trend starts that ends with the privatization of profits and socialization of losses. In their wake lie despoliation of the landscape and exploitation of human beings. This is Termite Economics.

The many fallacies involved in this process are caught by one of the best jokes I keep in my small repertoire of jokes. There is this fortyish Harvard-graduate CEO who has this exchange with a fisherman on a Caribbean island:

> I could make you rich!
> How?
> By helping you buy a bigger boat.
> And what would I do with a bigger boat?
> Why, you could catch more fish.
> And why would I want to catch more fish?
> Because you can sell your catch for a lot of money.
> And what would I do with the money?
> You could build up a business of many small boats like yours.
> Why?
> So as to make even more money and spend your winters on a Caribbean island.
> Sir, you must not be very smart. I am spending my life on a Caribbean island!

Sadly, this is not a joke. This is economic development philosophy these days. And unfortunately, this approach does not remain at the level of philosophy. It is practiced. It is shoved down the throats of people.

It is not necessarily riches that are dangled in front of the eyes of the community to make it gradually loosen the traditional moral restraints against human exploitation and environmental degradation. A more benign, a more alluring target is proposed in the technical textbooks of economics and the polite conversation of politics. The aim of economic development is supposed to be the amelioration of poverty and the acquisition of economic freedom. Neither aim has ever been achieved yet. One failure after another, one dismal failure after another during the last four to five hundred years will not stop economists and politicians from promising that both aims are just around the corner — what we need, perhaps, is only a little more taxation and/or a little more economic freedom. Even those who realize that poverty has increased for the many and economic freedom is reserved for the few, even these clear-sighted minds fall into the trap of believing that the age of plenty for all is just around the corner. Sooner or later a critical mass of the population will realize that the problem is systemic and that the solution has also to be systemic.

The root of the problem is the monochromatic vision of both economists and political scientists who have reduced the systemic issues of economic development to the simple mantra of money and freedom. True economic development is community development. It is not emphatically the poor who have to become financially rich and freedom has not to be reserved for the few. It is the entire community that, if necessary, has to be developed by paying attention to all four factors of production (land, labor, physical, and financial capital). It is all the faculties of all the people that have to be engaged and integrated into an organic whole — as in ancient Egypt, Israel, Greece, Rome, Tikal, Teotihuacán, Cusco, Peking, Florence, Istanbul, and wherever the human race reached a peak in its development.

It is for these reasons that in the essays presented here the emphasis has been — ideally, in equal parts — on broad issues of culture, physical environment, financial institutions, and managerial development. Very very briefly, while civilizations of the past paid much attention to the needs of the individual genius, civilizations of the future will have to pay attention to the relationships between the genius and the rest of the community. We have to stop repeating the errors of the past, namely assuming that by "throwing the rascals out" things will improve automatically by themselves. No, human relationships will have to be fully considered ahead of time in order to obtain the right result: enough of everything for everybody.

This goal can be achieved by organically implementing the four sets of economic rights and responsibilities emphasized throughout these essays. This goal can be achieved because "an invisible hand" has so arranged things that the four sets of economic rights and responsibilities, to be properly implemented will keep the complex issues of freedom and morality, freedom and authority, order and chaos in constant movable balance. This goal can be achieved because "an invisible hand" has so arranged things that, if hoarding is eliminated from the range of activities open to the civilized human being, there is indeed enough for everybody.

Yes, that is the essential reason for the emphasis on the belief in God in these essays. Believe in God and all things that you really need will come to you.

No. Belief in God is not an essential precondition for the implementation of the prescribed four sets of economic rights and responsibilities. You will achieve the same results if you behave as a civilized person: if you do not believe you deserve more than others; if you do not believe you are a genius and all other human beings are fools who deserve to be exploited; if you do not believe in the need to control other people. You will have enough if you believe that it is enough to control yourself.

There is a very simple reason why those who try to control other people's lives should cease and desist at the earliest possible opportunity. (And the process of disengagement might not be that automatic and easy.) The reason is self-interest. Sooner or later, they are necessarily going to be deceived by those whom they try to control. Why not give up the dastard enterprise sooner rather than later? Why prolong the agony for the controlled and the self-deceit for the controllers?

To have enough and to be happy with what one has is the very essence of frugality. And, therefore, yes, I do believe that Gloucester is fit to implement the four sets of economic rights and responsibilities that are the very essence of organic community development. Gloucester is capable of showing the world the ways of frugality. Gloucester is capable of this much because it is still largely an intact community. Gloucester is the land where the people still largely have enough self-control and respect for each other, respect for the diversity of each other opinions, to make life mostly livable here, pleasantly livable.

Let us briefly put it another way. The prevailing type of economic development has led to an immoral and inefficient form of capitalism: Five Percent Capitalism, capitalism for at most 5% of the population. Since the conscience of the world could not possibly abandon 95% of the population to the wolves, it has relied on the vague promises of the "social contract" to set things right. But "sociology" cannot deal with economics. The social contract has transformed us into a world of beggars: the rich beg for lower taxes; the middle classes beg for higher taxes (on the rich) that, in the administration of the social contract through government jobs and contracts, form the backbone of their income; and the poor beg for entitlements.

We must get out of this corrupting form of thinking in which there are no rights, and responsibilities are transformed into responsibilities of third parties: the responsibility of "the state" to provide jobs and insurance against financial risk (the "too-big-to-fail" syndrome). Both policies lead to all sorts of well-known acts of irresponsibility; both are fostered on the basis of unfounded fears. The specter of lack of jobs and the specter of the impending credit crunch will vanish as soon as we change our monetary policy. The Federal Reserve System, rather than accepting all sorts of worthless collateral to extend loans to failed financial institutions, ought to let them go by the way free market theory tells us they should go. The Federal Reserve System would then extend loans to American enterprises, loans that are approved by American banks, on the basis of the full faith and credit of American entrepreneurs.

The right form of economics, Concordian economics, will gradually lead us to a regimen of economic rights and responsibilities. Economic rights and economic responsibilities will be lodged into the same person. From a nation of beggars we will be transformed into economically interdependent persons and ultimately financially independent human beings. Is not this the American Dream? Is not this the promise of America to the world?

Let us pick up the task from where our Founding Fathers were compelled to leave it. Let us transform the faulty program enveloped in the formula "life, liberty and the pursuit of happiness" back into the safe and sound millennial great social, economic, and political program that is enveloped in the formula "life, liberty, and property."

Rather than exporting dollars and the Hollywood Dream, this program of economic rights and economic responsibilities is what America should give back to the rest of the world. The American Dream, after all, is the creation of the entire world — not America's alone. And when this program of action is going to be implemented in all the Gloucesters of the world, then America will have solved its "immigration problem." And the rest of the world will have solved its emigration problem: the need to export people, people who necessarily end up being the most able-bodied, the most enterprising. With their "brain drain," all the Gloucesters of the world are destined to fall into deeper despair. All the little oligarchs of the world are destined to play in a smaller and smaller, drier and drier pond.

All the pain and sufferance involved in the way things are going are unnecessary. If Gloucester can do it, the rest of the world can do it also. Let us create economic freedom and economic morality all over the world.

And the economic aspects of the overall picture are truly secondary. It is what happens to the spirit of each human being and the spirit of a civilization going through the exercises of Termite Economics that counts much more. David Lebedoff has just published a study of two famous English writers, George Orwell and Evelyn Waugh, both born in 1903, one wealthy, the other voluntarily poor, one looking at society from the top down, the other from the bottom up. Lebedoff concludes that they are "the same man" and they are the same because they land on substantially identical positions, which Michael Dirda has recently summarized in few sentences penned for his review of the book in the *Wall Street Journal*. Both writers fought against "our age's frenzied pursuit of vacuous pleasure.... the aimlessness of life without faith, the impossibility of living without tradition, the absence of fairness, the triumph of might." They both "loathed the rise of narrow specialists, middle managers, conformist salarymen and ruthless overachievers. In their eyes such experts and functionaries were creating a society hardly worth living in, a robotic world that encouraged people to act and think alike, a world divorced from the land, tradition and history."

This is not an idiosyncratic view. The literature is replete with such observations. The acute Dick Meyer has recently remarked: "Our litany of complaints, big and small, reflects an enduring social mood disorder. On the collective level, our distrust in politics and government has prevented us from solving solvable problems. On the private level, the toxicity of pop culture, the hyperactive communicating that new technology lures us into, and the stunning disappearance of basic manners has made it more difficult to savor everyday life and get happy."

One can disagree about the degree of pervasiveness of this type of life in the modern society; one can disagree about the choice of focus on specific segments of society to the neglect of others; one even can disagree about the characterization of this type of life: for some people all modern life is the wonderful life. Certainly you will not catch me inveighing against the Internet. One cannot disagree, however, about the cause-effect relationships that lead to this modern type of society. Once embarked upon, the road cannot lead but there. Here in Gloucester we have not yet embarked upon the conscious road of destroying the traditional life that is linked to the fisheries, even though we are on the verge of taking such a momentous decision. Here in Gloucester we have a real choice. We can choose upon improving the forms of life of the past *from within*. We can respect tradition; we can change what needs to be changed; and we can show full respect for whatever goodness modernity has brought along. This is indeed the best of all possible worlds. But we have to work hard to get there; we have to work fast to get there; we have to work, as much as possible, harmoniously with one another while getting there.

Am I hopeful that we will make the right decisions? Yes! There is a fundamental reason why I am hopeful. The fishing community still has its soul largely intact. This is certainly the deepest fountainhead of the tolerance and respect for others and for nature that exudes from Gloucester. There is deep, true religiosity here. "Cape Ann is a deeply spiritual place," Lindsay Crouse has said while gathering up to 300 people for special Buddhist events. There is deep respect for the land: the newspaper is full of stories of people who pick up trash daily and people can be seen daily taking care of traffic islands throughout the city. And the fishermen are not afraid to show their religiosity, as exemplified by the respectable statues of the Madonna or Jesus in front of tiny yards — statues that, even though I can still see their faint image, immediately disappear when the houses are sold to newcomers. When you are in a tiny vessel surrounded in a dark night by ten-to-twenty foot waves, you know how small you are. You know that you do not get back home on your own powers. You rely on the visible powers of Nature and the invisible powers of the Spirit; and the Spirit of God holds you in the palm of His hand.

Most days I pass under the statue of the Lady of Good Voyage and furtively I say hello to the Madonna, the patroness of the United States, my spiritual mother; once I was so taken by my own thoughts, I went by and did not acknowledge her presence. I got worried. Immediately, her voice whispered in my soul, "I am always with you." But, as I say, when in public I offer my prayers rather furtively. There I was one day driving with a burly fishing captain easily twice my size. We pass under the statue and he crosses himself with a generous gesture!

That is faith. That is active faith. That is faith that instills respect for nature; it is faith that instills respect for other people. If you are in a dark night on a fishing vessel and the man at the wheel falls asleep, you know you will not get back home. And the man at the wheel knows it; reciprocally, he expects that you will do your share when you are climbing the mast to chop the ice encrusted there; you will do your share when hauling the net.

My friend, the burly fishing captain daily emulates the great fisherman of the Bible. When Peter, at the Transfiguration of Jesus, sees the splendor of God face to face, he simply and powerfully says: *Lord, it is good to be here.*

Lord, it is good to be in Gloucester.

Atlantic Herring

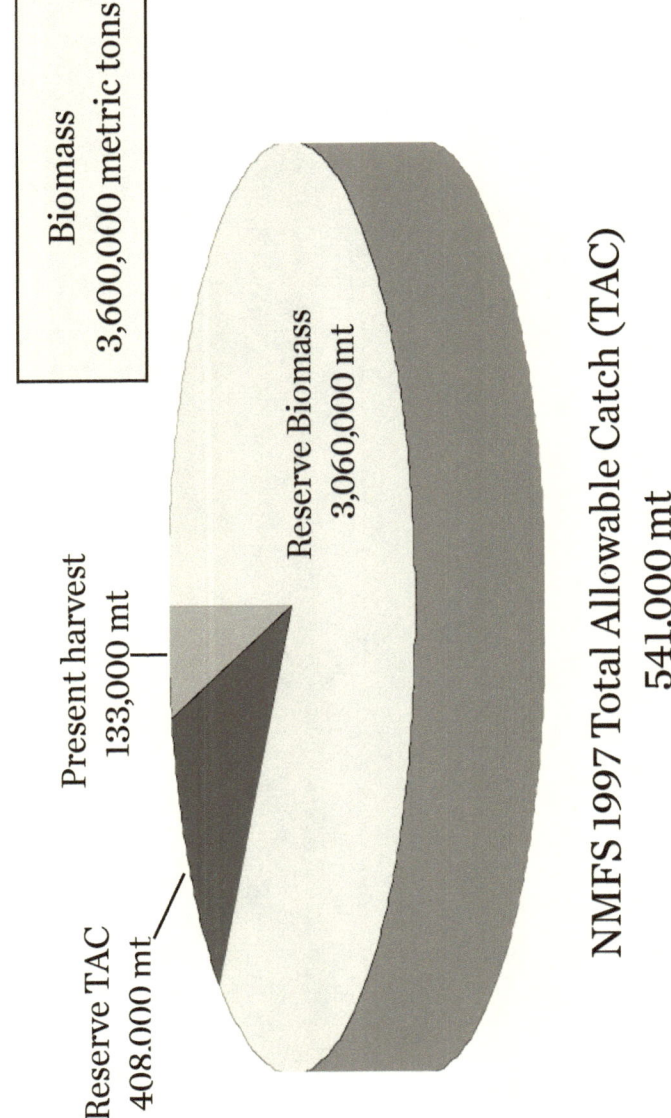

Biomass
3,600,000 metric tons

Present harvest
133,000 mt

Reserve Biomass
3,060,000 mt

Reserve TAC
408,000 mt.

NMFS 1997 Total Allowable Catch (TAC)
541,000 mt

Source: Gloucester Herring Corporation, Atlantic Herring, Final Report, July 1997

Atlantic Mackerel

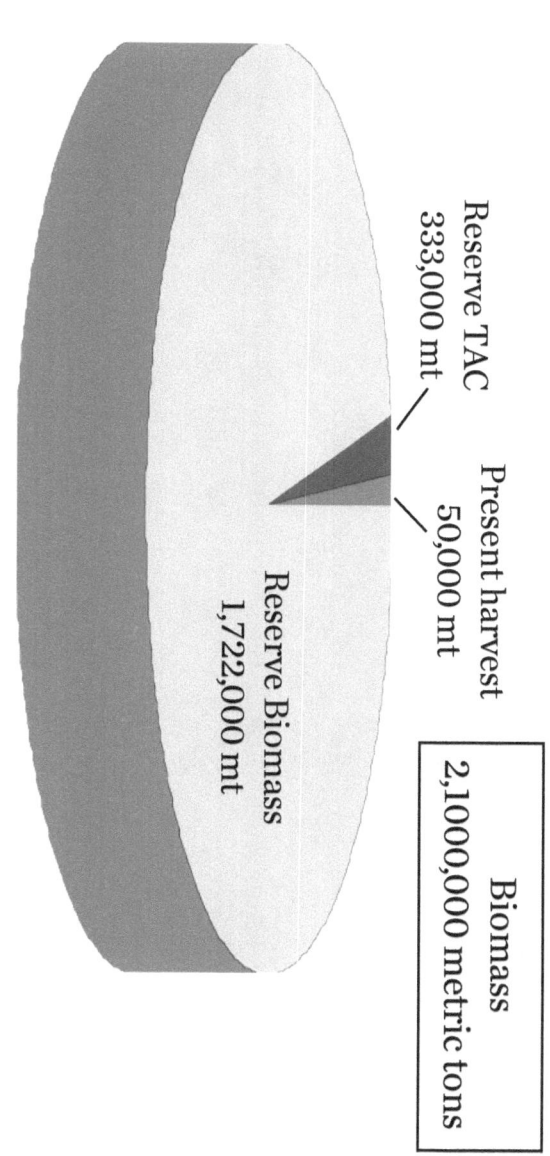

Reserve TAC
333,000 mt

Present harvest
50,000 mt

Reserve Biomass
1,722,000 mt

Biomass
2,1000,000 metric tons

NMFS 1997 Total Allowable Catch (TAC)
383,000 mt

Source: Gloucester Herring Corporation, Atlantic Herring, Final Report, July 1997

www.ingramcontent.com/pod-product-compliance
Lightning Source LLC
Chambersburg PA
CBHW031816170526
45157CB00001B/76